Israel, Globalism & The 2nd Coming of Christ

Understanding Current World Events
in Light of Bible Prophecy

RICK McGOUGH

Copyright © 2023 Rick McGough

All rights reserved.

ISBN- 9798386383602

"Scripture quotations taken from the New American Standard Bible® (NASB), Copyright © 1960, 1962, 1963, 1968, 1971, 1972, 1973, 1975, 1977, 1995 by The Lockman Foundation Used by permission. www.Lockman.org
(Unless otherwise noted)

TABLE OF CONTENTS

ISRAEL, GLOBALISM AND THE 2ND COMING OF CHRIST
(Understanding Current World Events In Light of Bible Prophecy)

Table of Contents	
Acknowledgments	i
INTRODUCTION - WHY ARE THESE THINGS IMPORTANT?	1
SECTION 1 - WHAT IS HAPPENING IN THE WORLD?	
Chapter 1 - An Overview of End Times Bible Prophecy	7
Chapter 2 - Israel, God's Timepiece	11
Chapter 3 - Jerusalem and The Nations	39
Chapter 4 - The Rebuilding of the Temple	49
Chapter 5 - False Christs and False Prophets	61
Chapter 6 - False Wonders and Deception (Be Alert!)	71
Chapter 7 - Wars and Rumors of Wars	97
Chapter 8 - Earthquakes, Famines and Plagues	101
Chapter 9 An Increase of Immorality and Wickedness	107
Chapter 10 - The Book of Daniel and The New World Order (Globalism)	119
Chapter 11 - The Roots of the New World Order (1945-1948)	127
Chapter 12 - The European Union and The New World Order	135
Chapter 13 - A Sustainable World and "The Great Reset"	155
Chapter 14 - Globalism and the United States	179
Chapter 15 - Globalism and the Pandemic	211
Chapter 16 - Mark of the Beast, 666 & Current Developments	253
Chapter 17 - Gog and Magog (Ezekiel 38 & 39)	269
Chapter 18 - The Antichrist & The Mystery of Lawlessness	281
Chapter 19 - As In the Days of Noah (Nephilim & UFOs)	295

Chapter 20 - Matthew 24 and The Seals of Revelation 307
Chapter 21 - Spiritual Battles 313

SECTION 2 - WHAT HAS GOD PROMISED?
Chapter 22 - God's Plans For The Last Days 319
Chapter 23 - Jesus Christ Will Come Again! (He Shall Reign!) 335
Chapter 24 - All Things For Good (Romans 8:28) 345

SECTION 3 - HOW SHOULD WE THEN LIVE?
Chapter 25 - Ready For Eternity 349
Chapter 26 - Awake, Alert and Sober Minded 355
Chapter 27 - Attached to the Heart of God 359
Chapter 28 - Be Heavenly Minded! 369
Chapter 29 - Leaning Into God's Grace 371

CONC. - LIFT UP YOUR HEAD, YOUR REDEMPTION IS NEAR! 387

ACKNOWLEDGMENTS

Thanks to my lovely wife Val for her love and support throughout our 40+ years of marriage and ministry. Val, your patience over the years and your willingness to humbly serve in the background is what has allowed me to pursue the things to which God has called me. We truly are a team! You are a great example of someone with a Christ-like spirit! I Love You Val!

Thanks to the directors, team members and financial supporters of Local Church Apologetics. After more than seven years now of pursuing this God directed ministry we continue to be amazed at what the Lord is doing through LCA. Without each of you, we could not function as a ministry and accomplish our God given mission.

Thanks to Pastor Dale Crall, my mentor and friend. Dale, your passion for the study and proclamation of end time prophecy inspired me 40 years ago and continues to impact me today!

Thanks to Willie Herath for your friendship and help in designing the cover for this book and others I have written. Thanks for teaching me how to typeset and publish a book! What a valuable gift of time you have given, allowing me to communicate much of what the Lord has given me to share!

Thanks to my 3 sons, my daughter-in-laws, and my grandkids for bringing joy to my life in so many ways! I pray that you all grow in your faith and accomplish much in this life for Jesus and His Kingdom! Always trust Jesus and be ready for His return! Love you lots!

Thanks to my wonderful Mom & Dad who raised me to know and serve Jesus Christ! I am forever grateful for your love, example and training!

INTRODUCTION

Why Are These Things Important?

Each of us desires to understand why things are happening in the world we live in today as they are. Oftentimes it makes it easier to face things in life if we have an understanding of how specific things fit within the bigger picture. Understanding Bible prophecy concerning the end times helps us to understand the things that are transpiring in the world we live in. It also helps us to know what to expect, what to beware of and how to react. Most importantly, it helps us to know what to stay focused on!

Some have said that over 25% of the verses in the Bible contain predictive prophecy. I have not taken the time to confirm this but I can affirm that there is a great deal of predictive prophecy in the Bible. This fact confirms the importance of understanding these prophecies and how they relate to each of us and the world we live in today.

In over 40 years of Christian ministry I have found that people are hungry to learn about Bible prophecy. We seem to instinctively know that something big is unfolding in the events happening around us. We desire to know what God has told us in advance about these things. Our faith in the Bible is strengthened as we see Bible prophecy coming to pass, even in our own lifetime!

As a young pastor in the mid 1980s I wrote a booklet called "One Minute Till Midnight" that dealt with the events in the world today that are fulfilling end time prophecies of the Bible. To my utter surprise I soon began receiving letters from all around the United

INTRODUCTION

States requesting various numbers of copies of the booklet. I even received letters from a few other countries requesting copies. All this before the internet, facebook or cell phones existed to spread the word about my booklet. We produced these simple booklets at the church and shipped them out as requests came in from near and far. I then realized how interested Christians around the world were in understanding world events and their relationship to Bible prophecy.

After 34 years of pastoring the same church in Moline, IL. I stepped away from pastoring in January of 2016 to devote the rest of my life to a ministry in apologetics. We began a ministry entitled "Local Church Apologetics". I now travel and speak, write and develop resources to equip believers, and put together apologetics conferences.

You may wonder why someone with a passion for apologetics (presenting evidence to defend the Christian faith and teach believers why we believe what we believe) would also have a passion for teaching matters related to Bible prophecy and the end times. Actually, there is an overlapping principle. Both Christian apologetics and fulfilled Bible prophecy confirm the reality of the things that we believe as Christians. Unbelief and skepticism within our culture is a great concern of mine. Both apologetics and fulfilled prophecy are great resources in helping unbelievers come to faith and helping believers strengthen their faith. Actually, teachings related to the fulfillment of Bible prophecy are an aspect of apologetics.

Understanding what the Bible says about the end times helps us see how the Bible deals with the real world that we live in. It strengthens our faith! It also helps us to be better prepared to face difficult times that we may encounter, understanding the big picture. It helps us to see that the coming end results are clear. Jesus will overcome all the powers of darkness and He will come again to earth! God's eternal kingdom will be established!

Originally, I intended to include both a study of what the Bible teaches regarding various aspects of the end times and a study of what we see happening in the world today related to Bible prophecy in one book. I then realized that this would be too much material for one book. I decided to write two books.

The first of the two was published in 2021. It is entitled "Rapture First or Rapture Later? And Why It Matters". This first book is an overview of Biblical eschatology and dives deeper into the Bible's teachings of various aspects of the end times such as "The Rapture", "The Second Coming of Jesus Christ", "The Day of the Lord", "The Great Tribulation", "The Abomination of Desolation", "The Seals, Trumpets and Bowls of Wrath", "The Two Witnesses", "The Antichrist", etc. I did include a chapter in the first book on Israel which is repeated and expanded in this book. Some of the things you might expect in this book may not be included because they are included in depth in the first book. "Rapture First or Rapture Later? And Why It Matters" is available on our website at LOCALCHURCHAPOLOGETICS.ORG or on Amazon. I encourage you to get the first book and study what the Bible tells us prophetically about the events that will take place leading up to, and following the glorious return of Jesus Christ. A greater understanding of these Biblical teachings will help you to gain a better understanding of the topics covered in this book.

Revelation 22:7 indicates that we are blessed if we study and

respond to Bible prophecy.

> *"And behold, I am coming quickly. Blessed is he who heeds the words of the prophecy of this book."*
> *Revelation 22:7*

Seeking to know and understand world events of our time and how they relate to the prophecies found in the book of Revelation and elsewhere in the Bible would seem to be an important step in being blessed as referenced in this verse.

Studying Bible prophecy and prayerfully observing the events transpiring in the world around us can help us to have wisdom related to what we should do in these days. There is a verse in 1 Chronicles that comes to mind related to this. Notice what is said about some of the tribe of Issachar here.

> *"Of the sons of Issachar, men who understood the times, with knowledge of what Israel should do, their chiefs were two hundred; and all their kinsmen were at their command."*
> *1 Chronicles 12:32*

A true understanding of the times we live in can only come through knowing Bible prophecy. Only God is Sovereign over all world history and only He knows the end from the beginning. The more we understand what He says about the end times the more we will understand what is taking place in the world. More importantly, the more we can know what to do and how to help others know what to do!

I believe that this is especially true within families. Parents and grandparents who understand the relationship of current world events to Bible prophecies can help their children and grandchildren understand and face this world with faith, hope and wisdom!

As I write in 2022 and 2023 our nation and our world face unprecedented questions and challenges. Individuals and families face uncertainties about health, finances, education, freedom and the future. It appears that the agendas of elites who aim to establish a global system which looks radically different than anything we in America have ever experienced are moving forward at alarming rates.

Apart from the anchor of Bible prophecy it would be nearly impossible to face these times with calm, peaceful hearts. Yet, for those who look to the Bible for understanding and guidance, we harken back to Jesus' words in Matthew 24:25 where He said, "Behold, I have told you in advance!". What we are seeing today is not a shock or surprise. These things are what Jesus warned us about. Not only does the Bible warn us about these things, it gives us direction as to what we should do in these days. We can face these times with peace, hope, faith and love in our hearts!

For those who have understanding through Bible prophecy there is great opportunity to help others. Isaiah 60:1-3 speaks prophetically of a time of darkness and yet a great opportunity for those who know God to let their light shine.

> *"Arise, shine; for your light has come, And the glory of the LORD has risen upon you. (2) "For behold, darkness will cover the earth And deep darkness the peoples; But the LORD will rise upon you And His glory will appear upon you. (3) "Nations will come to your light, And kings to the brightness of your rising."*
> *Isaiah 60:1-3*

My prayer is that God will use this book to help bring light to those who are in darkness and to those who are in the light but are struggling to understand what is going on in the world.

INTRODUCTION

I encourage Christians who read this book to use Bible prophecy as a way to converse with, reach out to, and help those who do not know Jesus. People are looking for answers and those answers are all found in Jesus Christ and His Word!

The Bible tells us that the end will not come until "this Gospel is preached as a testimony to all the nations!" Sharing Bible prophecy with others is a part of sharing the gospel of Jesus Christ, the One Who will soon come again and turn confusion into peace!

I pray that the Lord will bless, inform, inspire and challenge you as you read and as you study the Scriptures!

Finally, I pray as I'm sure you do, "even so come quickly Lord Jesus! Amen!"

P.S. - Many of the topics covered in this book involve controversial issues, of which people have greatly differing opinions and views. I will attempt to address these issues and express how they fit within Bible prophecy with enough boldness and directness to be helpful, but with enough sensitivity and humility so as not to alienate people with various viewpoints. The truth is, none of us knows for sure how every aspect of what is happening in our world fits within Bible prophecy. Still, we can glean extremely valuable insight into what is really going on by looking to Bible prophecy for our foundational understanding. I will include portions of researched information I have discovered on various topics. Of course, an attempt to prove every point on the multiple complex issues would be futile. My aim is to show how what is happening in the world today fits with Bible prophecy, not to promote a political or social agenda. My goal is to turn the reader's attention to Jesus, our only hope and our coming King! I encourage you to learn about, and speak about world events in these days with love, hope and faith in your heart! Let's seek to glorify Jesus in these days!

Israel, Globalism
and The 2nd Coming of Christ
(Understanding Current World Events
in Light of Bible Prophecy)

SECTION 1
What Is Happening In the World?

CHAPTER 1

"An Overview of End Times Bible Prophecy"

The Bible has much to say about what will take place in the world in the years leading up to the second coming of our Lord Jesus Christ!

The two books of the Bible that particularly address issues related to end times Bible prophecies are the book of Daniel in the Old Testament and the book of Revelation in the New Testament. The Olivet Discourse by Jesus in Matthew 24-25 also speaks directly to issues related to the end times. It is in this passage that Jesus says to us, "Behold, I have told you in advance." (Matthew 24:25) First and Second Thessalonians also contain a number of passages that speak about the end times, as does Second Peter. These are by no means the only places that prophecies concerning the end times are found in the Bible but they give us a foundational understanding of the end times that is supplemented by numerous other passages of Scripture throughout the Bible.

A few key themes emerge when we look at the book of Daniel, the book of Revelation, the Olivet Discourse, etc. Here is a partial list of key end times prophetic themes.

- The Reestablishment of the Nation of Israel
- The Struggles Over the City of Jerusalem
- The Development of a New World (Global) Order
- The Development of a Global Economic System
- The Increase of Deception Globally
- The Increase of Immorality and Wickedness

- The Rise of the Spirit of Antichrist
- The Alignment of Nations Against Israel
- The Persecution of Christians and Jews
- The Testimony of the Gospel to All Nations
- God's Patience, Not Willing For Any to Perish

In this book we will look at these key end times prophetic themes and at various details and/or aspects of these key themes. In doing so we will be able to see how the events taking place in the world today correspond to prophecies found in the Bible which describe the end times which lead up to the glorious return of our Lord Jesus Christ.

If we were to attempt to summarize even more the end times prophetic themes found in the Bible we might end up with these six categories to place end times prophecies in.

- The Nation of Israel
- The City of Jerusalem
- The Rise of the New World Order
- Deception and Increase of Wickedness
- Persecution and Battles Against God's People
- End Time Harvest of Souls

Seeing the world today through the lens of Bible prophecies brings so many things into perspective and can help us see the big picture of what is going on in the world.

Looking at the world through the lens of Bible prophecies is a part of having a Biblical Worldview. In order to understand what is going on, what is right and wrong, and how we should respond and live, we should pursue an understanding of Bible prophecies. With so much deception in the world today, which was spoken of much in the Bible, we need solid ground to build our lives upon. That solid ground is the Bible! Interpreting what is happening in the world through the lens of Bible prophecies is a part of building our lives on that solid ground!

Many warnings about massive deception in the end times are given in the Bible! I believe we are now living in the times when those warnings must be heeded in order to not be led astray. Individual believers and Christian families need to view world events today through the lens of Bible prophecies as a part of their defense against the deception that continues to saturate cultures throughout the world today!

> *"But the Spirit explicitly says that in later times some will fall away from the faith, paying attention to deceitful spirits and doctrines of demons,"*
> 1 Timothy 4:1

As we look together at various aspects of Bible prophecies concerning the end times we will gain understanding that can help us love the truth of God's Word and avoid the deception of deceitful spirits and the doctrines of demons promoted in the end times.

Before closing this chapter I want to mention a prophetic passage that I find fascinating. I mention this here because it doesn't really fit in any of the other chapters and would not merit a separate chapter on its own.

The book of Daniel is very prophetic in its contents. Chapters 7-12 are almost completely prophetic. Towards the end of Daniel's prophesying he is given some curious information along with some instructions. In Daniel 12:4 we read this.

> *"But as for you, Daniel, conceal these words and seal up the book until the end of time;* **many will go back and forth, and knowledge will increase."** Daniel 12:4

It is interesting to note that this curious piece of information given to Daniel 2500 years ago describes so accurately the changes in the world over the past 100 years, that have led us to a time when the whole world is connected like never before since nations developed across the globe. I think most would agree that the two most striking advances that have brought great change into the world over the past 100 years are the increase in travel and the increase in knowledge. A hundred years ago men could not travel faster than the speed of a horse. Today, traveling around the world is commonplace. The world is a smaller place because of the increase of travel. The increase of knowledge since the development of computer technology is just as staggering, if not more. The ability for people around the world to know and believe the same things has been greatly increased in the age of the internet.

    The Bible predicted these things millennia ago along with so many other things we will speak of that comprise the landscape of the world scene today!

CHAPTER 2

Israel, God's Timepiece

There are many things that have happened, and are happening in the world today that are fulfillments of Bible prophecy. These things give indication that we are living in the latter years.

None of these world events are more significant than what we can see has happened with the Jewish people and the nation of Israel within the past 125 years of world history. We are actually watching biblical prophecies being fulfilled before our very eyes. In this chapter I will present an overview of the fulfilled prophecies concerning the nation of Israel that we have witnessed in the world in recent years.

Israel (The Jewish People) - God's Chosen People

The Bible makes it clear that the Jewish people have been chosen by God to fulfill His purposes. They are God's people and are the apple of His eye. Note the following examples of passages that present this truth.

> "But now, thus says the LORD, your Creator, O Jacob, And He who formed you, O Israel, "Do not fear, for I have redeemed you; **I have called you by name; you are Mine!**" *(Isaiah 43:1)*

> *"For you are a holy people to the LORD your God, and* **the LORD has chosen you to be a people for His own possession** *out of all the peoples who are on the face of the earth."* *(Deuteronomy 14:2)*

> *"Remember these things, O Jacob, And Israel, for you are My servant; I have formed you,* **you are My servant, O Israel, you will not be forgotten by Me**.*"*
> *(Isaiah 44:21)*

> *"Hear this word which the LORD has spoken against you, sons of Israel, against the entire family which He brought up from the land of Egypt: "***You only have I chosen among all the families of the earth***; Therefore I will punish you for all your iniquities."* *(Amos 3:1-2)*

> *"For thus says the LORD of hosts, "After glory He has sent me against the nations which plunder you,* **for he who touches you, touches the apple of His eye**.*"*
> *(Zechariah 2:8)*

In addition to these Old Testament passages we are given great insight into God's purposes for Israel in Romans, chapter 9 in the New Testament.

> *"Who are Israelites, to whom belongs the adoption as sons, and the glory and the covenants and the giving of the Law and the temple service and the promises, (5) whose are the fathers, and from whom is the Christ according to the flesh, who is over all, God blessed forever. Amen."* *(Romans 9:4-5)*

So, the Jews are God's people because He has chosen them to be His people and they are the apple of His eye. Also, the Jews are God's people because He has chosen to use them to accomplish His purposes for all people and all nations. In Romans

9:4-5 we are told that to the Israelites belong -

    (1) the adoption as sons
    (2) the glory and the covenants
    (3) the giving of the law and temple service
    (4) the giving of God's promises
    (5) the fathers of the faith
    (6) the Christ, came for the world through them

As Christians, we are the beneficiaries of all of these things. We and all the nations of the world benefit from that which God has brought into the world through the nation of Israel. Our Savior, Jesus Christ, Who is the Messiah for all people and nations came to us through Israel. Apart from Him we would have no hope! We should have a deep love and appreciation for the Jewish people since our Savior came to this world through them.

> *"**In your seed all the nations of the earth shall be blessed**, because you have obeyed My voice."*
> *(Genesis 22:18)*

> *"Now the promises were spoken to Abraham and to his seed. He does not say, "And to seeds," as referring to many, but rather to one, "**And to your seed," that is, Christ**."*
> *(Galatians 3:16)*

Land Given To The Jewish People By God

The land of Israel was given to the Jewish people by God as an everlasting possession. Those who say that the Israelis are "occupiers" fail to recognize that God gave the land of Israel to the Jewish people over 3,000 years ago as a permanent possession.

> *"I will give to you and to your descendants after you, the land of your sojournings, all the land of Canaan, for an everlasting possession; and I will be their God."*
> *(Genesis 17:8)*

"The covenant which He made with Abraham, And His oath to Isaac. (10) Then He confirmed it to Jacob for a statute, To Israel as an everlasting covenant, (11) Saying, "To you I will give the land of Canaan as the portion of your inheritance," *(Psalms 105:9-11)*

"And behold, the LORD stood above it and said, "I am the LORD, the God of your father Abraham and the God of Isaac; the land on which you lie, I will give it to you and to your descendants."
(Genesis 28:13 - Spoken to Jacob)

In these passages and other Old Testament passages it is clear that God has given the land of Israel, formerly called the land of Canaan, to the Jewish people. In modern history the fact that the Jews legally own the land of Israel has been confirmed by the nations of the world. We will look at that in a moment.

Many today claim that the land of Israel does not belong to the Jews and they point to the name "Palestine" as proof that the land properly belongs to the Palestinians. Because of this it is important to know the source of the name "Palestine".

The truth is, the name "Palestine" is not Arab and has nothing to do with the Palestinians who live in and around Israel today. The name "Palestine" was given to the land in the 2nd century A.D. by the Roman Emperor Hadrian. After 3 Jewish-Roman wars over the control of the land, Hadrian realized that as long as the land was referred to as "Judea" the Jews would be ready to fight for the land, even unto death. He perceived that if the land was named "Palestine" (from Palestina, a reference to the Philistines) the Jews might lose their deep affection for the land.

Actually, Jews who lived in the area before World War 2 (WW2) were called Palestinian Jews. Even "The Jerusalem Post" newspaper was called "The Palestine Post" prior to WW2.

THE HOLY LAND

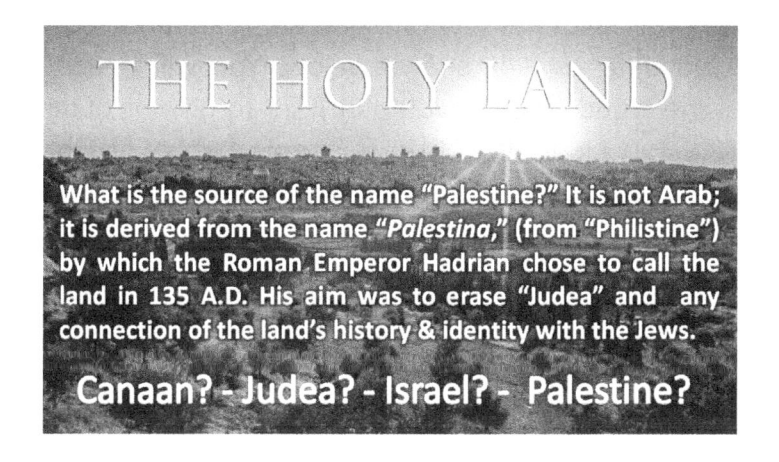

What is the source of the name "Palestine?" It is not Arab; it is derived from the name *"Palestina,"* (from "Philistine") by which the Roman Emperor Hadrian chose to call the land in 135 A.D. His aim was to erase "Judea" and any connection of the land's history & identity with the Jews.

Canaan? - Judea? - Israel? - Palestine?

During World War I the British and French armies defeated the Ottoman army and took control of much of the middle east after the Ottoman Empire had possessed this land for 400 years. After the war the victors gathered in San Remo, Italy to discuss what they would do with the land they now had gained control of. On April 24, 1920 they approved the "Mandate for Palestine" that designated the boundaries of the land in which the Jewish National Home was to be reconstituted. Notice on the two illustrations below the amount of land that was designated for Israel. The second illustration is designed to show that the amount of land was substantially more than ancient Israel.

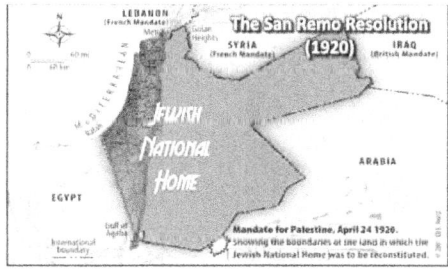

Over the next 2 years disagreements between Britain and France led to substantial alterations to the original mandate plans. The adjusted mandate plan was voted on by the League of Nations in 1922. On July 24, 1922 fifty one nations voted and approved the adjusted mandate as it is shown below. You will notice that the nations of the world officially voted in 1922 to give all of the ancient land of Israel back to the Jewish people, while giving a larger portion of land east of the Jordan River to the Arab people.

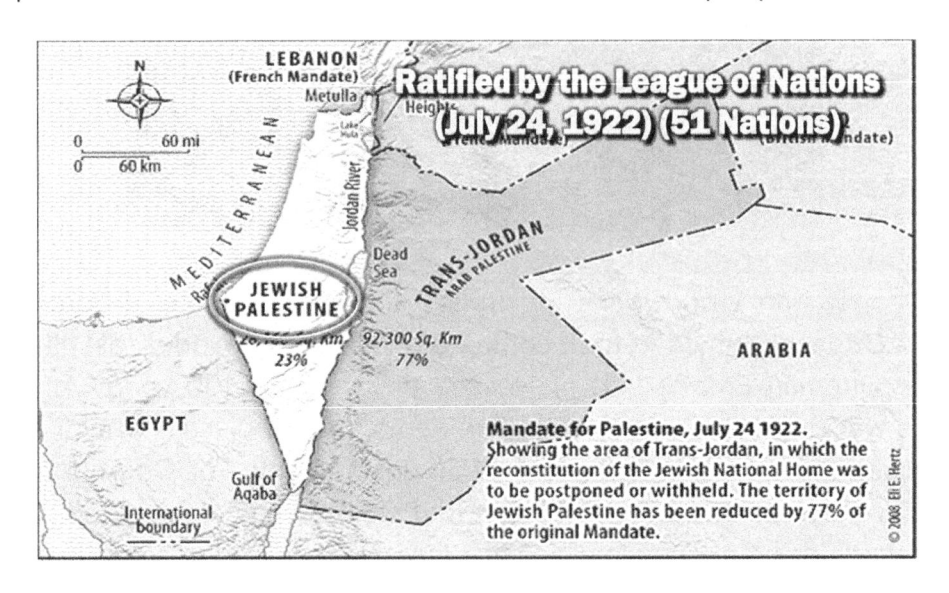

Mandate for Palestine, July 24 1922.
Showing the area of Trans-Jordan, in which the reconstitution of the Jewish National Home was to be postponed or withheld. The territory of Jewish Palestine has been reduced by 77% of the original Mandate.

After World War II, in November of 1947, the newly formed United Nations also officially designated the land of Israel as a homeland for the Jewish people, though they again reduced the amount of land designated for the Israelis. In reality the United Nations, according to their own guidelines, should not have overridden a League of Nations mandate. All of ancient Israel was given to the Jews by God. Since it was then approved as a homeland for the Jewish people by the League of Nations in 1922, the United Nations should have simply confirmed the League of Nations mandate. Nevertheless, the United Nations did again acknowledge officially that at least a portion of the land of Israel, belongs to Israel.

So we see that the Jewish people are God's people and the land of Israel belongs to them because it was given to them by God as an inheritance.

Throughout the history of the world, Israel has been the key to God bringing about His purposes on earth. It is no surprise that this is still true today.

The Fig Tree (Israel - 1948)

As Jesus spoke about His second coming and the end of the age in Matthew 24, He spoke of the parable of the fig tree and indicated that He was giving us something to look for as a sign of the nearness of His coming.

> *"Now learn the parable from the fig tree: when its branch has already become tender and puts forth its leaves, you know that summer is near; (33) so, you too, when you see all these things, recognize that He is near, right at the door."* (Matthew 24:32-33)

It is commonly accepted that Jesus was referring to the nation of Israel when He spoke of the fig tree. I believe that this is a proper conclusion for a number of reasons including the fact that within the last year before His crucifixion, Jesus spoke another parable of a fig tree that had not produced fruit in three years. In the parable He says that when the owner said it should be cut down the vine keeper asked him to leave alone for that year as well to see if it would bear fruit. (Luke 13:6-9) Then in the last week of His time on earth He sees a fig tree which has no fruit on it and curses it for bearing no fruit, causing it to wither. (Matthew 21:19-21)

Putting these two passages together along with the

timeframe in which they were spoken seems to indicate that they were a veiled reference to Israel and her lack of response to Jesus' ministry.

If Israel is the fig tree of Matthew 24:32-33 then we are directed to look at the redevelopment of the nation of Israel as a sign of the nearness of the coming of Christ.

Israel began to come back into existence in the 1890s and the early 1900s. Israel became a nation again in 1948 fulfilling a prophetic word found in Isaiah 66:8 that speaks of a nation being born in a day. Israel regained control of Jerusalem again in 1967. Since 1967 Israel has emerged as a prosperous, vibrant nation. This appears to be the sign of the fig tree that Jesus spoke about. Some make a point concerning the coming of Jesus that for centuries people have thought that they were in the end times. The biggest and most profound difference however, is that Israel, the fig tree has now put forth its leaves.

Prophecies - Israel to be Scattered and Brought Back

I believe that the most profound prophecies in the Bible that deal with human history are the prophecies concerning the scattering and regathering of the nation of Israel. No other nation or people group in the history of the world have ever been known to be scattered for hundreds of years to other nations and then regathered to their homeland to reestablish a nation again. Yet, this is exactly what the Bible prophesied would happen to the Jewish people. Most of these prophecies are around 2,500 years old with some of them being as much as 3,500 years old. I believe that every Christian needs to be familiar with these prophecies and of their fulfillment in modern times. These prophecies and the fulfillment of them provide wonderful confirming evidence that the Bible truly is the inspired Word of God!

First of all the Bible predicted that the Jewish people would be scattered throughout the world and that the land of Israel would become desolate.

> *"I will make the land desolate so that your enemies who settle in it will be appalled over it. (33)* **'You, however, I will scatter among the nations** *and will draw out a sword after you, as your land becomes desolate and your cities become waste."*
> (Leviticus 26:32-33)

> *"Moreover,* **the LORD will scatter you among all peoples, from one end of the earth to the other end of the earth**; *and there you shall serve other gods, wood and stone, which you or your fathers have not known."* (Deuteronomy 28:64)

> *"'I will make them a terror and an evil for all the kingdoms of the earth, as a reproach and a proverb, a taunt and a curse* **in all places where I will scatter them**.*"* (Jeremiah 24:9)

> *"So they will know that I am the LORD* **when I scatter them among the nations and spread them among the countries**.*"* (Ezekiel 12:15)

> *"***When I scatter them among the peoples***, They will remember Me in far countries, And they with their children will live and come back."* (Zechariah 10:9)

This in itself is profound, although some might say that you could guess that eventually a nation or people group might be defeated and scattered to the nations of the world. These prophetic words were fulfilled in the first and second centuries A.D. after the

Romans conquered the Jewish people, destroyed Jerusalem and the Jewish Temple. After the third of three Jewish-Roman wars ended with the defeat of the Jews in 135 A.D., they were left with no other options but to scatter to the nations of the world, abandoning their homeland. The next eighteen hundred years would be difficult and would include further rejections and scattering after events like the Spanish Inquisition in the late 1400s. Yet, Jewish people miraculously survived and somehow retained at least a portion of their Jewish heritage.

Certainly the more profound aspect of the prophetic words about the scattering and regathering of Israel are the many prophecies that clearly state that in the latter years God would bring the Jewish people back to their homeland and reestablish them there. I'm sure that someone reading these prophetic passages in the 1800s would have found it very difficult to believe that such a thing would be possible. The Jews had been scattered for over seventeen hundred years and the land of Israel had been under the control of the Ottoman (Islamic) Empire for nearly four hundred years. The idea of Jews returning to the area would have been hard to imagine. Yet the Bible had clearly prophesied that the Jewish people would return and Israel would become a nation again.

> "Do not fear, for I am with you; **I will bring your offspring from the east, And gather you from the west. (6) "I will say to the north, 'Give them up!' And to the south, 'Do not hold them back.' Bring My sons from afar And My daughters from the ends of the earth**," *(Isaiah 43:5-6)*

> "**I will whistle for them to gather them together, For I have redeemed them**; And they will be as numerous as they were before. (9) "When I scatter them among the peoples, **They will remember Me in far countries, And they with their children will live and come back**." *(Zechariah 10:8-9)*

"For I will take you from the nations, gather you from all the lands and bring you into your own land."

(Ezekiel 36:24)

"Then it will happen on that day that **the Lord Will again recover the second time with His hand The remnant of His people**, who will remain, From Assyria, Egypt, Pathros, Cush, Elam, Shinar, Hamath, And from the islands of the sea. (12) **And He will lift up a standard for the nations and assemble the banished ones of Israel, And will gather the dispersed of Judah From the four corners of the earth.**"

(Isaiah 11:11-12)

"'Thus says the Lord GOD, **"When I gather the house of Israel from the peoples among whom they are scattered**, and will manifest My holiness in them in the sight of the nations, **then they will live in their land which I gave to My servant Jacob**. (26) **"They will live in it securely; and they will build houses, plant vineyards** and live securely when I execute judgments upon all who scorn them round about them. Then they will know that I am the LORD their God."'"

(Ezekiel 28:25-26)

"**And I will bring my people Israel back from exile. "They will rebuild the ruined cities and live in them. They will plant vineyards and drink their wine; they will make gardens and eat their fruit. I will plant Israel in their own land**, never again to be uprooted from the land I have given them," says the LORD your God.

(Amos 9:14-15 NIV)

"Therefore behold, days are coming," declares the LORD, "when it will no longer be said, 'As the LORD

> *lives, who brought up the sons of Israel out of the land of Egypt,'* **but, 'As the LORD lives, who brought up the sons of Israel from the land of the north and from all the countries where He had banished them.' For I will restore them to their own land which I gave to their fathers.*"* *(Jeremiah 16:14-15)*

> *"I will bring them out from the peoples and gather them from the countries and bring them to their own land; and I will feed them on the mountains of Israel, by the streams, and in all the inhabited places of the land."* *Ezekiel 34:13*

All of these passages foretell the return of the Jewish people to the land of Israel by the hand of Almighty God! Jeremiah 29:11-14 also has something to say about this. Let me first show you verses 11-13. Many christians are very familiar with these verses and some may very well have them, or a portion of them, hanging on their refrigerator. My wife and I have a part of this passage hanging on our bathroom wall.

> *"'For I know the plans that I have for you,' declares the LORD, 'plans for welfare and not for calamity to give you a future and a hope. 'Then you will call upon Me and come and pray to Me, and I will listen to you. 'You will seek Me and find Me when you search for Me with all your heart."* *(Jeremiah 29:11-13)*

Now let me add the next verse so that we can see who these famous verses were spoken to and what the context of this wonderful promise actually is.

> *'I will be found by you,' declares the LORD, 'and I will restore your fortunes* **and will gather you from all the nations and from all the places where I have driven you,' declares the LORD, 'and I will bring you back to the place from where I sent you into exile.'**

(Jeremiah 29:14)

Wow, so the famous promise of God's plans for welfare, a future and a hope that we all claim as followers of Christ is actually a part of a specific promise to Israel, to bring them back from their exile to the nations back into their homeland! I do believe that we can hold to the promises in verses 11-13 by faith as a part of our inheritance in Christ, but it is also important to see the significance of these promises within the context of God's promise to Israel.

One other prophetic word about the return of Israel that I want to include is actually spoken to warring nations that God will call up against Israel in the last days for the battle of Gog and Magog. Notice the description given of the people that will be attacked by these nations.

> *"After many days you will be summoned;* ***in the latter years*** *you will come into the land that is restored from the sword,* ***whose inhabitants have been gathered from many nations to the mountains of Israel which had been a continual waste; but its people were brought out from the nations****, and they are living securely, all of them.* (Ezekiel 38:8)

So the prophecies are clear. God said that He would bring His people back to their homeland **in the latter years**. Let's look now at how these amazing prophecies have been coming to pass in the modern world in the past 125 years and are still coming to pass year by year, even today.

On August 29, 1897 the first Zionist congress meeting opened in Basel, Switzerland. Theodor Herzl, the founder of the Zionist movement chaired the 3 days of meetings. The purpose of the meetings was to discuss and develop an implementation plan for the goals of reestablishing a home for Israel. The stated goals of Zionism are seen in the statement,

Theodor Herzl

"Zionism seeks to establish a home for the Jewish people in

Palestine secured under public law."[1]

Zionism was opposed by the majority of Jewish voices around the world originally until the revelation of the Holocaust during World War II. The advancement of Zionism in its early years was slow and difficult. Ancient Israel, then called Palestine, was under control of the Ottoman Empire which increased the difficulties.

Looking back over the past 100+ years it is easy to see that both World War I and World War II played significant roles in bringing about the fulfillment of God's promises to regather the Jewish people to the land of Israel. This should serve as a reminder to us that the sovereignty of God is key in all the events of history.

During World War I the British troops in Palestine conquered Ottoman forces in 1917 and freed the region from the control of the Ottoman Empire. During the same period of time that these battles were taking place the Balfour Declaration (see below) was signed in which the British Government declared its support of the establishment of a Jewish national home in Palestine. By the end of 1917 all of this had come together, dramatically changing the prospects for Jewish people to return to the land of Israel and establish it as their home.

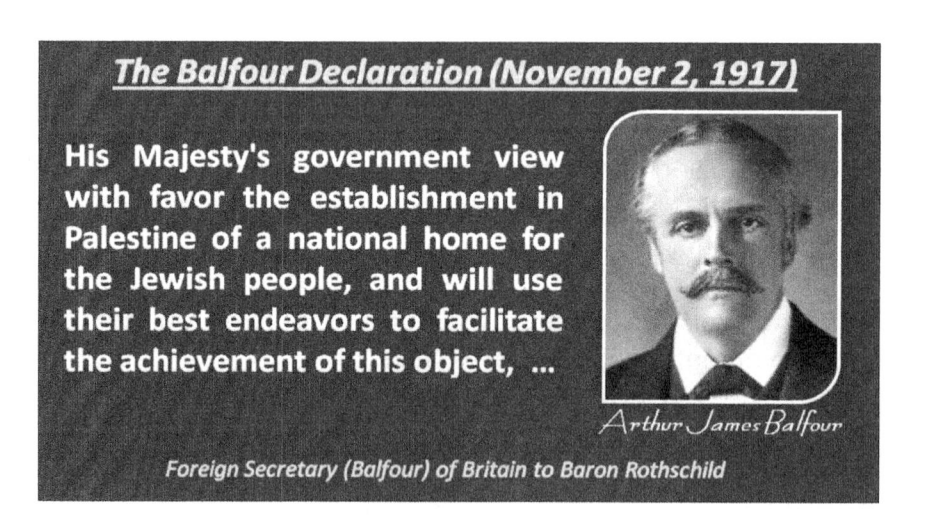

The Balfour Declaration (November 2, 1917)

His Majesty's government view with favor the establishment in Palestine of a national home for the Jewish people, and will use their best endeavors to facilitate the achievement of this object, ...

Arthur James Balfour

Foreign Secretary (Balfour) of Britain to Baron Rothschild

---

[1] Wikipedia on First Zionist Congress - https://en.wikipedia.org/wiki/First_Zionist_Congress

With these new developments Zionism gained momentum and many more Jewish people made "Aliyah" (Hebrew for "Ascent") and came home to Israel. By 1920 about 76,000 Jews lived in the land of Israel which constituted just over 5% of all Jews worldwide.

Under the British mandate established in the wake of World War I British soldiers remained in the region for over 25 years helping to maintain a stable environment in the area.

The events of World War II would involve some of the most tragic moments in the history of the world. One of the results of Darwinian theory was the rise of a belief in Eugenics which in simple terms involved selective breeding of human beings and the elimination of those humans who were deemed to be less advantageous to the advancement of civilization. One of the believers in the Darwinian theory of evolution and proponents of Eugenics was Adolf Hitler. Hitler believed that Jews were an inferior race and that they should be eradicated from the face of the earth. He sought to accomplish this goal and to establish a superior, aryan race. As a result he and his Nazi forces instituted the Holocaust and over 6 million Jews were brutally and systematically murdered over a time period of about 3 ½ years from the fall of 1941 until the spring of 1945.

Once World War II had ended and news of the Holocaust had spread, Jewish acceptance of Zionism increased greatly. Jews now felt in increasing measure that their only hope for security and safety was to gather together again in their ancient homeland. Many more Jews decided to leave their homes in Europe and other parts of the world to return to the land of Israel. From 1948 - 1957 over 900,000 Jewish people immigrated to Israel, making it their new home.[2]

On May 14, 1948 the British mandate ended and British troops departed from the region. That afternoon, in anticipation of the ending of the British mandate at midnight, Jewish leaders gathered together in Tel Aviv and Jewish Agency Chairman David Ben-Gurion

---

[2] https://www.jewishvirtuallibrary.org/total-immigration-to-israel-by-year

proclaimed the State of Israel, establishing the first Jewish state in 2,000 years. This amazing moment fulfilled the prophetic words of Isaiah 66:8 that said, "Who has ever heard of such things? Who has ever seen things like this? Can a country be born in a day or a nation be brought forth in a moment? Yet no sooner is Zion in labor than she gives birth to her children."

The picture here captures some of the headlines of May 15, 1948 recounting this historic moment. Not only did Israel declare itself a nation on May 14, 1948 but within minutes of their declaration, U.S. President Harry Truman sent notice to Israel of the United States' acknowledgment and approval of their declaration. All of this took place within moments, fulfilling what Isaiah had prophesied.

The New York Times headline included these words, "Tel Aviv is Bombed, Egypt Orders Invasion". Israel was attacked by multiple nations the first day of her newly declared statehood. Though vastly outnumbered and poorly equipped, Israel survived and defeated her attackers. Israel's army did not have a single cannon or tank and only 18,000 trained soldiers, ready for battle. Israel's air force had only nine obsolete planes. Still, with God's help Israel emerged from the war victorious. This same scenario has played out numerous times since that war of independence in 1948.

Jewish immigrants continued to arrive from all around the world and Bible prophecy continued to be fulfilled.

On June 12, 1987 President Ronald Reagan famously said to Soviet Union President Mikhail Gorbachev, "Mr. Gorbachev, tear down this wall!" He spoke these words in Berlin, Germany and was referring to the wall that separated East and West Germany, the wall that prevented people living in the Soviet Union from leaving if they wanted to. In November of 1989 the world was shocked as Reagan's demands were fulfilled and the wall came down. The Soviet Union relinquished its hold on people and allowed people to travel in and out of the Soviet Union.

As shocking as these events were, the full story was not spoken of by many or understood. Behind these events, the God of heaven and earth was fulfilling His promises to the Jewish people who lived behind the iron curtain in the Soviet Union. Amazingly, over the next two years (1990-1991), **about 375,000 Soviet Jews made their way back to the land of Israel**, continuing the fulfillment of 2,500 year old Bible prophecies, **and within the next decade almost another million Jews immigrated back to Israel**, joining those who were already living there.[3]

It continues to happen today. Each year Jewish people are moving back to Israel. "The Law of Return" has been established, helping those who return to quickly become citizens, find jobs and homes, learn the language of Hebrew, and become active participants in the country.

Consider what took place in Ethiopia in May of 1991. Over fourteen thousand Ethiopian Jews were longing to move to Israel but their circumstances prevented their departure. A few were so desperate that they actually departed on foot, determined to make the fifteen hundred mile trip across desert terrain, in order to make Israel their home. On May 24-25, 1991 a covert Israeli military operation called "Operation Solomon" was conducted, using 35 Israeli aircrafts, including C-130s and Boeing 747s, to airlift 14,335 Ethiopian Jews to Israel in a thirty six hour period! In some cases, seats were removed from aircraft in order to fit more people on board. One of the flights carried 1,088

---

[3] https://www.jewishvirtuallibrary.org/total-immigration-to-israel-by-year

passengers, including two babies who were born during the flight. That flight holds the world record for number of passengers on an aircraft.[4]

When checking for updates on "Aliyah" of Jewish people returning to Israel I discovered that there was an increase of over 30% of Jews immigrating to Israel in 2021 compared to 2020. Even with COVID-19 restrictions Jews continue to return to Israel. In 2022 an even greater increase took place as 70,000 Jewish people immigrated to Israel from 95 different countries, the largest number of immigrants in one year since 1999, and bringing the total number of Jewish people living in Israel to just over 7,000,000.[5]

The miracle of the regathering of the Jewish people back to their ancient homeland and the reestablishing of the nation of Israel is an incredible testament to the fact that the Bible is the Word of God! The fact that these unprecedented events are foretold in Scripture should greatly encourage believers and should cause unbelievers to reconsider their beliefs about the Bible and the nearness of the 2nd coming of Jesus Christ. The magnitude of the return of the Jews to Israel can be seen in the picture below.

1920 – 5.4% of the World's 14.2 Million Jews Lived in Israel
(76,000)
(Almost all had entered since 1880)
(Prior to 1850 there were only a handful of Jews in Israel)
2021 – 47% of the World's 14.7 Million Jews Lived in Israel
(6,894,000)

wikipedia & jewishvirtuallibrary.org

From 5.4% of the world's Jewish population living in Israel in 1920 to 47% of the world's Jewish population living in Israel in 2021.

---

[4] https://www.guinnessworldrecords.com/world-records/most-passengers-on-an-aircraft
[5] https://www.jns.org/70000-people-from-95-countries-make-aliyah-in-2022/

This seems to be the most incredible fulfilled prophecy in the history of the world other than the resurrection of Jesus!

This amazing fulfillment of Bible prophecy certainly indicates that we are now living in the end times, with the Jews now living back in their ancient homeland. Ezekiel 38:8 indicated that this would take place "in the latter years."

The Land Will Blossom!

The Bible not only predicted that the Jewish people would return to Israel in the last days. It also proclaimed that the land itself would blossom and become fruitful while the cities would be rebuilt and reinhabited.

> *"'But you, O mountains of Israel, you will put forth your branches and bear your fruit for My people Israel; for they will soon come. 'For, behold, I am for you, and I will turn to you, and you will be cultivated and sown. 'I will multiply men on you, all the house of Israel, all of it; and the cities will be inhabited and the waste places will be rebuilt."* (Ezekiel 36:8-10)

> *"I will multiply the fruit of the tree and the produce of the field, so that you will not receive again the disgrace of famine among the nations. ... 'Thus says the Lord GOD, "On the day that I cleanse you from all your iniquities, I will cause the cities to be inhabited, and the waste places will be rebuilt. "The desolate land will be cultivated instead of being a desolation in the sight of everyone who passes by. "They will say, 'This desolate land has become like the garden of Eden; and the waste, desolate and ruined cities are fortified and inhabited.'"* (Ezekiel 36:30-35)

To see the fulfillment of these 2,500 year old prophecies let's start by observing what the ancient land of Israel was like before the Jews began to return to their homeland.

In 1867 Mark Twain wrote a book entitled "The Innocents Abroad" in which he chronicles his journey to the holy land. He describes the region of Palestine in this book. He describes it in this way. "The further we went the hotter the sun got, and the more rocky and bare, repulsive and dreary the landscape became...There was hardly a tree or a shrub anywhere. Even the olive and the cactus, those fast friends of a worthless soil, had almost deserted the country". [6] In another place he described it in this way, "It is a hopeless, dreary, heart-broken land ... Palestine sits in sackcloth and ashes... desolate and unlovely ." [7]

From Mark Twain's eye-witness account we can see that as late as the mid nineteenth century the land of Israel did not resemble what Ezekiel had described in the least. Yet, God's Words have now come true and the blossoming of the land of Israel is a reminder to us that we are living in the latter years. Since Mark Twain penned those words over 150 years ago and the Jews made their way back to Israel in the twentieth century the land has truly blossomed. Over four hundred million trees have been planted in Israel, the rains have returned, world class irrigation systems have been installed, and Israel has become a fruit exporting nation. Cities have been built and populated, and the country has developed rapidly technologically. The changes in the country over the past

---

[6] https://blog.nli.org.il/en/mark-twain-in-palestine/
[7] https://www.jewishl.com/mark-twain-s-visit-to-palestine-in-1867/

one hundred years are remarkable and speak again to the fact that the Bible which foretold these things is the Word of God.

There is much more that can be said about the fulfillment of God's promise to bring the land of Israel to life in the last days. In addition to what we have already addressed there are numerous other important developments that can be seen.

Massive amounts of natural gas have been discovered in the Mediterranean Sea off the coast of Israel. As a result, Israel began processing huge amounts of natural gas recently in 2013. Additional natural gas fields have been opened since then, including "Leviathan" which was opened in 2019, and Israel continues to increase the amount of natural gas that they are processing each year. "Leviathan" alone is believed to contain more than twenty one trillion cubic feet of natural gas! Israel has gone from an energy dependent country to an energy exporting country almost overnight.

Prophecies in Genesis 49 and Deuteronomy 33 also appear to indicate that large amounts of oil will be discovered and harvested in a specific part of the land of Israel.

- Blessings of the deep that lies beneath will rest on the head of Joseph   (Ephraim and Manasseh)
  (Genesis 49:22-26) (Deuteronomy 33:13-16)
- Asher will dip his toe in oil
  (Deuteronomy 33:24-25)
- Issachar and Zebulun will draw out hidden treasures of the sand (Deuteronomy 33:18-19)

The map here showing land divisions for the tribes of Israel in ancient times reveals the significance of these prophecies in Genesis 49 and Deuteronomy 33. As you can see, the land area for Joseph (Manasseh and Ephraim, his two sons) looks much like a head. *(Note - I added the mouth and eye to help show how the land mass is shaped like a head.)* The prophecies said that the blessing of the deep that lies beneath will rest on the head of Joseph. The land mass for Asher, which is just above Joseph, looks like a leg with the foot and toes pointing downward. The prophecies said that Asher will dip his toe in oil. The land masses for Zebulun and Issachar are just beside Asher's toe and just above Joseph's head. The prophecies said that Zebulun and Issachar will draw out hidden treasures of the sand. When you put this all together it certainly appears that the land in this region will be a place where oil will be found and drawn out from beneath the sand. Amazing!

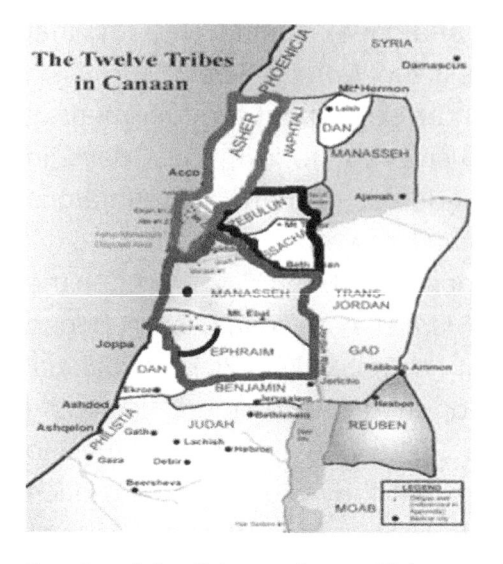

Based on these prophecies, the Zion Oil Company from the state of Texas has now been working in Israel for a number of years, searching for oil, based on 3,500 year old biblical prophecies. The company gives regular updates on their work. To date they have not struck oil but they have discovered massive amounts of oil in the very area that they searched, based on the Bible's words. The oil is very deep and they have not been able to tap into it yet but their test results have revealed that it is certainly there in great quantities. I believe that the timing of them actually striking oil will be dictated by God's last days timeline. Israel with massive amounts of oil, along with massive amounts of natural gas, may be the hook in the jaw of the Gog and Magog nations that will one day attack Israel according to Ezekiel 38 and 39.

Even the restoration of the Hebrew language was prophesied in Scripture and has now been fulfilled. As a colloquial language Hebrew had become extinct. It was only used in literary and liturgical applications. Yet in Zephaniah 3:9 the prophet predicted that God would restore the purity of the Hebrew language to the Jewish people.

> *"For then I will restore to the peoples a pure language, That they all may call on the name of the LORD, To serve Him with one accord."*   *(Zephaniah 3:9 NKJV)*

In fulfillment of this prophecy the Hebrew language has been restored in the nation of Israel today and is the official language of the country. Immigrants are taught Hebrew as they come from around the world back to their ancient home. Hebrew is the only language to be revived from extinction. This is one more aspect of the modern miracle of the nation of Israel.

The City of Jerusalem

Prophetic Scripture not only has much to say about the nation of Israel, but speaks specifically of the city of Jerusalem as well. The prophetic words in the Bible about the city of Jerusalem are significant enough that we will look at them separately in the next chapter. The fulfillment of biblical prophecies concerning the city of Jerusalem is another part of the restoring of the nation of Israel.

A Blessing To The Nations

There is no question that the Jewish people and the nation of Israel are unique in the world. Despite having been exiled for over 1800 years and having been persecuted more than any other people, the Jewish people have not only survived, they have become a tremendous blessing to the world in many ways.

At least four different times in the book of Genesis God proclaimed that the descendants of Abraham, Isaac and Jacob would be a blessing to all the nations.

"And I will make you a great nation, And I will bless you, And make your name great; And so you shall be a blessing; And I will bless those who bless you, And the one who curses you I will curse. **And in you all the families of the earth will be blessed."** *(Genesis 12:2-3)*

"And through your offspring all nations on earth will be blessed*, because you have obeyed me."*
(Genesis 22:18 NIV)

"I will multiply your descendants as the stars of heaven, and will give your descendants all these lands; **and by your descendants all the nations of the earth shall be blessed***;"*   *(Genesis 26:4)*

"Your descendants will be like the dust of the earth, and you will spread out to the west and to the east, to the north and to the south. **All peoples on earth will be blessed through you and your offspring.***"*
(Genesis 28:14 NIV)

God spoke this promise to Abraham in Genesis 12 and Genesis 22. He spoke this promise to Isaac in Genesis 26 and to Jacob in Genesis 28. When we look at the world today we can again see Bible prophecy publicly fulfilled in our lifetime. Though a very young nation, Israel and the Jewish people have been a blessing to the nations of the world in many ways.

To illustrate this fact we can look at Nobel prize winners. Nobel prizes are given to individuals who contribute things to the world that bless the people of the world. The motto of the Nobel prize is "For the Greatest Benefit to Mankind." With the Jewish population being at approximately 0.2% of the world's population it would stand to reason that there would be very few Nobel laureates of Jewish descent. Yet, this is not at all the case. Men and women of

Jewish descent have contributed to the world greatly in every field represented by Nobel prizes and the number of Nobel laureates of Jewish descent is greatly out of proportion to their percentage of population within the world. Since Nobel prizes began to be

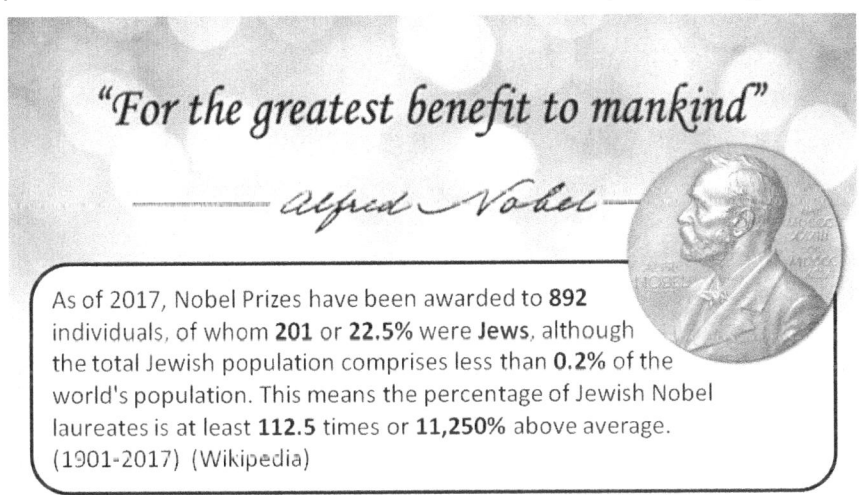

> "For the greatest benefit to mankind"
> — Alfred Nobel
>
> As of 2017, Nobel Prizes have been awarded to **892** individuals, of whom **201** or **22.5%** were **Jews**, although the total Jewish population comprises less than **0.2%** of the world's population. This means the percentage of Jewish Nobel laureates is at least **112.5** times or **11,250%** above average. (1901-2017) (Wikipedia)

awarded in 1901 over 20% of all recipients have been of Jewish descent. That is over 11,000% above average based on their population! Just as God said 3,500 years ago, the descendants of Abraham, Isaac and Jacob have become a blessing to the peoples of the world.

Israel has contributed much to the world in the way of medical, technological and agricultural advances. Israel is number one in the world in expenditures for human research and development per capita. Israel is number one in the world per capita for medical device patents.

Note the list here of some of the medical techniques and devices developed in the nation of Israel.

(1) "Apifix" system to correct severe curvature of the spine
(2) "Rewalk" robotic exoskeleton to enable paraplegics to walk
(3) "Gamida Cell" stem-cell therapy to treat blood cancers
(4) "GI-View Aer-O-Scope" disposable colorectal screening
(5) "IceSense3" removes benign breast lumps in 10 minutes

(6) "ExAblate OR" uses MRI-guided focused ultrasound to destroy tumors and uterine fibroid cysts without surgery
(7) "Bio-Weld1" bonds surgical incisions using cold plasma
(8) "Bio-Retina" a tiny implantable device inserted into the retina in a 30-minute procedure, turns into an artificial retina that melds to the neurons in the eye.
(9) "OrSense's NBM-200", a non-invasive monitor is relied upon by blood donation centers in 40 countries for measuring of potential donors' hemoglobin level (to check for anemia) and other blood parameters.
(10) "NeuroEndoGraft" flow diverters redirect blood flow from a brain aneurysm, so that a stable clot can form and the potentially fatal aneurysm no longer is in danger of rupturing.
(11) "Pill-Cam" miniature camera in a pill to visualize and detect disorders in the GI-Tract
(12) "Endo-Pat" A heart-smart device that uses a fingertip test to measure cardiac health, and can even predict whether the patient will suffer a heart attack in the next seven years.

These medical breakthroughs are just examples of the multitudes of breakthrough devices and treatments developed in Israel that are blessing the nations.

The same type of thing is true in other technological fields. For example, cell phone technology was developed in Israel along with flash drives for computers. Desalination, which allows salt water from the ocean or sea to be purified into drinking water and flowing from the home faucet within ninety minutes was developed in Israel. Desalination is now used in over 40 countries.

In agriculture, Israel has provided some of the most advanced systems and technologies used throughout the world including Drip Irrigation Systems now used in over 100 countries around the world.

There is no question that the nation of Israel and the Jewish people have been a tremendous blessing to the nations, just as the book of Genesis said they would be!

God has fulfilled His promises to bring the Jewish people back to the land of Israel in the last days, make the land to blossom, keep Israel safe from her enemies, restore the Hebrew language, and make the Jewish people a blessing to the nations! All of this is a sign that the fig tree has put forth its leaves and the coming of Jesus Christ is getting oh so near!

The Eastern Gate

Before closing this chapter I want to mention one more biblical prophecy related to the city of Jerusalem and to the 2nd coming of Jesus Christ. This prophetic word is found in the book of Ezekiel, chapter 44. Here the prophet spoke very specific words about one particular gate in the walls of the city of Jerusalem.

> *"Then He brought me back by the way of the outer gate of the sanctuary, which faces the east; and it was shut. The LORD said to me, "This gate shall be shut; it shall not be opened, and no one shall enter by it, for the LORD God of Israel has entered by it; therefore it shall be shut. "As for the prince, he shall sit in it as prince to eat bread before the LORD; he shall enter by way of the porch of the gate and shall go out by the same way."* (Ezekiel 44:1-3)

Ezekiel is given a vision of the gate which faces east in the walls of the old city of Jerusalem. He saw that it was shut. The prophetic vision that he is shown reveals this important message. "This gate will be shut and will remain shut until the prince, the messiah, returns and again enters by way of this gate."

That's pretty specific! One gate in the walls of the city will be shut up. It will remain shut until Jesus, the messiah, comes back and enters by this gate into the city.

The Eastern (or Golden) Gate

Those who have had the privilege of traveling to Israel and visiting the city of Jerusalem have been able to see the fulfillment of this prophecy before their very eyes, at least the first part of the prophecy. The eastern gate, which is also called the "golden gate" and "the beautiful gate", in the ancient wall of the city of Jerusalem has been walled shut for nearly five hundred years. It is shut today, and it will remain shut until Jesus returns! Praise God!

Israel, the fig tree that Jesus spoke of, has put forth its leaves! So many Bible prophecies have been fulfilled in Israel over the past 125 years and are still being fulfilled today! All of this reminds us that the Bible is the Word of God and that Jesus is coming back soon!

Though many other fulfilled prophecies indicate that Jesus Christ is coming back soon, none are more significant than these prophecies concerning the nation of Israel and the Jewish people!

CHAPTER 3

"Jerusalem and The Nations"

What do you think the chances would be of predicting one city in all the world to be the focus of world attention 2,500 years ahead of time? Probably not much chance of selecting the correct city, right?

The Bible made some bold predictions concerning a city in prophecies written about 2,500 years ago. Notice what Zechariah, chapter 12 and chapter 14 boldly proclaim.

> *"Behold, I am going to make Jerusalem a cup that causes reeling to all the peoples around; and when the siege is against Jerusalem, it will also be against Judah. (3) "It will come about in that day that I will make Jerusalem a heavy stone for all the peoples; all who lift it will be severely injured.* **And all the nations of the earth will be gathered against it."**
>
> *Zechariah 12:2-3*

> **"For I will gather all the nations against Jerusalem to battle**, and the city will be captured, the houses plundered, the women ravished and half of the city exiled, but the rest of the people will not be cut off from the city. **Then the LORD will go forth and fight against those nations, as when He fights on a day of battle. In that day His feet will stand on the Mount of Olives, which is in front of Jerusalem on the east;**

and the Mount of Olives will be split in its middle from east to west by a very large valley, so that half of the mountain will move toward the north and the other half toward the south." Zechariah 14:2-4

The Bible prophecies of a day when the armies of the nations of the world will gather for battle, surrounding the city of Jerusalem. In that day Jesus will return to the earth, stand on the Mount of Olives outside the city of Jerusalem, and join in this battle referred to as the "Battle of Armageddon".

Obviously, these prophecies have not yet come to pass. Yet we can easily see that the focus of the nations is upon the city of Jerusalem in our time, more than any other city in the world. This can be seen in many ways.

An International Zone

In November of 1947, just after WW2, the newly formed United Nations passed U.N. Resolution 181 which amended and updated the "Mandate For Palestine" ratified on July 24, 1922 by the League of Nations which designated all of ancient Israel as a homeland for the Jews. In U.N. Resolution 181, some of what had been given back to the Jewish people in 1922 by the nations of the world was now taken from them and given to Arab Palestinians who had been given a larger landmass east of the Jordan river in 1922 by the League of Nations. (see Chapter 2 for more details on these matters). U.N. Resolution 181 did confirm part of the measure passed in 1922 by the League of Nations and designated a part of the land of Israel as a homeland for the Jewish people.

U.N. Resolution 181 also reveals the tension surrounding the city of Jerusalem at that time. Not knowing how to deal with the tensions between Arabs and Jews concerning the city of Jerusalem, the United Nations separated Jerusalem and the area around the city and designated it as an "International Zone".

It is difficult to see the details on the map shown here but if you look closely you can see that the area around Jerusalem is designated differently that the Arab or Jewish areas and that there is an "International Boundary" established around the city.

According to a paper dealing with the city of Jerusalem, prepared by the United Nations in 1997, the primary reasoning for the designation of Jerusalem as an International zone was the need for protection of Holy places within the city and surrounding areas. In addition to this was the demographics of the city area at that time. By December 1946 an estimated 102,000 Jews, 104,000 Muslims and 46,000 Christians were in the Jerusalem sub-district.[1]

I find it interesting that the area included in the International zone designation includes both the city of Jerusalem and the town of Bethlehem. The birthplace of Jesus and the place of His death and resurrection are both in the crosshairs of world attention 2,000 years after His first coming and His work of redemption was accomplished. I have included a blowup of the designated International zone to show this.

The United Nations paper prepared in 1997 entitled "The Status of Jerusalem" says much about the city of Jerusalem that helps us to understand its significance and the tensions that surround it. Note the following statements:

---

[1] https://www.un.org/unispal/wp-content/uploads/2016/07/The-Status-of-Jerusalem-Engish-199708.pdf (page 5)

"The status of Jerusalem is one of the most sensitive and contentious issues in the Arab-Israeli conflict, with ramifications well beyond the parties themselves. Because of its emotional and potentially explosive significance, negotiations on Jerusalem have been postponed to the negotiations on the permanent status between Israel and the Palestine Liberation Organization (PLO)." [2]

"Jerusalem, Al-Quds in Arabic, Jerushalayim in Hebrew, is the site of the Western (Wailing) Wall, the last remnant of the second Jewish Temple; the Church of the Holy Sepulchre and the Passion of Crucifixion; and the Al-Aqsa Mosque, the first kibla and third holiest sanctuary of Islam. Accordingly, the City holds enormous religious significance for millions of believers of the three monotheistic religions throughout the world. One of the oldest cities in the world, throughout history Jerusalem has been at the crossroads of cultures and civilizations, and a destination for pilgrims and conquerors. Since antiquity, innumerable battles for its control have been fought by different peoples and groups, which have left a city of unique cultural and religious depth and texture. Since the nineteenth century, the City has been the object of conflicting claims by Jews and Palestinian Arabs; those claims have acquired a political and territorial dimension in addition to the religious one, since both peoples consider the City the

---

[2] https://www.un.org/unispal/wp-content/uploads/2016/07/The-Status-of-Jerusalem-English-199708.pdf (page 3)

embodiment of their national essence and right to self-determination." [3]

The importance of the city of Jerusalem within the world today is hard to overstate. Some would attempt to minimize the Bible's prediction of this importance by bringing attention to the fact that Jerusalem is a key location for 3 major religions which naturally brings it into attention and controversy. It is true that Jerusalem's importance to 3 major world religions is a key to the tensions that surround the city, but it must be noted that when the prophecies in the Bible concerning the city of Jerusalem were written only Judaism existed of these 3 monotheistic world religions. Christianity was established about 500 years later and Islam over 1,100 years later.

Capital City

Jerusalem was in essence the capital of the nation of Israel in ancient times and has been the capital of modern Israel since its beginning in 1948. This fact angers many who do not believe that Israel has a right to the city.

On May 14, 2018 the United States officially moved its embassy from TelAviv to Jerusalem and acknowledged the city of Jerusalem as the capital of the nation of Israel. This act sparked celebration by some and great anger in others. Though it is the common practice around the world to place foreign embassies in the capital of the country they are in, this has not been true in Israel, where most foreign embassies have been located in the TelAviv area. A few other nations followed the United States' lead and moved their embassy to Jerusalem while most refused to make such a move.

Palestinians have sought acknowledgment of a Palestinian State by the United Nations for a number of years and have stated

---
[3] ibid

that when they achieve statehood Jerusalem will be their capital. The Palestinian flag has flown in front of the United Nations headquarters, along with other national flags since 2015. All of this adds to the tensions regarding the city of Jerusalem and shows the great potential for even greater turmoil in the near future since Israeli leaders have indicated they are resistant to the thought of Jerusalem being the capital of a Palestinian State.

The United Nations and Jerusalem

While the United States has shown support for Israel and its right to Jerusalem as its capital, the United Nations has continually stood in opposition to Israel and blamed Israel for the tensions between them and Palestinians.

There is a long history of this. As recently as December 1, 2021 this can be seen. Three resolutions were passed on December 1st by a vote of 129-11 with 31 nations abstaining. All 3 of the resolutions pointed blame and criticized Israel for issues related to the land of Israel and the city of Jerusalem.

The text of the UNGA's "Jerusalem resolution," however, threw the most mud at Israel. The text made no mention of the holy city's ties to Judaism or Christianity. It referred to the Temple Mount only by its Arabic name, *al-Haram al-Sharif*. It "deplored" Israeli settlement activity in and around Jerusalem, and Israeli "acts of provocation and incitement" at the city's holy site. [4]

The votes came on the heels of the UN's annual "Day of Solidarity With the Palestinians" on November 29. November 29th was the day in 1947 when the UN General Assembly endorsed the Partition Plan, a recommendation to divide British Mandate Palestine into Jewish and Arab states.

---

[4] https://unitedwithisrael.org/at-un-129-countries-erase-jewish-ties-to-jerusalem/

The attention of the nations of the world to Israel and the city of Jerusalem is undeniable.

A Chilling Chant

Of all the examples of escalating tensions regarding the city of Jerusalem that I have come across in recent years, none have been more telling it would seem than what took place in Egypt on May 1, 2012.

Excitement was in the air as Egyptians met in large numbers to show support for their soon to be elected leader, President Mohamed Morsi. Within 2 months from this night Morsi would become the first member of the Muslim Brotherhood to become the president of Egypt and the first person to be elected as Egyptian president in a democratic election.

As supporters of his candidacy gathered in Cairo on the evening of May 1, 2012 for a massive outdoors rally, Islamic Cleric Safwat Hegazi served as a keynote speaker. During his speech he included these words.

"We can see how the dream of the Islamic Caliphate is being realized. ... Our capital shall not be Cairo, Mecca or Medina. It shall be Jerusalem. ... Yes, Jerusalem is our goal! We shall pray in Jerusalem or we shall die as martyrs on its threshold![5]

After speaking these things he led the massive crowd in a chant that they repeated over and over again. They chanted, "Millions of martyrs march toward Jerusalem! Millions of martyrs march toward Jerusalem! ..."[6]

Though they did not act upon these words, what they chanted reveals something in the heart of many Muslims today. That is a dream of a worldwide Islamic Caliphate (Kingdom)(United States

---

[5] https://www.memri.org/tv/egyptian-cleric-safwat-higazi-launches-mb-candidate-mohamed-morsis-campaign-morsi-will-restore

[6] ibid

of the Arabs), with Jerusalem as its capital.

What are the chances of all of this attention upon the one city in the world that the Bible predicted over 2,500 years ago would be the focus of the nations in the last days?

The chances would be practically zero except for the fact that the Bible is the Word of God and He knows the end from the beginning!

All that is happening in the world related to Jerusalem is another indicator of the end times and the soon coming return of Jesus Christ!

The Year of Jubilee and Jerusalem

According to Leviticus 25 every 50th year is to be a Year of Jubilee among the Jews. Debts are canceled, land is restored to its original owner, etc. The Year of Jubilee is very significant in Judaism and in Christianity.

I want to share some information here with you concerning the city of Jerusalem and the Year of Jubilee. What I am sharing here cannot be confirmed as fact and is contested by many. I share it because of its potential merit and because some of the details, which can be confirmed, are very interesting by themselves.

Rabbi Judah Ben Samuel lived from 1150 A.D. - 1217 A.D. It has been reported that he wrote a prophecy concerning the city of Jerusalem in 1217 A.D. This prophecy can be obtained from numerous sources. One of those online sources is quoted here.

> *"When the Ottomans conquer Jerusalem they will rule over Jerusalem for eight jubilees. Afterwards Jerusalem will become no-man's land for one jubilee, and then in the ninth jubilee it will once again come*

back into the possession of the Jewish nation — which would signify the beginning of the Messianic end time." [7]

This becomes very interesting when we look at some verifiable dates related to the city of Jerusalem.

- Control of Jerusalem was taken by the Ottoman Empire (1517)
- Jerusalem came under control of the British (WWI) (1917)
- Jerusalem came under Jewish control (Six Day War) (1967)
- The U.S. acknowledged Jerusalem as Israeli Capital (2017)

From these dates we can see that Jerusalem was under the control of the Islamic Ottoman Empire for exactly 400 years, from 1517-1917. This would be 8 Jubilee cycles. Jerusalem was controlled by the British under the British Mandate from 1917-1948 and under international control still from 1948-1967. So for 50 years, from 1917-1967 Jerusalem was under the control of Gentiles and was like a no-man's land. Its' final status continued in a wait and see posture during those 50 years. Then in 1967 during the Six Day War the Jews took control of Jerusalem for the first time since the days before the Babylonian captivity more than 500 years before the time of Christ. Israel has had control of the city of Jerusalem since 1967. 50 years after Israel gained control of Jerusalem the United States publicly acknowledged Jerusalem as the Israeli capital as President Donald Trump announced this acknowledgment on December 6, 2017 and also announced that the planning and work toward the moving of the U.S. embassy from TelAviv to Jerusalem would now move forward. This was accomplished on May 14, 2018, exactly 70 years after the establishment of the State of Israel.

There are problems with reports of Judah Ben Samuel writing this prophecy in 1217 A.D., including the fact that the Ottoman Empire did not exist during his lifetime. Still, whether or not he wrote

---

[7] https://z3news.com/w/800yearold-prophecy-claims-israel-lose-control-jerusalem/

these prophetic words in 1217 A.D. or not, the timeline of the modern history of the city of Jerusalem is fascinating as it relates to the 50 year jubilee cycles spoken of in the book of Leviticus.

The city of Jerusalem, which means "foundation of peace" will be a place of great and wonderful peace someday! Jesus Christ will return to Jerusalem and defeat those who have gathered there with evil intent. For now, all that we see developing concerning the city of Jerusalem in our time serves as a reminder that the end times are upon us!

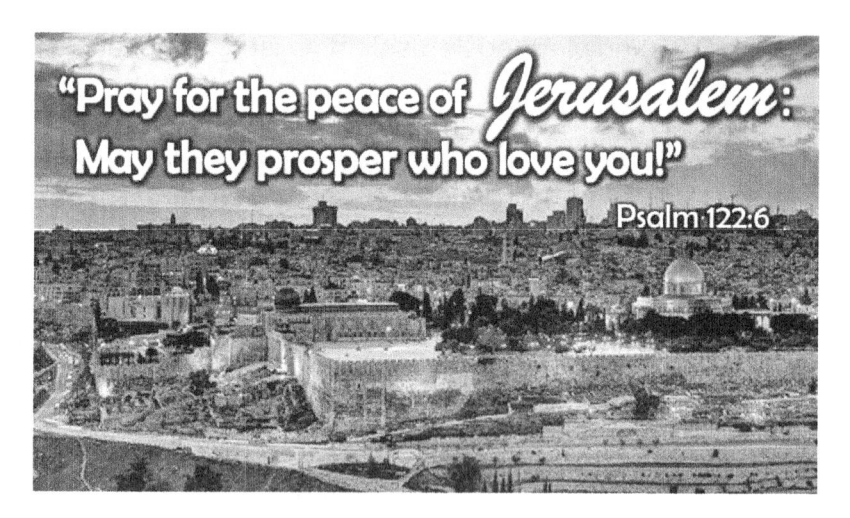

"Pray for the peace of *Jerusalem*: May they prosper who love you!"
Psalm 122:6

CHAPTER 4

"The Rebuilding of the Temple"

Within the nation of Israel and the city of Jerusalem we find activity today that provides another indication that we are in the end times leading to the second coming of Jesus Christ. This activity has to do with the plans to rebuild the Jewish temple and reestablish temple worship as it was prescribed in the Old Testament 3,500 years ago.

Before we look at some of the specific things that have happened in recent years and are happening today, let's examine why the rebuilding of the Jewish temple and reestablishing of temple worship is important in relation to end times Bible prophecy.

Though the Bible never says, "In the last days the temple will be rebuilt in Jerusalem", many who study Bible prophecy have long considered the rebuilding of the temple as a necessary development to allow other key prophecies to be fulfilled. Here are some of the reasons for this understanding.

In Daniel 9:24-27 there is a key prophetic passage regarding "The 70 Weeks of Daniel." The significance of this prophecy is discussed in my previous book, "Rapture First or Rapture Later and Why It Matters." In verse 26 of this passage the destruction of the Jewish temple is spoken of prophetically. This destruction took place In 70 A.D. (or C.E. if you're into the B.C.E. and C.E. revision).

The Roman armies destroyed the temple and the city of Jerusalem. The temple has not been rebuilt since. Verse 27 of this passage speaks of a time when a "prince who is to come" will "put a stop to sacrifice and grain offering". This will be a part of what the Bible refers to as "the abomination of desolation". It would appear that in order for this to take place the temple must be rebuilt and temple worship must be restored. Daniel 11:31 also speaks prophetically of the doing away of the regular sacrifices and the setting up of the abomination of desolation.

> "Forces from him will arise, desecrate the sanctuary fortress, and do away with the regular sacrifice. And they will set up the abomination of desolation.
> Daniel 11:31

Daniel 12:11 refers to this as well.

> "From the time that the regular sacrifice is abolished and the abomination of desolation is set up, there will be 1,290 days."
> Daniel 12:11

Jesus also referred to this "abomination of desolation" in Matthew 24:15 & 21 when gave this warning.

> "Therefore when you see the ABOMINATION OF DESOLATION which was spoken of through Daniel the prophet, **standing in the holy place** (let the reader understand), ... "For then there will be a great tribulation, such as has not occurred since the beginning of the world until now, nor ever will."
> Matthew 24:15, 21

It would appear that the abomination of desolation is set up just before the start of the great tribulation, in the middle of the 70th week of Daniel according to Daniel 9:27. Since this appears to involve both the halting of temple worship and the setting up of something abominable in the temple of God, ("standing in the holy place") it would seem to necessitate the rebuilding of the Jewish temple and the reestablishing of temple worship in the end times.

Second Thessalonians 2:3-4 also speaks prophetically about something that would appear to necessitate the rebuilding of the temple.

> *"Let no one in any way deceive you, for it will not come unless the apostasy comes first, and the man of lawlessness is revealed, the son of destruction, (4) who opposes and exalts himself above every so-called god or object of worship, so that **he takes his seat in the temple of God**, displaying himself as being God."*   2 Thessalonians 2:3-4

We are told here that when the man of lawlessness is revealed (referred to as "that lawless one" in verse 8) he will exalt himself and will take his seat in the temple of God, displaying himself as being God." There are those who believe that this is all a picture of something spiritual and that it is simply referring to the coming man of lawlessness (or antichrist) establishing himself as the one that people will worship in their hearts. I believe, as do many others, that this is referring to a literal temple. If the coming antichrist will take his seat in the literal, physical temple of God, there will have to be a temple of God in existence at the time he rises to power and sets up the abomination of desolation.

For these reasons, many, or most of those who study Bible

prophecy have looked for the rebuilding of the Jewish temple on the Temple Mount in Jerusalem as a key development in the fulfillment of end times Bible prophecy.

As of the writing of this book, early in 2023, the Jewish temple has not been rebuilt. Though this is true, it is also true that many developments and preparations for the rebuilding of the Jewish temple have occurred in recent years.

DEVELOPMENTS AND PREPARATIONS FOR REBUILDING THE TEMPLE

Growing Movement Among Jews to Rebuild the Temple

The first development involves a general growing sentiment among Jews that the Jewish temple should be rebuilt on the Temple Mount. As we have already discussed, Jews have been returning to the land of Israel for the past 125 years from all around the world. Though a majority of these immigrants are secular Jews who have little interest in the rebuilding of the temple, there are growing numbers of Jews who believe that the temple should be rebuilt and that this should take place soon.

A 2014 internet article from Israel365News entitled "We're Ready to Rebuild the Temple" says that there is growing interest in seeing the temple rebuilt in Jerusalem. Here is a portion of that article.

> *Indeed, there is a growing "Temple Movement" in Israel today with thousands of Jews working to rebuild the Temple. According to a poll taken last year in a leading newspaper Ha'aretz, one third of Israelis believe that Israel should erect the Temple on the Temple Mount. Israel's Housing Minister called publicly for the rebuilding of the Temple, "We've built many little, little temples," MK Uri Ariel said, referring to synagogues, "but we need to build a real Temple on the Temple Mount."* [1]

---

[1] https://www.israel365news.com/19539/ready-rebuild-temple/

The growing number of Jews working to rebuild the Temple is a key development toward the fulfillment of the Bible's indication that there will be a Jewish temple in Jerusalem in the end times before Jesus comes again.

Another interesting potential connection between the rebuilding of the Jewish Temple and the fulfillment of end times Bible prophecies is seen in an April 2022 article from the Jerusalem Post entitled: "When Blood Spills on Passover and Easter, It's Time to Rebuild the Temple." In this article responding to the violence which occurred on Passover at the Temple Mount the following statement is made. *"Responsible Jewish, Christian and Muslim leaders should use this recent wave of Islamic violence to immediately begin discussing practical and peaceful steps for the rebuilding of the Temple on the Temple Mount. It could be done without damaging or disrespecting the Dome of the Rock or Al Aqsa,* **as part of a future peace plan between Israel and her Arab neighbors** *to end the plague of Islamic terror once and for all."* [2]

It is interesting to consider that a potential future 7 year peace treaty, which Daniel 9:24-27 speaks of could include permission for Jews to rebuild the temple on the Temple Mount. I don't believe this is actually being considered as of now but as we see here it is in the hearts of some in Israel. If this were to happen the temple could be built very quickly since many preparations have already been completed.

The Temple Institute

An organization has emerged within Israel over the past few decades that is dedicated to the work of rebuilding the Jewish temple. The Temple Institute is intricately involved in many aspects of preparing for the rebuilding of the temple, from preparing

---

[2] https://m.jpost.com/christianworld/article-704445/amp

blueprints, preparing the priestly garments and the items used in temple worship, to the training of priests to serve in the new temple.

The Temple Institute's Holy Temple Museum includes a state-of-the-art presentation of the Temple-ready sacred vessels, garments of the High Priest, oil-paintings depicting aspects of the Divine service of the Holy Temple and a model of the Holy Temple. Visitors come from around the world to see the displays included at the museum and visitor's center.

Over sixty sacred Temple vessels have been produced by the Temple Institute, including some of the most difficult and complicated items, such as the Menorah and the High Priest's breastplate, including the precious stones of the breastplate. The recently created stones of the breastplate were investigated with the help of professional gemologists, geologists and other experts.

The Temple vessels that have been produced by the Temple Institute are not just for display, they are made to Bible specifications so that they can be used in temple worship in the new temple. Included in these vessels is the menorah which weighs one-half ton. It contains forty five kilograms of twenty four karat gold and it now stands for the public to see in Jerusalem's old city Jewish Quarter, overlooking the Temple Mount.

Here is a listing of some of the vessels that the Temple Institute has prepared along with their purposes or uses.

Sacred Vessels Prepared by the Temple Institute according to Exact Biblical Requirements

ITEM	PURPOSE
Copper Laver	For Priests to wash at start of day
Mizrak	Holds blood from sacrificial animals
Large Mizrak	Holds blood from larger sacrificial animals
Three-pronged Fork	To arrange offerings on altar
Measuring Cup	To measure meal offerings
Copper vessel for Meal Offerings	To prepare meal offerings
Silver Shovel	To remove ashes from altar
Silver Vessel for Wine Libation	For wine accompanying offerings
Lottery Box	For Yom Kippur (Day of Atonement)
Silver Altar Cup for Water Libation	For Sukkot (Feast of Tabernacles)
Silver Libation Vessels	For Sukkot (Feast of Tabernacles)
Sickle	To reap the Omer barley
Other Offering Implements	To offer the Omer barley
Abuv	To roast the Omer barley
Menorah Cleansing Vessel	To clean the Menorah
Oil Pitcher	For replenishing the Menorah
Small Golden Flask	For replenishing individual Menorah lamps
Frankincense Censer	
Incense Chalice	For Ketoret (Incense Offering)
Incense Shovel	For Ketoret (Incense Offering)
Menorah	For light by burning of Olive Oil
Table of Showbread	To display Showbread
Incense Altar	For Ketoret (Incense Offering)
Ark of the Covenant (Mock Up)	For the Most Holy Place
Crown	To be worn by the High Priest
Garments of the High Priest	To be worn by the High Priest
Silver Trumpets	Announce special occasions and offerings
Gold-plated Shofar	For Rosh Hashanah (Feast of Trumpets)
Silver-plated Shofar	For fast days
Harp	For choir of Levites singing Psalms
Lyre	For choir of Levites singing Psalms

Some of these items are quite large and others are very small but all have been made with great care. Gold and silver have both been used in great quantities in order to make these items in accordance with the Bible's directions so that they can be used in the rebuilt temple. From the Copper Laver that the priests would wash their hands in each morning, to the gold-plated shofars to be blown each year during the Feast of Trumpets, to the Table of Showbread used to hold the special Showbread in the temple, to the Mizrak used to hold the blood of animal sacrifices. All of these have been completed and are on display in the Temple Institute's Museum.

Training of Levitical Priests

As mentioned above, priestly garments are among the items for temple use that have been prepared by the Temple Institute, as well as a crown to be worn by the High Priest. Also, the breastplate with precious stones, to be worn by the high priest has been prepared and is ready to be worn when temple worship is restored.

The identifying of potential priests of the lineage of Aaron, as well as the training of those priests is another part of the mission of the Temple Institute.

The Nezer HaKodesh Institute for Kohanic Studies has been established by the Temple Institute in order to train young priests ("Kohanim") so that they will be ready to serve in the temple when it is rebuilt. This training is taking place even now.

Also, in 2009 a field school was built in Mizpe Yericho to prepare Kohanim (priests) and Levites for service in the Third Temple. "The Third Temple Academy" in Mitzpe Yericho is about a 20-minute drive from Jerusalem on the road that leads to Jericho and the Jordan Valley. By building a replica of the Temple, the school has been able to give the priestly students a hands-on experience of Temple sacrificial worship. Kohanim are also being trained to perform the regular Temple duties or the daily Tamid service that is performed in the Holy Temple.[3]

Modern science has also played a role in the preparations for the reestablishing of temple worship. It is important that those who serve as priests in the new temple be descendants of Moses' brother Aaron. Aaron and his family were chosen by God to serve as priests and to perform temple worship.

In recent decades advancements in DNA technology have helped to confirm men from various parts of the world who are descendants of Aaron. Y-Chromosome data is used in determining this, helping to identify men who are qualified to train to serve as priests. Some, when realizing that they are descendants of Aaron, have been so stirred that they moved to Israel and have begun training to become priests.

"Techelet" Special Blue-Violet Dye

The Bible prescribed the use of a specific shade of blue (or violet) to be used in the curtains of the temple (see Exodus 26:1, 31), the priestly ephod (see Exodus 28:6, 31), the priest's breastplate (see Exodus 28:15), and the tassels on the edge of their garments to remind them of the law of God (see Numbers 15:38-39). The Hebrew word often translated "blue" in all of these passages as well as in many others regarding instructions for the tabernacle curtains, temple curtains and priestly garments is "tekeleth", "techelet" or "tekhelet". It means blue or violet but specifically means "the cerulean mussel, that is, the color (violet) obtained therefrom or stuff dyed therewith: - blue."[4]

This color dye is obtained from a medium sized sea snail identified as *"Hexaplex trunculus".*

---

[3] https://free.messianicbible.com/feature/Israels-priests-prepare-third-temple/
[4] Strong's Exhaustive Concordance (Hebrew Word - H8504)

The amazing thing about all of this is that the understanding of how to manufacture or obtain this color was lost hundreds of years ago. Only in recent decades has the secret been rediscovered and "techelet" blue dye is now being produced again in Israel. Because of these recent developments another important component to the necessary processes in rebuilding the temple and reestablishing temple worship is now in place.

A Red Heifer

Another important part of temple worship involved cleansing with a mixture that included the ashes of a Red Heifer.

> *"This is the statute of the law which the LORD has commanded, saying, 'Speak to the sons of Israel that they bring you an unblemished red heifer in which is no defect and on which a yoke has never been placed. (3) 'You shall give it to Eleazar the priest, and it shall be brought outside the camp and be slaughtered in his presence."*   *Numbers 19:2-3*

> *"Now a man who is clean shall gather up the ashes of the heifer and deposit them outside the camp in a clean place, and the congregation of the sons of Israel shall keep it as water to remove impurity; it is purification from sin."*   *Numbers 19:9*

Because of these instructions in the book of Numbers, it is critical for true temple worship that there be a pure Red Heifer available to be a sacrifice so that the ashes can be used for cleaning. Since the destruction of the Temple in the 1st century A.D. there has not been a pure Red Heifer available for use in temple worship and cleansing.

Jewish tradition has included the belief the next Red Heifer to be burned and its ashes used will be sacrificed by the Messiah.[5]

Today, in Israel there is ongoing work in breeding to produce a pure Red Heifer. The Temple Institute gives updates on the process that is being used. In September of 2022 a shipment of 5 young red cows that have been inspected by Jewish Rabbis and determined to be pure and unblemished arrived in Israel from the United States.[6] These 5 young heifers are now being kept and cared for in Israel. If in the fall of 2023, when they are 2 years old, they still have only red hairs and are judged to be unblemished, they will be the first available red heifers in nearly 2,000 years! This is another development that may point to the fact that we are now in the end times.

The Ark of the Covenant

In 1981 the movie "Raiders of the Lost Ark" was released and became what many consider one of the greatest films of all time. Though the movie was fiction, the mystery of the location of the actual Ark of the Covenant has been the subject of much discussion for decades.

The discovery of the Ark would certainly be something that would advance the cause of rebuilding the Jewish temple.

On their website, the Temple Institute speak of a vast system of corridors and chambers built by King Solomon under the 1st Temple. They indicate that they believe the Ark was stored in a chamber underneath the Temple by King Josiah as he saw the destruction of the 1st Temple coming. They indicate that there are some today who know where the Ark is stored and that it is still undisturbed. They say that the Islamic Wakf, a governing body that controls the Temple Mount area will not allow excavation that would

---

[5] https://templeinstitute.org/red-heifer-the-tenth-red-heifer/
[6] https://allisrael.com/red-heifer-sacrifice-could-take-place-in-about-a-year-in-jerusalem

reveal the Ark. [7]

If this is true, obviously it could change quickly and the Ark could become available for use in a newly built temple.

Important Developments

In addition to all of these developments it is interesting to note the following events that have occurred in recent times.

In 2007 the six and a half ton Menorah which was built to Bible specifications by the Temple Institute was moved to the Jewish Quarter, overlooking the Temple Mount with great celebration and singing about "the Temple will be rebuilt".

In 2010, uncut stones were collected from the Dead Sea for the construction of the Temple altar. Such pristine stones are believed to fulfill the injunction that such building material be free from contact with metal tools. *(Deuteronomy 27:5)* [8]

A group in Israel called "The Temple Mount and Land of Israel Faithful Movement" has prepared a six and a half ton cornerstone and, since 1989, has attempted numerous times to place it on the Temple Mount, only to be forbidden by the Israeli government. Still, a cornerstone has been made ready and can be put in place whenever permission is granted. [9]

All of these developments and preparations for the rebuilding of the Jewish temple seem to indicate that the fulfillment of end times Bible prophecies concerning the man of lawlessness taking his seat in the Temple of God and the setting up of the abomination of desolation may take place very soon!

---

[7] https://templeinstitute.org/frequently-asked-questions/
[8] https://free.messianicbible.com/feature/israels-priests-prepare-third-temple/
[9] https://templemountfaithful.org/articles/the-cornerstone-is-ready.php

CHAPTER 5

False Christs and False Prophets

Of all the things that Jesus warned us about concerning the last days in Matthew 24 there is one thing that He warned us about three times in this same chapter.

> *And Jesus answered and said to them, "See to it that no one misleads you. "For many will come in My name, saying, 'I am the Christ,' and will mislead many."*
> *Matthew 24:4-5*

> *"Many false prophets will arise and will mislead many."*
> *Matthew 24:11*

> *"Then if anyone says to you, 'Behold, here is the Christ,' or 'There He is,' do not believe him. "For false Christs and false prophets will arise and will show great signs and wonders, so as to mislead, if possible, even the elect. "Behold, I have told you in advance."*
> *Matthew 24:23-25*

Three times He warned of many false Christs and false prophets that will come forth in the last days. Three times He warned that these false Christs and false prophets will mislead many. He even warned that these false Christs and false prophets will be so convincing through their deceptive signs and wonders that even the elect would be misled if that were possible. It should be noted that these last days "false Christs" and "false prophets" may not all be religious per say. Secularism has become so pervasive in the world today that many who claim no religious nature speak about issues as though they were prophetic and have answers that would make them appear as though they were "anointed ones" or "Christs".

Certainly, the appearance of many false Christs and false prophets is a sign of the end times or last days. This is another sign that we can see has come, and is coming to pass in our time.

Wikipedia has a page entitled "List of people claimed to be Jesus". On this page they list 39 different people who have claimed to be Jesus Christ themselves or who have been claimed to be Jesus Christ by others. [1]

Most of those listed on this page have lived within the past 100 years. Among those listed in this list are names that many are familiar with, such as Sun Myung Moon, Jim Jones and David Koresh.

There are other names not as familiar such as Sergey Torop (1961–), a Russian former traffic cop who claims to be "reborn" as "Vissarion", Jesus Christ returned, which makes him not "God" but the "Word of God". Also known as "Jesus of Siberia," Torop has an appearance similar to depictions of Jesus. [2]

One of the most recent examples of those claiming to be Jesus Christ is Alan John Miller (1962–), more commonly known as A.J. Miller, a former Jehovah's Witness Elder and current leader of the Australia-based Divine Truth movement. Miller claims to be Jesus Christ reincarnated with others in the 20th century to spread messages that he calls the "Divine Truth". [3]

Wikipedia has another page entitled "List of Messiah Claimants". On this page they list 50 individuals who have claimed to be the Messiah. Jesus, the true Messiah is listed along with 49

---

[1] https://en.wikipedia.org/wiki/List_of_people_claimed_to_be_Jesus
[2] ibid
[3] ibid

others who have claimed to be the Messiah. [4]

Sun Myung Moon is certainly one of the most influential individuals to claim to be the Christ. Moon started the Unification Church in 1954 which claims to have 3 million adherents. He spoke to large crowds including a crowd estimated at 1.2 million at a gathering in 1975 in Yeouido, South Korean. Moon wrote a religious text entitled "The Divine Principle" which became the main theological textbook of the Unification Church, now referred to as "The Unification Movement." Followers of Sun Myung Moon have often been referred to as "moonies".

Moon believed that Jesus was able to create the conditions necessary for humanity's spiritual salvation, but that He did not complete God's plan because He did not marry. The Unification Church identified Moon as the Messiah who will implant God's heart of love in his followers and complete Jesus' works. [5]

Jim Jones promoted teachings of "apostolic socialism" and began to claim his own divinity before leading over 900 people into a mass murder-suicide in Jonestown, Guyana.

David Koresh was originally named Vernon Howell. He claimed as a young adult that he had the gift of prophecy and eventually changed his name to David Koresh. Koresh is the Biblical name of Cyrus the Great, a messianic figure to many for freeing the Jews during the Babylonian captivity. David was King of Israel from whose lineage the Messiah would come. Koresh became the cult leader of the "Branch Davidians". In 1993 Koresh and 78 others died in their compound during an FBI raid.

Gurus

Hundreds of gurus, who are spiritual leaders from various types of Eastern religions have been followed by millions of people over the past century. Wikipedia has a page entitled "List of Hindu

---

[4] https://en.wikipedia.org/wiki/List_of_messiah_claimants
[5] https://www.britannica.com/topic/Unification-Church

gurus and sants" that lists over 200 gurus just from Hinduism. [6]

Modern gurus, sometimes referred to by other names, are numerous in other forms of Eastern religions as well.

Though gurus are not necessarily referred to as "Christ" or as a "Messianic figure", they are revered by many and considered to be much more than a simple teacher. They certainly would hold status equal to a prophet in the eyes of those who look to them for wisdom and guidance.

Perhaps the guru in modern times who has had the greatest influence and gained the most followers was Maharishi Mahesh Yogi. He lived from 1918-2008 and had influence around the world. He is known for developing and popularizing Transcendental Meditation. He is reported to have trained more than 40,000 TM teachers, taught the Transcendental Meditation technique to "more than five million people" and founded thousands of teaching centers and hundreds of colleges, universities and schools. [7]

Included in those who looked to the Maharishi for spiritual guidance were the Beatles who stayed with him for a number of weeks, listening to him and learning from him.

Maharishi Machech Yogi also founded a university in Fairfield, Iowa that is still there today and is now called Maharishi International University, along with universities in India and in the Netherlands.

Another guru who had a great following in the United States and beyond was Bhagwan Shree Rajneesh. He lived from 1931-1990. At one point after he moved to the United States and developed a great following, he and his followers bought land in the state of Oregon. He became famous for his fleet of over 90 Rolls-Royes.

Rajneesh promoted religious views that were a blend of many sources and that included a form of sexual liberation. At one point he spoke of his 10 commandments. Among them were "There is no God, other than life itself" and "Truth is within you, do not search for

---

[6] https://en.wikipedia.org/wiki/List_of_Hindu_gurus_and_sants
[7] https://en.wikipedia.org/wiki/Maharishi_Mahesh_Yogi

it elsewhere." [8]

Many young people from the west sought for truth in Eastern religion in general from the 1960s forward, and from various gurus in particular. Many combined the teachings of gurus from the east with the cultural movements resisting traditional views in the west.

The New Age Movement

During the 1980s I began to study a movement that appeared to be gaining momentum and seemingly had end times significance called "The New Age Movement". This movement certainly blended teachings from Eastern religions with modern cultural views of the west, along with views openly exalting Lucifer in some cases.

As I studied what was happening in various places and what was being taught about a great spiritual hierarchy leading mankind into a new age of reason, I could see how the roots of this, that seemed to be growing at an alarming rate, had been around for some time. I remember coming to the realization that a song I had heard in the 1960s as a kid was really a new age mantra. Some of you may remember the song. The chorus said, "This is the dawning of the age of aquarius."

New age teachings and thoughts were, and are, hard to pin down since they are all over the board. One theme that seemed pretty consistent went something like this, "Jesus of Nazareth came as a great spiritual master to lead the world into the age of pisces and now greater spiritual masters are coming to lead the world into the next age of human evolution, the age of aquarius." This kind of thinking obviously opened many up to the search for a new Messiah.

One example of new age thought related to a new age christ was found in the words and actions of a man named Benjamin Creme. Creme was considered by many to be a modern day John the Baptist, preparing the way for the arrival of the new Messiah. Creme boldly proclaimed often that the Christ was now on the earth

---

[8] https://en.wikipedia.org/wiki/Rajneesh

and was ready to lead mankind into the new age. He did interviews about this. He spoke at gatherings about this. He wrote books about this and he proclaimed this through many different ads and articles in major publications. One of those ads was a full page ad in the USA Today newspaper in 1980. It boldly proclaimed that "THE CHRIST IS NOW HERE".

The text within the portion of the ad entitled "WHO IS THE CHRIST?" is very revealing. It reads -

"Throughout history, humanity's evolution has been guided by a group of enlightened men, the Masters of Wisdom. They have remained largely in the remote desert and mountain places of earth, working mainly through their disciples who live openly in the world. This message of the Christ's reappearance has been given primarily by such a disciple trained for his task for over 20 years.

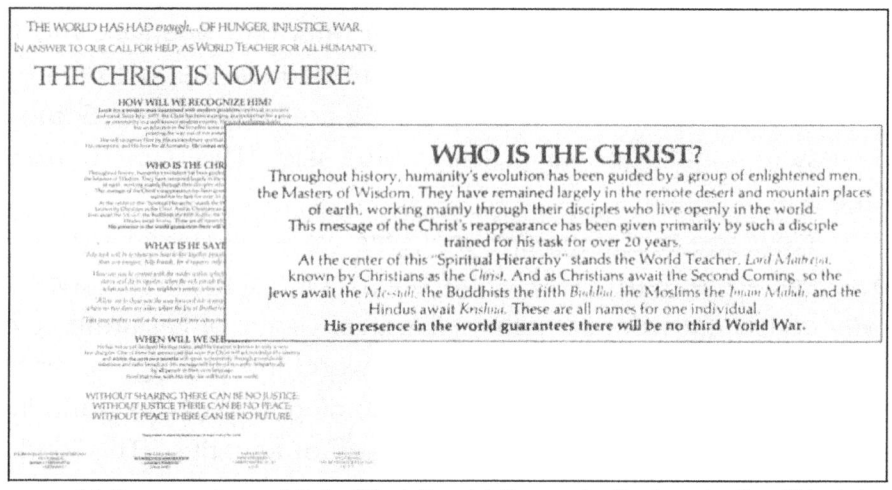

At the center of this "Spiritual Hierarchy" stands the World Teacher, *Lord Maitreya*, known by Christians as the Christ. And as Christians await the Second Coming, so the Jews await the Messiah, the Buddhists the fifth Buddha, the Moslims the Imam Mahdi, and the Hindus await Krishna. These are all names for one individual. His presence in the world guarantees there will be no third World War."

Creme claimed that the Christ had been living in London since 1977 and was ready to reveal himself to the world when the world was ready and asking for him.

Though we can see, the New Age Movement involved some false Christs and false prophets, it may be that the New Age Movement brought an even broader fulfillment of Jesus' warnings about the last days. Within new age teachings there is a belief that the Christ is not a specific individual but that the Christ is actually a consciousness that each of us can tap into, allowing each of us to become a Christ.

In an online article by the Apologetics Resource Center entitled "The New Age Jesus" author Douglas Groothuis speaks of new age belief that we can all become Christs, using quotes from new age teachers.

> "*Many argue (within the new age movement) for the separation of Jesus the individual person of history from the universal and impersonal Christ Consciousness, or Christ Principle.* His consciousness of God and miracles were evidence he tapped into a higher level of consciousness. But if Jesus tapped into this cosmic power, he did not monopolize it. New Age philosopher David Spangler, echoing the ancient Gnostics, said that, "The Christ is not the province of a single individual. As Joseph Campbell put it in his best-selling book *The Power of Myth* (1988), "We are all manifestations of Buddha consciousness or Christ consciousness, only we don't know it." Christhood comes through self-discovery; we may all become Christs if we tap into the universal energy, the Christ consciousness." [9]

So today there are not only many who have come saying "I

---

[9] https://arcapologetics.org/the-new-age-jesus/

am the Christ", but there are teachings that say, "We are all Christs" if we simply tap into the Christ consciousness within us through self-discovery."

I would be remiss if I did not include mention in this chapter of the obvious failures within the Christian church to have accurate prophetic voices speaking God's Word in these tumultuous times. I feel no ill will toward those who claimed to have prophetic words about major national and world events in recent times. I certainly am in no position to point a finger of judgment toward them. I actually have applauded those who have spoken boldly about what they felt the Lord was saying to them while much of the church has been virtually silent, watching sinister plans move forward to affect every aspect of life. Still, the fact is many of the prophetic words and visions that have come forth publicly from some Christian leaders in the past few years do not appear to be accurate and have not, at least at this point, come to pass.

As a result many have labeled a number of those who have spoken words they felt were from the Lord as false prophets within the Christian church. I am not prepared to make that judgment but would certainly agree that accurate prophetic words have been hard to come by. Because of this, it is clear at this time as I write in early 2023 that there is currently little or no confidence in prophetic voices of our time. This, I believe, adds to what Jesus spoke about, allowing for many to be misled since they are not being assisted by accurate prophetic words.

I believe that this may be happening within the church because the Lord is not pleased with many of us having become so dependent upon someone else hearing from God for us. He may be nudging us toward a realization that each of us needs to learn to hear God's voice for ourselves as we study His Word, the Bible and as we are led by the Holy Spirit Who lives inside of each believer.

Jesus said many false Christs and false prophets will come in the last days and many will be led astray. We can see that this is being fulfilled in our time.

In the next chapter we will expand upon this and speak of the alarming levels of deception at work within our world today through false religion, education, political leaders, news media, internet outlets, etc. Jesus spoke about this deception that would come in the last days, as did the Apostle Paul and others.

CHAPTER 6

False Wonders and Deception (Be Alert!)

In the last chapter we spoke of the fact that in Matthew 24 Jesus warned us three times of false Christs and false prophets and who will come forth in the last days and mislead many. He said that they will show great signs and wonders.

In Matthew 24:4 Jesus specifically said **"See to it that no one misleads you!"** Then after the third warning in verses 23-25 Jesus says this, **"Behold, I have told you in advance!"** These two statements, along with the three specific warnings of coming false Christs and false prophets, make it clear that Jesus wants us to understand that we must be alert and be on guard against misleading, deceptive people in the last days.

As we look at the world we live in today it is clear that those people and various entities that mislead and seek to deceive others abound! This is certainly one of the most identifying characteristics of the day that we live in.

There is so much happening in the world today in this vein that an entire book could be written from the title of this one chapter. We will only be able to scratch the surface of all that is happening but will be able to confirm that the Bible prophecies about deception in the world in the days prior to the return of Christ are now being fulfilled openly and abundantly!

In addition to the warnings that Jesus gave us in Matthew 24 consider the following passages that speak of deception, false signs and wonders, etc. in the end times.

*"Then that lawless one will be revealed whom the Lord will slay with the breath of His mouth and bring to an end by the appearance of His coming; that is, the one whose coming is in accord with the activity of Satan, **with all power and signs and false wonders, and with all the deception of wickedness for those who perish**, because they did not receive the love of the truth so as to be saved. For this reason God will send upon them **a deluding influence so that they will believe what is false**, in order that they all may be judged who did not believe the truth, but took pleasure in wickedness."* 2 Thessalonians 2:8-12

*"But the Spirit explicitly says that **in later times** some will fall away from the faith, **paying attention to deceitful spirits and doctrines of demons**,"*
1 Timothy 4:1

*"But realize this, that in the last days difficult times will come. ... But evil men and impostors will proceed from bad to worse, **deceiving and being deceived.** You, however, continue in the things you have learned and become convinced of, knowing from whom you have learned them,"* 2 Timothy 3:1, 13-14

*"Then I saw another beast coming up out of the earth; and he had two horns like a lamb and he spoke as a dragon. He exercises all the authority of the first beast in his presence. And he makes the earth and those who dwell in it to worship the first beast, whose fatal wound was healed. **He performs great signs, so that he even makes fire come down out of heaven to the earth in the presence of men. And he deceives those who dwell on the earth because of the signs which it***

> *was given him to perform in the presence of the beast,* telling those who dwell on the earth to make an image to the beast who *had the wound of the sword and has come to life."*   Revelation 13:11-14

> *"By smooth words he will turn to godlessness those who act wickedly* toward the covenant, but the people who know their God will display strength and take action."   Daniel 11:32

In all of these passages we see indications that the end times will be a time when great amounts of false signs and wonders along with great amounts of deception are prevalent. It is this aspect of the end times that I believe to be the most dangerous. Persecution and turmoil are temporary difficulties but being deceived to the point of turning away from faith would have eternal consequences. I believe this is why another passage dealing with the end times says this.

> *"For you are all sons of light and sons of day. We are not of night nor of darkness; so then let us not sleep as others do, but **let us be alert and sober**. For those who sleep do their sleeping at night, and those who get drunk get drunk at night. But since we are of the day, **let us be sober**, having put on the breastplate of faith and love, and as a helmet, the hope of salvation."*
>   1 Thessalonians 5:5-8

Avoiding deception and not being misled must certainly be a priority for every Christian living in the end times! Helping our loved ones to avoid deception and not be misled must also be a priority! We must be alert and sober minded! We must be committed to that which we have been taught from the Bible, God's Holy Word!

It is not surprising that lies and deception would be a distinguishing mark of the end times. As mankind strays away from

God and evil becomes more predominant throughout the world, the character and nature of Satan will be increasingly identifiable in the lives of those who will eventually be ready to follow the antichrist, or lawless one, whose coming is in accordance with the activity of Satan. The very nature of Satan is that of a liar and deceiver! Note what we are told in these two passages.

> *"You are of your father the devil, and you want to do the desires of your father. He was a murderer from the beginning, and does not stand in the truth because **there is no truth in him. Whenever he speaks a lie, he speaks from his own nature, for he is a liar and the father of lies**."* John 8:44

> *"For such men are false apostles, deceitful workers, disguising themselves as apostles of Christ. No wonder, for even **Satan disguises himself as an angel of light. Therefore it is not surprising if his servants also disguise themselves** as servants of righteousness, whose end will be according to their deeds."* 2 Corinthians 11:13-15

As we look at examples of deception in our world today we should remember that the Bible indicates that this deception will increase more and more, leading to a time when all the world, except for those who know Christ, will be ready to accept an evil, false Christ who sets himself up to be God.

Modern Lies Leading To Great Deception

Deception has been around since the beginning of time. The serpent deceived Adam and Eve in the garden of Eden all the way back in Genesis, chapter 3. It was deceptive lies and twisted half truths that led to sin coming into the world. The father of lies is ultimately behind all the deception found in the world today and he has been deceiving people since the creation of man.

Understanding this, we could not expect to identify a modern starting point for all the deceptive lies that are believed and promoted in the world today. Having acknowledged this, I do want to point to a critical development in world history that has had huge ripple effects, paving the way for many deceiving views and ideas to gain acceptance in the world.

In 1859 Charles Darwin published his book "On Origin of Species" which promoted the idea of evolution. This was not the beginning of intellectual attempts to get rid of God or to explain the origins of life without a creator. Still, this was an amazingly significant moment in history since Darwin's ideas and explanations of origins were and are accepted and promoted by much of the world as though they were scientific law. Some promoters of evolutionary ideas today with broad influence say as much. I have heard influential professors and scientists compare not believing in evolution to not believing in the law of gravity. Darwin's ideas about the origin and significance (or lack thereof) of life underpin many of the deceptive lies that are now readily accepted by many throughout the world.

In reality, there are major flaws within the theory of evolution and there are great numbers of scientists from around the world, many of whom teach at major universities, who do not accept the theory of evolution as being scientifically reliable. The Discovery Institute has a secondary website at dissentfromdarwin.org, at which a list of over 1,000 scientists from around the world expressing their doubts in the accuracy of darwinian evolutionary theory can be seen.[1] (For much more information on the issues related to Creation vs. Evolution you may want to obtain a copy of my book "Faith & Reason Made Simple", available at localchurchapologetics.org or on amazon.com.)

Still, through propaganda and sometimes outright deceit, evolutionary ideas, which in most cases eliminate God's role in creation, have been successfully promoted for over 150 years.

This deceptive idea that life came about through an explosion billions of years ago, and through random, unguided processes, has taken root in modern culture around the world and has opened the door to many other deceptive ideas.

One major error in thought that has come to prominence through the acceptance of Darwin's ideas of evolution is a false understanding concerning the nature and purpose of man. If evolutionary ideas were correct then man would have no essential value or place of prominence within the world. If man is not created by God in His image and likeness, then man is nothing special and has no more rights than any other living thing. If man is created by God in His image and told by God to rule over all of creation, then man has great purpose, privilege and responsibility.

Many deceptive ideas have sprung forth from the erroneous view of humanity that springs forth from evolutionary ideas. The destructive idea of Eugenics, which in essence is the idea that governments or a few powerful people should be able to determine who can have children and who cannot, has been accepted and promoted by some who embrace evolutionary ideas over the past 150 years. The deceptive, horrible and inhumane practice of abortion is a result of evolutionary ideas. Babies in the womb are not considered to be worthy of living if they are deemed inconvenient.

---

[1] https://dissentfromdarwin.org/

Even many of the emerging views on man's relationship with the earth are affected by evolutionary ideas. If man is created to rule over the earth then his being here is obviously a good thing. The truth found in Genesis 1:26-28 makes it clear that this is the case.

> *"Then God said, "Let Us make man in Our image, according to Our likeness; and let them rule over the fish of the sea and over the birds of the sky and over the cattle and over all the earth, and over every creeping thing that creeps on the earth." (27) God created man in His own image, in the image of God He created him; male and female He created them. (28) God blessed them; and God said to them, "Be fruitful and multiply, and fill the earth, and subdue it; and rule over the fish of the sea and over the birds of the sky and over every living thing that moves on the earth."* Genesis 1:26-28

Notice here that mankind is created distinctly as male and female. Notice that mankind is blessed by God and is charged by God to (1) be fruitful and multiply, (2) fill the earth, (3) subdue the earth, and (4) rule over the earth and all the other living creatures on the earth. According to the truth found in God's Word, the earth is for mankind, not mankind for mother earth!

In contradiction to this, if humans are a random life form that just happens to have evolved here then they may be considered a cancer on the earth, which is a growing sentiment among some entrenched in climate change mentality. For example, David Foreman, the co-founder of three environmental organizations: Earth First!, the Wildlands Project, and the Rewilding Institute said, *"I believe that human overpopulation is the fundamental problem on Earth Today"* and, *"We humans have become a disease, the Humanpox"*. [2] He also said, *"Our environmental problems originate*

---

[2] https://www.azquotes.com/quote/609353

in the hubris of imagining ourselves as the central nervous system or the brain of nature. We're not the brain, we are a cancer on nature." [3] I'll speak more about this later in this chapter.

It stands to reason that any thinking that involves not giving thanks and praise to God for life can only lead to bad results. Romans 1:18-22 warns of this negative outcome.

> *"For the wrath of God is revealed from heaven against all ungodliness and unrighteousness of men who suppress the truth in unrighteousness, because that which is known about God is evident within them; for God made it evident to them. For since the creation of the world His invisible attributes, His eternal power and divine nature, have been clearly seen, being understood through what has been made, so that they are without excuse. For even though they knew God, they did not honor Him as God or give thanks, but they became futile in their speculations, and their foolish heart was darkened. Professing to be wise, they became fools,"*   *Romans 1:18-22*

Not giving God honor and thanks as Creator, even though He has clearly made Himself known through the things He has made, will lead to foolish hearts embracing a darkened and warped understanding of truth and life.

This passage continues in verse 23-32 to describe what will take place in any culture, nation or people who decide to no longer honor God as God and as Creator. America's history over the past 75-80 years since evolution began to be taught as truth in public schools mirrors the prophetic words of Romans 1:18-32.

For these reasons I believe that though deception has been prevalent throughout history, the acceptance of the theory of evolution in the mid 19th century has set the course for a host of

---

[3] ibid

modern day deceptive ideas to come to prominence. Apart from God man is prone to believing every lie Satan puts forth.

In America today those things that are considered "politically correct" are almost always views that are erroneous or flawed. Those who allow these views to set the course of their life are deceived and being led astray. Among these deceptive views are religious views like "universalism" which promotes the erroneous idea that all religions are basically the same and all provide paths that will lead people to heaven.

Lies believed within American culture today also include lies about the raising of children, with the idea that it is harmful and wrong to lovingly but firmly discipline your child. Then there is the lie that men and women are no different and that men should no longer be the leaders within marriages and within families.

Lies concerning sexuality abound, including the false idea that sex before marriage (fornication) is not a sin, or sex outside of marriage (adultery) is not a sin. These deceptive views about sexuality also include the view that homosexuality is not a sin.

Of course, the deceptive lies that Satan promotes among people, as society moves further from God, are designed to destroy people. It is no wonder that deception causing people to flounder in their understanding of who they were created to be has become more and more common. The promotion of the deceptive idea that a person being born male or female does not determine their gender confuses and wounds many. Children in America today are often encouraged to question the biological realities of who they were created to be. So-called experts boast that they have identified 60+ gender identities or even 80+ gender identities. The deceptive confusion is rather mind boggling. Beyond this we now see some indications of people "identifying" as animals or even striving to be transhuman, part human and part computer. All of these confusing ideas are deceptive and destructive as they are promoted in society as being good and normal.

Let me pause to make it clear that I believe it is the role of Christians to reach out in love to those affected by these lies and seek to bring them into wholeness. Truth and love are not enemies, but companions! Jesus told us to love our neighbor as ourselves. When Christians encounter people who are impacted by the lies which are being promoted as truth today, they must choose to show Christ-like love and compassion.

Increasing Deception

It has become clear that since 2020 the level or intensity of deception has increased greatly! I plan to deal with many of these issues in later chapters. The deception driving much of what is taking place among the nations at this time is actually one of the primary themes of this book. I believe that many of the issues related to the COVID-19 pandemic and the move toward a "great reset" of global governance are driven by the spiritual deception which is prevalent in the world today.

If there were any question that there are at least some in the world today with radical views about what the world should look like and be like, spawned out of spiritual deception, we need only to consider a mysterious granite monument which was erected in 1980 in Elbert County, Georgia. The structure is called "The Georgia Guidestones" and it involves four very large granite pillars and a large granite capstone. The capstone has these words engraved upon it, "Let these be the guidestones to an age of reason." Engraved on each side of the granite pillars are the 10 proposed guiding principles or 10 commandments for this so-called "age of reason" in the 8 most widely spoken languages in the world.

Looking at just a few of the guiding principles listed on the Georgia Guidestones is very telling.

> #1 - Maintain humanity under 500,000,000 in perpetual balance with nature
> #2 - Guide reproduction wisely improving fitness and diversity
> #3 - Unite humanity with a living new language
> #4 - Rule passion - faith - tradition - and all things with tempered reason
> #8 - Balance personal rights with social duties
> #10 - Be not a cancer on the Earth - Leave room for nature - Leave room for nature

Some might say that this must be the work of a rich "kook". If there were not such obvious similarities between these "guiding principles" and the statements of powerful people today promoting global governance, climate control, and a "great reset" that would seem correct. Unfortunately, the truth is that these same principles are being encouraged, at least in part, by many powerful people today.

Notice guiding principle number 1, "Maintain humanity under 500,000,000, in perpetual balance with nature." The world's population today has just surpassed eight billion. This means that for guiding principle number one to be accomplished the world's population has to be reduced by seven and a half billion. This would mean that 15 out of every 16 people on the planet would need to die. There is an obvious connection between this and number 10 of their guiding ideas, "be not a cancer".

It is difficult to conceive of anyone actually believing this sort of thing. One thing is clear. This kind of thought comes from a rejection of God's stated purpose and role of mankind on earth to fill the earth, subdue the earth, and rule over the earth. This kind of thought comes from the ideas of Darwinian evolution that mankind is a random evolutionary creation, with no more importance or privilege than any other living thing.

As crazy and concerning as it might seem, there are quotes by numerous powerful people in recent years that confirm that there are many who believe in this guiding principle, at least in some manner. Consider the following quotes.

"Depopulation should be the highest priority of foreign policy towards the third world, because the US economy will require large and increasing amounts of minerals from abroad, especially from less developed countries." [4] (Henry Kissinger)

"World population needs to be decreased by 50%" [5]
(Henry Kissinger)

"The United Nation's goal is to reduce population selectively by encouraging abortion, forced sterilization, and control of human reproduction, and regards two-thirds of the human population as excess baggage, with 350,000 people to be eliminated per day." [6]
Jacques Cousteau

"Should we eliminate suffering, diseases? The idea is beautiful, but perhaps not a benefit for the long term. We should not allow our dread of diseases to endanger the future of our species. . . . In order to stabilize world population, we need to eliminate 350,000 people a day. It is a horrible thing to say, but it's just as bad not to say it." [7]
Jacques Cousteau

"A total population of 250-300 million people, a 95% decline from present levels, would be ideal." [8] (Ted Turner)

---

[4] https://www.azquotes.com/quote/609356
[5] https://www.quotemaster.org/q4acd82e70bbefa2cd6246f4f3cc404ad
[6] https://www.azquotes.com/quote/1177963
[7] https://www.azquotes.com/quote/1177964
[8] https://www.azquotes.com/quote/1309522

"If I were reincarnated I would wish to be returned to Earth as a killer virus to lower human population levels." [9] (Prince Philip)

"The optimum human population of earth is zero." [10] (David Foreman)

"The world today has 6.8 billion people...that's headed up to about 9 billion. If we do a really great job on vaccines, health care, reproductive health services, we could lower that by perhaps 10 to 15 percent." [11] (Bill Gates)

There certainly is need for mankind to respect the gift and responsibility that God has given to him. Caring for the planet we live on is a part of ruling over it, as our God-given privilege and responsibility. The satanic deception of evolutionary theory leads to the view that man is a cancer on the earth and that the earth, and the creatures on the earth, would be better off without mankind being here, or at least without a significant portion of mankind being here.

Those who have a biblical worldview and view man from a biblical perspective tend to believe that issues regarding the diminishing amounts of available resources on the earth should be considered, but should not be used to depopulate the earth, and to control the lives of people around the world.

Guiding principle number 2 speaks of directing reproduction which is what "eugenics" is all about. Hitler was a proponent of eugenics. This idea would give elites the authority to say who can have children and who cannot.

Guiding principle number 3 speaks of a global language, which would obviously assist in establishing a new world order. The tower of babel in Genesis 11 comes to mind when thinking about this one.

Guiding principle number 4 speaks of some person, entity or

---

[9] https://www.azquotes.com/quote/604927
[10] https://www.azquotes.com/quote/789443
[11] https://www.azquotes.com/quote/604924

government ruling over what people are passionate about, including their religion. It is probably not a coincidence that many skeptics today argue that religion and faith need to be replaced with "reason". Some have even indicated that they think it should be considered a crime for parents to teach their religious views to their children.

Guiding principle number 8 is eerily similar to words of globalists and climate change activists who speak of a "sustainable" world which can only be achieved by the relinquishing of many of the personal "rights" those in western culture are used to such as owning your own home.

Guiding principle number 10 comes back to the starting point, suggesting that mankind is a cancer on the Earth and that people who are here should be bunched together more to leave more room for nature.

Whether you think these guiding principles are all the weird ideas of a "kook" or not, it is important to wake up to the fact that there are many people in powerful positions today who believe the basic things that were communicated in the 1980 inscriptions found in the Georgia Guidestones.

It should be noted that the Georgia Guidestones were mysteriously bombed and destroyed in July of 2022. Their beginning and their end both evoke many questions.

The deception found in these "guiding principles" and the "age of reason" that they supposedly will lead to, ultimately have a spiritual origin that explains the disregard for mankind, as well as the disregard for the needs and rights of people, all in the false pretense of "equality" and "sustainability". Satan hates people because people are created in the image and likeness of God. Satanically, or demonically inspired ideas always come to rob mankind of freedom, happiness, and ultimately of life. Jesus addressed this in John 10:10 where He said this.

"The thief comes only to steal and kill and destroy; I

came that they may have life, and have it abundantly."
John 10:10

Just as in the garden Adam and Eve were lied to and promised good things by the one who had come to steal, kill and destroy them, so today a world that has strayed away from God follows the voice of the deceiver, the one who comes to steal, kill and destroy.

Another place we find this same vein of deception, leading toward a global, Marxist system of government is in textbooks used within American universities to educate students.

A list of the top 10 books found to be required reading in America's top universities include almost exclusively books that speak positively of governing systems that differ greatly from the capitalist, republic form of government found in America.[12] Plato's "The Republic" tops the list followed by "Leviathan" by Thomas Hobbes, "The Prince" by Niccolo Machiavelli and "The Clash of Civilization" by Samuel Huntington. None of these books speak favorably of America and its form of government and commerce. Want to guess what number 9 is in this top 10 list of books that are required reading in the top American universities? It is hard to believe but true. Number 9 is "The Communist Manifesto" by Karl Marx and Friedrich Engels. Despite the fact that history shows that wherever Marxist principles have been embraced and followed it has led to destruction, poverty and even genocide, American Universities continue to promote Marxist ideas to young American students. I will speak further about these books in another chapter.

Yes, deception has reached a level in our world today where our universities teach our young people that America is bad and that we need a "great reset", a whole new form of government that will supposedly positively impact the entire world bringing equality and

---

[12] https://www.businessinsider.com/the-most-popular-required-reading-at-the-top-10-us-colleges-2016-1#10-the-politics--aristotle-1

sustainability to us and future generations.

As universities and global organizations such as "The World Economic Forum" and "The United Nations" call for a reset of governments and economies to make way for a global New World Order, even the Pope has chimed in with agreement.

In October of 2020 it was reported that Pope Francis said, "Market Capitalism has failed in pandemic, needs reform". [13] In the article by this title it is reported that the Pope said, "the pandemic, however, had confirmed his belief that current political and economic institutions must be reformed to address the legitimate needs of the people most harmed by the coronavirus." Later in the article it is reported that "Francis rejected the concept of an absolute right to property for individuals, stressing instead the "social purpose" and common good that must come from sharing the Earth's resources." [14]

From all fronts it seems, the deception comes, with calls for a global system based on a system of government and economy that has never worked in the history of mankind, yet now is desired by many on a broader scale than ever before.

Someone might ask, how can we know that an end times global system of government and economy would be a bad thing? How do we know that it will not be a good thing that truly creates a loving world of kindness, equality and goodness? These are good questions and speak to the main issue of this chapter which is deception.

We have already mentioned indicators from past history that tell us that the calls for the classless, utopian society which Karl Marx spoke of have never materialized where Marxism has become the dominant ideology. There is also the fact that the methods being used today to attempt to achieve a global socialist (Marxist) system are themselves hurtful and deceptive.

---

[13] https://apnews.com/article/virus-outbreak-pope-francis-archive-capitalism-bcde00533 14e65612add0709fada5519
[14] ibid

In addition to these things there is a current element within the push toward a global system that indicates the spirit and heart behind it. I will allude to this briefly here and cover it in detail in chapter 12.

The European Union is a major proponent of the advancement of a global system, maybe the greatest proponent. The European Union as we know it today began in 1948 as the European Movement. Since then the European Union and its member nations have been key in the movement towards a New World Order.

What is the spirit and motivation behind the European Union? On the surface the goals and objectives of the European Union and its humanitarian arm The Council of Europe appear good and commendable. To see underneath the stated goals we can look at the group's affinity with the Tower of Babel, the story of which is told in Genesis 11 in the Bible. We will look at this in more depth in chapter 12 but for now I will simply state that the European Union and the Council of Europe have openly shown an affinity for the Tower of Babel as though it represents a good thing, people coming together for a common purpose. Yet the Bible makes it clear that the Tower of Babel was not a good thing and that God was very much displeased with those who sought to build it and accomplish great and mighty things apart from God and His help.

Nothing about the movement toward a New World Order in Europe, the U.S., or in other parts of the world presents a call for people to honor and worship God or to look to Him in dependency as they seek to build a global society. This is in sharp contrast to the Founding Fathers of America who paused for 3 days of prayer and fasting before writing the Constitution of the United States, seeking to know and understand God's wisdom and plan as they laid the foundation for a new nation.

Other Forms of Deception

Certainly, deception is found in the world today in numerous other areas, including religious thought and scientific thought. I believe that ultimately all these veins of deception will come together globally. As I mentioned at the beginning of this chapter, an entire book could be written about this subject. For our purposes here we will briefly look at a few more examples of deception seen today.

Religious (Spiritual) Ideas

In the previous chapter we spoke of numerous false Christs and false prophets, as well as the New Age Movement which promotes the idea that we can all tap into the Christ consciousness. This tends to also encourage the deceptive idea that there are many paths to God.

Consider the words of a famous television personality who has had an enormous following and is known for her kindness, generosity and charisma. She has openly expressed views about Jesus Christ that are embraced by New Age Movement teachers. Consider the following quote from her on a televised discussion. Speaking of a book she says, "It points out that one of the mistakes human beings make is believing that there is only one way to live and that we don't accept that there are diverse ways of being in the world, that there are millions of ways to be human, and many ways, many paths to what you call God, and her path might be something else and when she gets there she might call it "the light" but her loving, and her kindness and her generosity, if it brings her to the same point that it brings you it doesn't matter whether she calls it God along the way or not." A few moments later during an interaction with a person in the crowd who says that Jesus is the only way, she says, "There couldn't possibly be only one way." [15]

In another program she says this about Jesus as she speaks of understanding she received from reading a book. "And up until then ... I thought Jesus came, died on the cross, that Jesus' being here was about His death and dying on the cross, when it really was about Him coming to show us how to do it, how to be, to show us the Christ consciousness that He had and that that consciousness abides with all of us. That's what I got." [16]

I have chosen not to use her name here because I do not want to appear to be attacking her, though you probably already know who I am quoting. She truly seems to be a nice person who cares about people. Still, deception is just as real, and maybe more so, when it comes through the words of a nice person. We need to remember to pray for others, including those who have great influence over many people. We need to pray against the deception that Satan brings to people and pray for the truth that is found in the Bible to penetrate hearts. Jesus said, *"If you continue in My word, then you are truly disciples of Mine; and you will know the truth, and the truth will make you free." (John 8:31-32)*

Blending of Science, Science Fiction and Eastern Religion

Before ending this chapter I want to draw your attention to some other forms of deception prevalent today in some circles that I believe to be significant. They may seem random and unrelated but I believe that they may blend together as a part of the global deception described in the Bible that will find a foothold in the days leading up to the second coming of Jesus Christ.

---

[15] https://www.youtube.com/watch?v=noO_dCWtB1E
[16] https://www.youtube.com/watch?v=OsjvGvNKCzo

Alternative Universe

Some very intelligent people are now considering the possibility that all of life that we are experiencing today is no more than a computer simulation being controlled by someone with advanced understanding and knowledge. This may very well be an example of what Romans 1:22 says when it proclaims, "Professing to be wise they became fools."

This idea can be better understood through the words of a prominent scientist in America who answered the question of an interviewer, "are we living in simulation?". He responded, "I find it hard to argue against that possibility." [17] He added later, "It's hard to argue against the possibility that all of us are not just the creation of some kid in a parent's basement, programming up a world for their own entertainment." [18]

This same simulation idea is the basis of a popular movie entitled "The Truman Show" in which the main character, Truman Burbank, played by Jim Carrey, has unknowingly spent his entire life as the main character of the television show, "The Truman Show". In the movie the television show is produced by a character named "Christof". I would say that is no accident. Eventually Truman figures out he is imprisoned in the television set he has called home and he begins to work to break free.

The Multiverse

In an attempt to explain the phenomenal fine tuning of the universe without giving credit to God, some scientists today have begun to promote the idea of "The Multiverse" though they admit there is no scientific data to support such an idea. The idea is

---

[17] https://www.youtube.com/watch?v=SYAG9dAfy8U
[18] ibid

that there may be millions of universes, not just one. With this idea the reality of one perfect universe, where every dial is randomly set exactly as it must be for galaxies, stars, planets and life to exist becomes a possibility to them.

The idea of a multiverse, typically is called "The Multiverse Theory". The fact that it is referred to as a theory though there is no scientific data available to support it, is another example of the deception that abounds today. This is seen even within the scientific community.

Those who espouse the idea of a multiverse become open to further deceptions, dealing with the thought of traveling from one universe to another.

Directed Panspermia and Alien Life

Dr. Francis Crick, along with Dr. James Watson won nobel prizes for their groundbreaking work in the 1950s after discovering the double helix structure of the DNA molecule. As a part of their discoveries, they came to understand the immensely complex nature of proteins, the DNA molecule, and life at the cellular level.

Dr. Crick came to the conclusion that the formation of life from non-living elements here on earth, even if given four and half billion years, was virtually impossible. He wrote about this in his book, "Life Itself, Its Origin and Nature".

Ruling out the development of life on earth by random, unguided processes, Dr. Crick developed a "theory" of how life may have come about here on earth.

His "theory" became known as "Directed Panspermia", which contends for the direct planting or seeding of life by highly evolved aliens from elsewhere in the universe.

Just like the multiverse idea, this idea also has no scientific data to confirm it. Still, it is viewed favorably by a number of scientists.

When God, the obvious source of creation, is ruled out by the bias of those who don't want Him to exist, the embracing of deception is inevitable.

Certainly, the acceptance of the ideas conveyed in "directed panspermia" provide fodder for the fascination with UFOs and for the search for alien life. I believe, as do many other Bible teachers, that the sightings of UFOs are no hox. I believe that people really do see and hear things that are beyond the earthly realm but I believe that these things are demonic rather than alien.

There are many today who are convinced that eventually we will contact intelligent, alien life. Many of these same people also believe that these aliens will direct us into the next steps of human evolution. The openness to these thoughts can be seen today in a number of ways. One way is in the great increase in emphasis on space travel in the past few years. In 2021 a number of new pioneering space projects were launched. From the China Mars Probe launched in May to the multiple space orbits by private billionaires including Jeff Bezos, Richard Branson and Elon Musk later in the year, 2021 was filled with exciting news for those interested in space exploration.

In the World Economic Forum's (WEF) 8 predictions for the world of 2030, number 7 states that, "You could be preparing to go to Mars. Scientists will have worked out how to keep you healthy in space." It then asks, "The start of a journey to find alien life?"

I believe it is very possible that a supposed encounter with alien life may provide a major boost to the demonic plan to deceive the world and lead the world toward the worship of the coming antichrist.

CERN

We would expect to see spiritual deception in the realms of false religion and such, but not in the realms of high tech science. Yet there is a strange blending of high tech science and eastern religion found at the CERN laboratories in Europe. CERN is the European Organization for Nuclear Research and is one of the world's largest and most respected centers for scientific research. CERN houses an underground circular facility called a "Large Hadron Collider". The Large Hadron Collider (LHC) is the world's largest and most powerful particle accelerator. It consists of a 27-kilometer ring of superconducting magnets with a number of accelerating structures to boost the energy of the particles along the way.

Through their colliding of particles at enormous speeds the scientists from around the world who work at CERN seek to understand what is the nature of our universe and what is it made of? It all sounds quite technical and scientific which it certainly is. Yet there are some strange elements to what takes place at CERN.

Between two of their main buildings in Switzerland CERN has a statue of "Lord Shiva", one of the three main hindu gods. The statue is a depiction of "the dance of destruction" by Shiva. In Hinduism the three main gods are "Brahma", considered as the creator, "Vishnu", considered the preserver, and "Shiva", considered the destroyer. The belief behind the dance of destruction is that destruction must come before renewal or new creation can come.

Not only is there a statue of a hindu god of destruction between two of the CERN buildings, there have been some strange videos produced by CERN that give clues to some of what they are considering as they pursue understanding of the universe.

In a video produced by CERN entitled "Symmetry" they

FALSE WONDERS AND DECEPTION (BE ALERT!)

depict workers within the Large Hadron Collider with hard hats dancing within the facility. The dance is classical in style, much like ballet. As the video progresses the main dancer is drawn into a circle in the desert sand by a figure in a dark outfit. The dancer is seen dancing in the circle. Then the scene is back inside the facility and as he and the other dancers dance they are drawn into a wormhole and sucked away, disappearing into another dimension, or another universe.

Remember, some scientists who speak of a multiverse refer to the possibility of being transported from one universe to another through a wormhole. Of course just as some think we might be able to go through a wormhole to arrive in a different dimension or universe, there are some who believe that aliens may be able to pass through a wormhole to get to us.

All of this certainly appears to be paving the way for even greater demonic deception associated with the false signs and wonders the Bible says will be accomplished by the antichrist and the false prophet who gives honor to the beast in Revelation 13.

One final thought before closing this chapter. Facebook CEO Mark Zuckerberg has announced the name change of Facebook to Meta Platforms Inc. and has explained their intent to be a major player in the "Metaverse". The metaverse is said to be a world where you can live in virtual reality, having a life that you design which includes virtual meetings and virtual activities. Holograms will be a major part of the metaverse which again involves making unreal things appear as if they were real.

The technology involved in Meta and other's vision for the metaverse is certainly impressive and it is pretty clear that with the right marketing strategy multitudes will gladly enter this new virtual world. In a sense they are offering what appears to be a new life to those who join with them, blending humanity with artificial intelligence and virtual reality. New terms like "virtual real estate", "virtual property" and "virtual currency" are becoming more common.

One major problem that seems probable based on Meta's (Facebook's) current tendency to try and control what people can communicate with others, is the danger of a group of people having even greater power to control how people think and what they say in the world that they create for others to live in.

If we have concerns now about the amount of time that people spend on their phones, tablets and laptops, imagine how this could increase massively when people no longer just view the internet, but rather, they are in the internet and become a part of it in a sense.

The Bible tells us that deception will be widespread and strong in the last days and we see deception growing all around us in the world we live in today.

Dads and moms, grandpas and grandmas, this is a time when a commitment to bringing the Bible, God's Word to the center of family life is paramount! Be alert! Be awake! Love your family enough to diligently work to help them stay connected to the truth of God's Word, the Bible.

CHAPTER 7

"Wars and Rumors of Wars"

One of the things Jesus warned of in Matthew 24 regarding the last days was wars and rumors of wars.

> *"You will be hearing of wars and rumors of wars. See that you are not frightened, for those things must take place, but that is not yet the end. "For nation will rise against nation, and kingdom against kingdom,"*
> Matthew 24:6-7a

Looking at the world today we can see that this is another prophesied area concerning the time leading up to the second coming of Christ that has been, and is being fulfilled.

Wars and rumors of wars have been a part of the human experience throughout history but it is also true that there has been an increase in the magnitude and intensity of wars over the past 100+ years. Also, the rumors of wars in the past 75 years have been much more profound since the era of nuclear war came into reality. Rumors of wars now involve the concern of war that potentially could wipe out humanity and the earth since various nations now possess enough nuclear bombs to destroy the entire planet.

The amount of human lives lost through wars over the past 100+ years is staggering!

Many have said that the 20th century was the bloodiest century in human history. Whether or not that is the case, it is clear that an enormous amount of human lives were lost in the 20th century due to wars and genocide. One estimate, by Piero Scaruffi, which includes a breakdown of individual wars throughout the 20th century, is 160 million killed in 20th century wars.[1] This includes millions killed by oppressive governments making war upon segments of their own people.

A 2002 online article in "The Guardian" by Eric Hobsbawm entitled "War and Peace" says, *"The 20th century was the most murderous in recorded history. The total number of deaths caused by or associated with its wars has been estimated at 187 million, the equivalent of more than 10% of the world's population in 1913."* [2] It goes on to say that from 1914 forward *"it was a century of almost unbroken war, with few and brief periods without organized armed conflict somewhere."* [3]

According to Wikipedia 16-40 million died in WW1 and 85 million died in WW2 alone.[4] WW2 is considered the largest and bloodiest war of all time. (The higher total for WW1 incorporates millions who died as a result of the Spanish Flu being transported by moving troops.)

Here is a list of 20th century wars in chronological order from ThoughtCo.com.[5] There are numerous other battles and skirmishes that are not included here. Some of those could be considered wars as well.

1898–1901 Boxer Rebellion
1899–1902 Boer War
1904–1905 Russo-Japanese War

---

[1] https://www.scaruffi.com/politics/massacre.html
[2] https://www.theguardian.com/education/2002/feb/23/artsandhumanities.highereducation#:~:text=The%2020th%20century%20was%20the,the%20world's%20population%20in%201913.
[3] ibid
[4] https://en.wikipedia.org/wiki/List_of_wars_by_death_toll
[5] https://www.thoughtco.com/major-wars-and-conflicts-20th-century-1779967

1910–1920 Mexican Revolution
1912–1913 First and Second Balkan Wars
1914–1918 World War I
1915–1918 Armenian Genocide
1917 - Russian Revolution
1918–1921 Russian Civil War
1919–1921 Irish War of Independence
1927–1937 Chinese Civil War
1933–1945 Holocaust
1935–1936 Second Italo-Abyssinian War (also known as the Second Italo-Ethiopian War or the Abyssinian War)
1936–1939 Spanish Civil War
1939–1945 World War II
1945–1990 Cold War
1946–1949 Chinese Civil War resumes
1946 1954 First Indochina War (also known as the French Indochina War)
1948 Israel War of Independence (also known as the Arab-Israeli War)
1950–1953 Korean War
1954–1962 French-Algerian War
1955–1972 First Sudanese Civil War
1956 - Suez Crisis
1959 Cuban Revolution
1959–1975 Vietnam War
1967 - Six-Day War
1979–1989 Soviet-Afghan War
1980–1988 Iran-Iraq War
1990–1991 Persian Gulf War
1991–1995 Third Balkan War
1994 - Rwandan Genocide

For Christians around the world, the 20th century was the most deadly in human history as well. According to statistics from David B. Barrett and the Center for Study of Global Christianity, there have been approximately 70 million Christians martyred between 30

A.D. and 2000 A.D. Of those 70 million, 45 million were martyred in the 20th century. [6]

The middle eastern part of the world, where Jesus spoke the prophetic words about wars and rumors of wars in the end times, is especially prone to the fulfillment of these prophetic words. Since Israel became a nation again in 1948 they have survived 8 defensive wars, as well as a number of intifadas and armed conflicts. In addition to the wars and conflicts involving Israel there have been numerous conflicts between other middle eastern countries. The threat of war seems to be a continual part of life for those living in this volatile part of the world.

Since September 11, 2001, new terms have now become commonly associated with war. The terms "terrorism" and "terrorist" are now very familiar to us all. These terms generate fear and describe tactics of war that are purposely barbaric and cruel. Even within times of war there have been rules for engagement that have been observed by warring forces which provided protection, at least to a degree, for innocent women and children. September 11th introduced a new level of threat to innocent civilians as attackers purposely killed as many civilians as possible and some reveled in their actions.

When we add to this the fears of the "Cold War" between Russia and the United States and the Cuban Missile Crisis, the concerns of a World War Three, and even the concern some have of space wars, it is clear that we live in a time when Jesus' prophetic words concerning wars and rumors of wars have come to pass.

---

[6]https://www.deseret.com/2011/9/2/20213382/christian-killed-every-5-minutes#:~:text=The%20majority%20of%20those%20martyrs,martyrs%20in%20the%2020th%20century.

CHAPTER 8

"Earthquakes, Famines & Plagues"

In Matthew 24 and Luke 21 Jesus also warned of difficulties upon the earth in the last days such as earthquakes, famines & plagues.

> *"... and in various places there will be famines and earthquakes."*   *Matthew 24:7b*

> *"and there will be great earthquakes, and in various places plagues and famines; and there will be terrors and great signs from heaven."*   *Luke 21:11*

According to the USGS (United States Geological Survey) there are about 20,000 earthquakes each year around the globe, about 55 each day.[1] On average this includes 16 major earthquakes within a given year, with 15 in the 7 magnitude range and 1 over 8 in magnitude.[2]

2021 was a very active period for global seismicity, including 19 major earthquakes 7 or above in magnitude and 3 that were above 8 in magnitude.[3]

The "Ring of Fire", as it is called, around the rim of the Pacific Ocean contains over 450 active and dormant volcanoes. These

---

[1] https://www.usgs.gov/faqs/why-are-we-having-so-many-earthquakes-has-naturally-occurring-earthquake-activity-been

[2] ibid

[3] https://en.wikipedia.org/wiki/List_of_earthquakes_in_2021

regions surrounding the Pacific Ocean are by far the most vulnerable to earthquakes. About 90 percent of earthquakes strike within the "Ring of Fire".

It does not appear for the most part that there is a marked increase in the occurrence of earthquakes in recent decades but there is certainly an increase in our awareness of earthquakes and their resulting damage tolls. It should be noted that Jesus did not say that "there will be an increase in earthquakes". He simply said that "there will be great earthquakes in various places." This sign is certainly being fulfilled each year around the world.

Earthquakes are a reminder to us that the things which seem the most solid and dependable to us are actually quite fragile. Only Jesus Christ and His Word provide a solid foundation for us to build our lives upon! Jesus spoke of this in Matthew 7:24-27.

> *"Therefore everyone who hears these words of Mine and acts on them, may be compared to a wise man who built his house on the rock. (25) "And the rain fell, and the floods came, and the winds blew and slammed against that house; and yet it did not fall, for it had been founded on the rock. (26) "Everyone who hears these words of Mine and does not act on them, will be like a foolish man who built his house on the sand. (27) "The rain fell, and the floods came, and the winds blew and slammed against that house; and it fell--and great was its fall."*   Matthew 7:24-28

Famines killed nearly 75 million people in the 20th Century worldwide.[4] Large-scale famines affected the Horn of Africa in 1984-85 and 1992, and North Korea in the mid-1990s. A large-scale famine creating a devastating crisis in southern Somalia in 2011 killed a quarter of a million people.[5]

Emergency food assistance needs were unprecedented in

---

[4]https://theconversation.com/famines-in-the-21st-century-its-not-for-lack-of-food-73587#:~:text=The%20last%20large%2Dscale%20famines,quarter%20of%20a%20million%20people.

[5] ibid

2017 with upwards to 70 million people in 45 different countries experiencing various levels of famine and food shortages.[6]

The Action Against Hunger Organization recently said, "After steadily declining for a decade, world hunger is on the rise, affecting 9.9 percent of people globally. From 2019 to 2020, the number of undernourished people grew by as many as 161 million.[7]

Famine is not something that has been a concern for the most part in the United States and other western countries but there are some indications of potential food shortages now, even in places where food concerns have been rare. In 2022, alarm in the U.S. over baby formula shortages became a reality.

When we think of "plagues" we tend to think back to the book of Exodus in the Bible. God sent plagues upon Egypt before He delivered His people from their bondages. The "plagues" seen in the book of Exodus were of the outward type as opposed to inward, bodily illnesses. We might call the type of plagues seen in the book of Exodus as "pestilences". It would appear that both illnesses and pestilences can be considered as plagues.

The term "plague" today primarily refers to bodily illness caused by bacteria. Plagues include 3 major types. "Bubonic" plague affects the lymphatic system and eventually the outer skin. "Septicemic" plague is seen when bacteria infect the bloodstream and thereby travel throughout the body. "Pneumonic" plague involves infection in the lungs.

Though modern medicine has helped to deal with plagues, two of the deadliest plagues in human history have occurred in just the past 40 years. HIV/AIDS has claimed an estimated 27-47 million lives since 1981 and COVID-19 claimed an estimated 5.17 million lives worldwide from early 2020 through spring of 2022.[8]

Just a few years ago our thoughts about "plagues" in the western world would have been primarily directed to far off places and something we would not have imagined touching our lives

---

[6] ibid
[7] https://www.actionagainsthunger.org/world-hunger-facts-statistics
[8] https://www.gavi.org/vaccineswork/historys-seven-deadliest-plagues#:~:text=SARS%2D CoV%2D2%20has%20officially,list%20of%20history's%20deadliest%20plagues.&text=A% 20masquerade%20historical%20scene%20reconstruction.

directly. Since the outbreak of COVID-19 in late 2019 the world we live in has changed drastically and the danger of infectious plagues is now something in the forethought of people all around the world.

Other types of plagues are also still seen today around the world, despite modern technology assisting in controlling the numbers of potentially destructive insects and such.

In 2019-2021 a locust infestation affected 23 different countries with East Africa being the epicenter of the infestation.[9]

In 2020 Kenya experienced the worst infestation of locusts in the past 70 years. A BBC article entitled "The Biblical locust plague of 2020" says that East Africa is seeing the worst swarms of locusts in many decades.[10] Desert locusts, or *Schistocerca gregaria*, have often been called the world's most devastating pest. These insects are able to multiply 20-fold in three months and reach densities of 80 million per square kilometer. Each can consume 2g of vegetation every day – combined, **a swarm of 80 million can consume food equivalent to that eaten by 35,000 people a day.**[11]

Mosquito-borne diseases are also examples of potential plagues, including Eastern Equine Encephalitis (EEE), West Nile Virus (WNV) and Jamestown Canyon Virus (JCV). A 2021 article entitled, "Michigan weather continues to be ripe for what feels like 'biblical plague' of mosquitoes" speaks of the recent increases in mosquito problems in the state of

---

[9] https://en.wikipedia.org/wiki/2019%E2%80%932021_locust_infestation
[10] https://www.bbc.com/future/article/20200806-the-biblical-east-african-locust-plagues-of-2020
[11] ibid

Michigan.[12] Another September 2021 online article speaks of death tolls from the West Nile Virus rising in the United States, even in places not normally known for mosquito problems like Arizona.[13]

There certainly are examples of earthquakes, famines and plagues that can be pointed out as fulfillments of Jesus' prophetic words concerning the end times but I believe that there will be an increase in these type of calamities during the coming years as we drawn nearer and nearer to the 2nd coming of Christ! Even today, we see enough of these things happening in the world to say that this Biblical prophetic indicator is coming to pass around us in our lifetime!

COVID-19 in particular has altered what life looks like around the world in just the past 3 years. Talk of future pandemics or plagues is abundant as well. This should serve as a reminder to us that we are living at a time when the 2nd coming of Jesus Christ is fast approaching!

---

[12] https://www.wxyz.com/news/michigan-weather-continues-to-be-ripe-for-what-feels-like-biblical-plague-of-mosquitoes#:~:text=State%20health%20officials%20say%20the,severe%20illness%2C%E2%80%9D%20said%20Dr.

[13] https://www.today.com/health/west-nlle-vlrus-2021-how-safe-deaths-rlse-some-spots-t232267

CHAPTER 9

"An Increase of Immorality and Wickedness"

Another characteristic of the end times that the Bible tells us of is the increase of immorality and wickedness. Second Timothy 3:1-5 speaks of this.

> *"But realize this, that in the last days difficult times will come. (2) For men will be lovers of self, lovers of money, boastful, arrogant, revilers, disobedient to parents, ungrateful, unholy, (3) unloving, irreconcilable, malicious gossips, without self-control, brutal, haters of good, (4) treacherous, reckless, conceited, lovers of pleasure rather than lovers of God, (5) holding to a form of godliness, although they have denied its power; Avoid such men as these."*
> 2 Timothy 3:1-5

> *"But evil men and impostors will proceed from bad to worse, deceiving and being deceived. (14) You, however, continue in the things you have learned and become convinced of, knowing from whom you have learned them, (15) and that from childhood you have known the sacred writings which are able to give you the wisdom that leads to salvation through faith which is in Christ Jesus. (16) All Scripture is inspired by God and profitable for teaching, for reproof, for correction, for training in righteousness;"*   2 Timothy 3:13-16

In both of these passages we see indications that there will be an increase of immorality and wickedness evidenced in the last days. I included verses 14-16 because we see in these verses the answer for believers who live in these times. Stay committed to the Scriptures! Only in the truth of God's Word, the Bible can we find the direction and strength that we need to live in these times.

Jesus refers to this characteristic of the end times in Matthew 24:12.

> "Because lawlessness is increased, most people's love will grow cold." Matthew 24:12

The word "lawlessness" here is translated "iniquity" in the King James Version and "wickedness" in the New International Version. The Greek word used here is "anomia" and it means "illegality, that is, violation of law or (generally) wickedness: - iniquity, transgression of the law, unrighteousness." Whether we call it "lawlessness", "wickedness" or "iniquity" it is clear that this is an increase of sinfulness that fills the world in the last days and is manifest in all sorts of immoral and ungodly behavior. Jesus indicates that this lawlessness will increase so much that most people will cease to be loving people. One interesting translation of this verse is found in the Complete Jewish Bible. It translates this verse this way.

> "and many people's love will grow cold because of increased distance from Torah." Matthew 24:12 (CJB)

Whenever a person strays from God's law and God's Word they will always gravitate toward wickedness.

Second Peter 3:3-4 adds this description about people in the last days. They are mockers and are following after their own lusts. They will mock the prophetic words of the 2nd coming of Christ.

"Know this first of all, that in the last days mockers will come with their mocking, following after their own lusts, (4) and saying, "Where is the promise of His coming? For ever since the fathers fell asleep, all continues just as it was from the beginning of creation." 2 Peter 3:3-4

Later in 2 Peter 3 we see that the Day of the Lord, the time of His judgment upon the sinfulness of this world will come like a thief, suddenly and swiftly. (2 Peter 3:10) This same truth is expressed in 1 Thessalonians 5.2-3 indicating that people will be hardened to the fact that Jesus is coming back and the judgment of God is coming upon all the earth.

"For you yourselves know full well that the day of the Lord will come just like a thief in the night. (3) While they are saying, "Peace and safety!" then destruction will come upon them suddenly like labor pains upon a woman with child, and they will not escape."
1 Thessalonians 5:2-3

In addition to these passages of Scripture there are related warnings we have already looked at in previous chapters that speak of many false Christs and false prophets, people believing doctrines of demons, deception and increases in war and violence. We can also add what Jesus said in Matthew 24:37-39.

"For the coming of the Son of Man will be just like the days of Noah. (38) "For as in those days before the flood they were eating and drinking, marrying and giving in marriage, until the day that Noah entered the ark, (39) and they did not understand until the flood came and took them all away; so will the coming of the Son of Man be." Matthew 24:37-39

AN INCREASE OF IMMORALITY AND WICKEDNESS

Genesis 6 describes the days of Noah in this way.

*"Then the LORD saw that the wickedness of man was great on the earth, and that **every intent of the thoughts of his heart was only evil continually.**"*

Genesis 6:5

In Noah's days people's hearts were full of wickedness and evil. That is one of the reasons judgment came upon the earth. Jesus said it will be like that again in the last days. Judgment will again come only this time it will be by fire instead of by water.

The increase of immorality and wickedness in these days can be seen throughout the world. Some of the outward manifestations of this are increases in pornography, fornication, adultery, homosexuality, sexually transmitted diseases, higher crime rates, gang violence, higher murder rates, abortion, obsession with gambling, drug abuse and alcoholism, increases in armed robbery and theft, mass murders in schools and public places, rioting and destruction of property, increases in lying and deceptive behavior, cursing and foul language, bullying, selfish behavior, irresponsible behavior, corruption in government, denying God as Creator, a disregard for human life, and a lack of respect for God and His Word. All of these things, and other related attitudes and behaviors, can now be seen openly and frequently all over the world.

The rapid decline in morality is obvious in America, which has been known for many decades as a "Christian nation". Think of how drastically culture has changed in just a few decades since the days of the Dick Van Dyke show and Andy Griffith show where no one would have ever considered showing a passionate bedroom scene.

The moral decline in America is indicative of a moral decline throughout the world. One way we can see the moral decline in America is to look at what has happened in major universities in America. In particular, Ivy league schools such as Harvard, Princeton, and Yale all now espouse views that reject Christian values and

Biblical principles. Secularism abounds. Yet these same universities were all founded to be places to train young people to be disciples and ministers of Jesus Christ and His Word.

A visit to the campus of Harvard University would reveal Scripture passages on buildings and gates all around. For instance the "1875 Gate" is engraved with the words from Isaiah 26:2 which reads "Open ye the gates, that the righteous nation that keepeth the truth, may enter in."

The "1881 Gate", which serves as the entrance to the Phillip Brooks House, named after the preacher who wrote the Christmas hymn "O Little Town of Bethlehem", bears both a cross and John 8:32, "Ye shall know the truth and the truth shall make you free." on its ironwork structure.

"1881 Gate"
"Ye shall know the truth and the truth shall make you free"

Another building on campus bears the words from Psalm 8, "What is man that Thou art mindful of him?"

The seal of Harvard, adopted in 1692, highlights the Latin word "Veritas" which means "Truth". On each side of the word "Veritas" are the words "Christo" (Christ) and "Ecclesiae" (Church). Thus the key motto for Harvard was "Truth for Christ and the church".

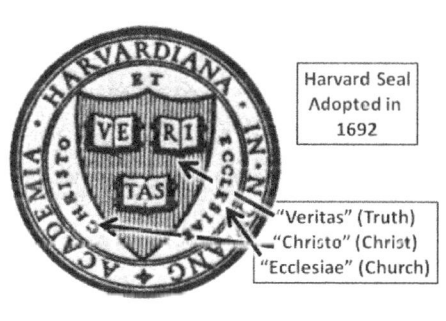

Harvard Seal Adopted in 1692
"Veritas" (Truth)
"Christo" (Christ)
"Ecclesiae" (Church)

Even more telling are words found in Harvard's Rules and Precepts written in 1646.

> Let every Student be plainly instructed, and earnestly pressed to consider well, the main end of his life and studies is, to know God and Jesus Christ which is eternal life (John

17:3) and therefore to lay Christ in the bottom, as the only foundation of all sound knowledge and learning. And seeing the Lord only giveth wisdom, Let every one seriously set himself by prayer in secret to seek it of Him (Prov. 2:3).

What is seen at Harvard of a massive departure from its Christian roots is indicative of much of American life and culture and is another indication that Bible prophecies concerning the end times are being fulfilled in these days.

The pinnacle of immorality and wickedness in the world today is seen through the practice of abortion. It is hard to fathom that over 64 million innocent babies have been killed within their mother's womb in America since 1973.[1] Over 1.6 billion innocent babies have been killed in their mother's womb worldwide since 1980.[2] All of these represent the killing of an innocent life but a percentage of them also represent murder of an unimaginable type, where little babies are actually torn apart limb by limb and removed from the womb, or they are partially born only to have a scissor type instrument used to pierce their head and skull so that their brain can be sucked out of their head. Kevin Sorbo and others have produced an animated video that can be seen on YouTube entitled "The Procedure" that chronicles the true story of an ultrasound technician who unwillingly assisted in one such procedure years ago, causing him to resign his position and suffer horrible memories of the gruesome procedure.[3]

Falling away from God and His Word in America and throughout the world has not been accidental. Purposeful steps have been taken to move away from Christianity and Biblical truth. For instance in 1962-1963 both public

---

[1] http://www.numberofabortions.com/?mid=5708452
[2] ibid
[3] https://www.youtube.com/watch?v=rTlrNEkwFW4

prayer in school and Bible reading in school were deemed to be unconstitutional and were outlawed (School Prayer in 1962 - Engel v Vitale)(Bible Reading in Public Schools in 1963 - Abington School District v Schempp).

The moral implications of these decisions proved to be staggering. In his 1988 book "America: To Pray? or Not to Pray?" David Barton revealed numerous statistics compiled from government agencies that showed the devastating implications of removing prayer and Bible reading from our public schools. Here are a few examples of the moral decline that followed the 1962 and 1963 decisions. (Some of these graphs are shown in alternate forms from the originals but the data comes from the information in the book.) (Note - Later printings of this book from 1991 forward are easier to locate at this time than copies of the 1988 version.)

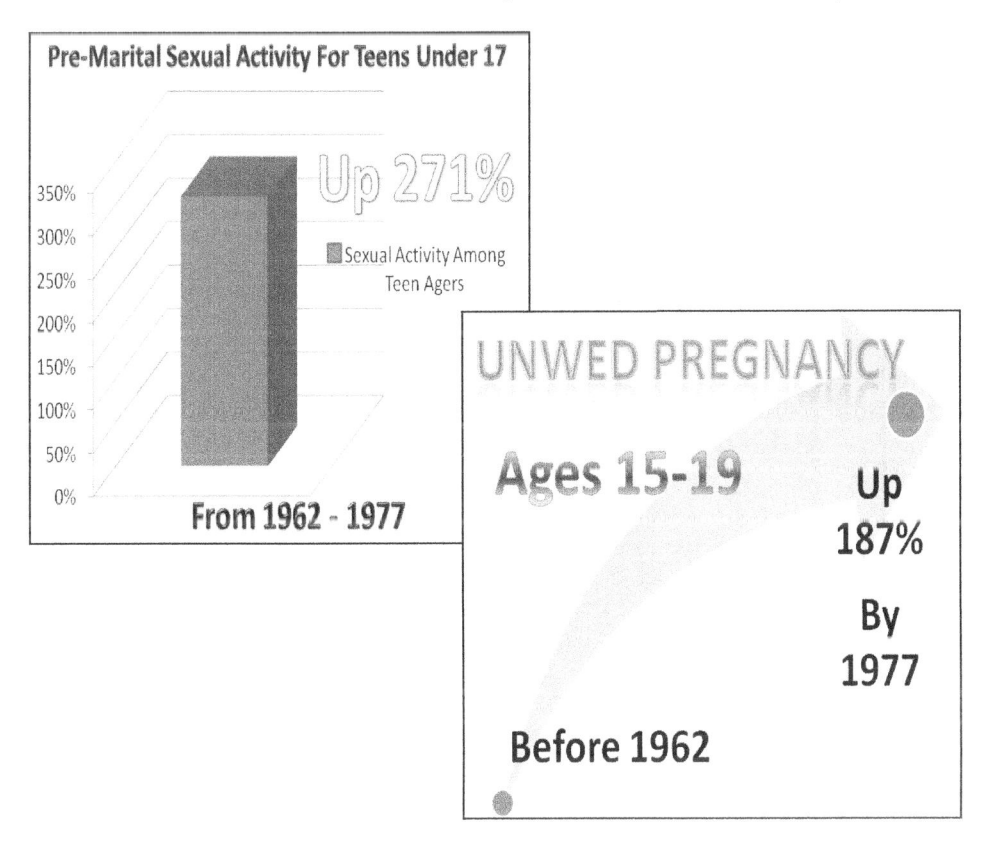

Pre-Marital Sexual Activity For Teens Under 17

Up 271%

Sexual Activity Among Teen Agers

From 1962 - 1977

UNWED PREGNANCY

Ages 15-19   Up 187% By 1977

Before 1962

AN INCREASE OF IMMORALITY AND WICKEDNESS

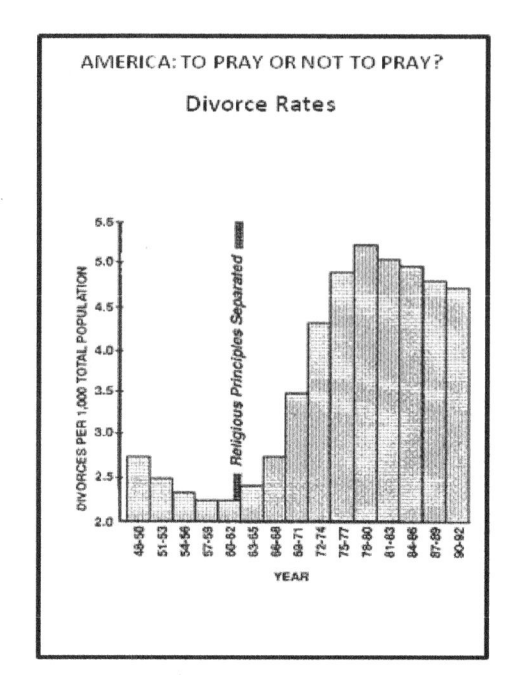

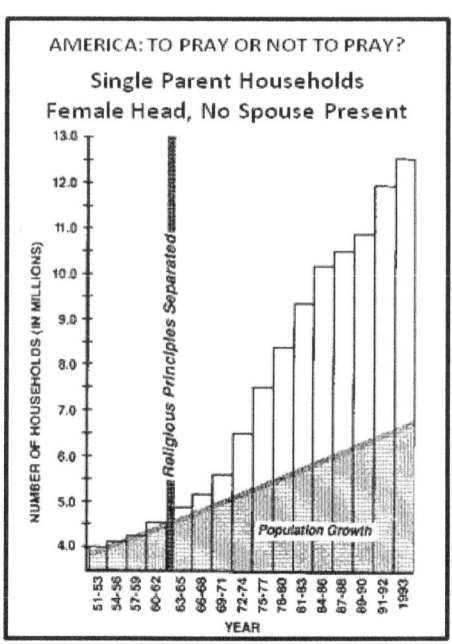

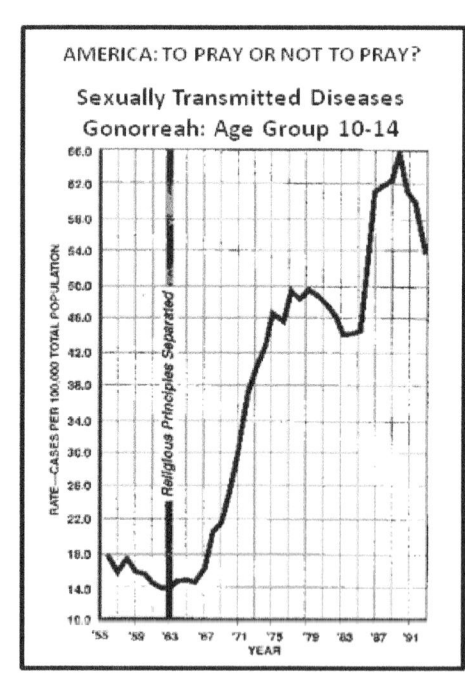

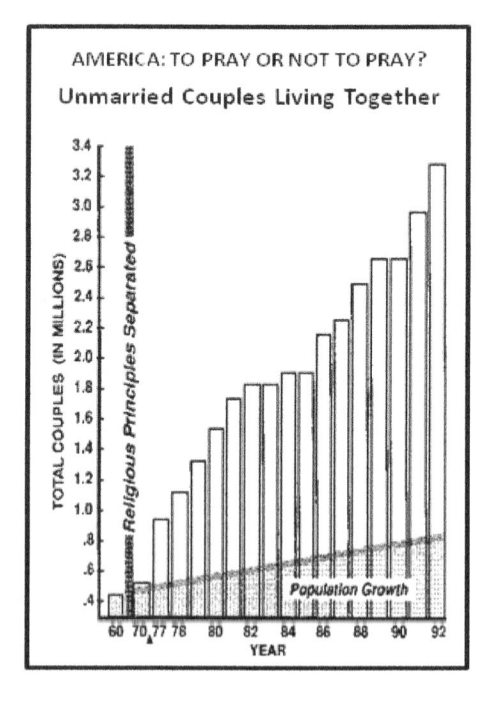

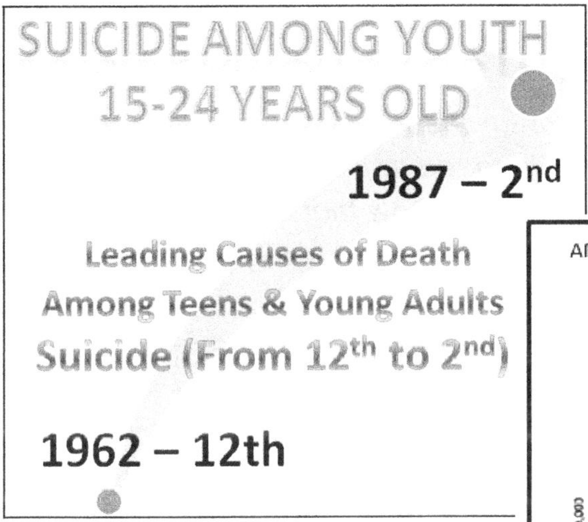

SUICIDE AMONG YOUTH 15-24 YEARS OLD

1987 – 2nd

Leading Causes of Death Among Teens & Young Adults Suicide (From 12th to 2nd)

1962 – 12th

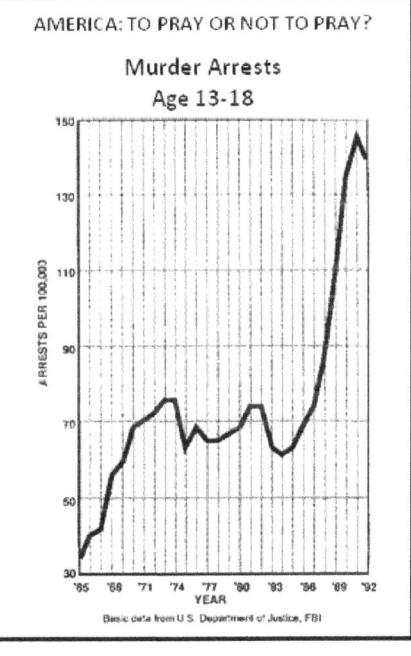

AMERICA: TO PRAY OR NOT TO PRAY?
Murder Arrests Age 13-18

It is easy to see from these statistics that the lives of many in America were affected by the decisions to pull away from God and His Word as a nation. Anyone living in America today can attest to the fact that the increase of immorality and ungodliness has continued in the past few decades. Violent crimes and murders have been increasing in major cities across America in recent years as well. Already high numbers of murders in 22 major cities in America rose by 44% from 2019 to 2021. [4]

All of this points to the fulfillment of Bible prophecies concerning the increase of immorality and wickedness in the last days.

I want to mention briefly in this chapter something related to the days leading up to the 2nd coming of Christ being as the days of Noah. We already saw that Genesis 6:5 speaks of the fact that evil filled the hearts and minds of people in the days leading up to the

---

[4] https://www.foxnews.com/us/murders-rose-study-2021

flood. Genesis 6:1-4 speaks of another thing that happened during those days.

> *"Now it came about, when men began to multiply on the face of the land, and daughters were born to them, (2) that the sons of God saw that the daughters of men were beautiful; and they took wives for themselves, whomever they chose. (3) Then the LORD said, "My Spirit shall not strive with man forever, because he also is flesh; nevertheless his days shall be one hundred and twenty years." (4) The Nephilim were on the earth in those days, and also afterward, when the sons of God came in to the daughters of men, and they bore children to them. Those were the mighty men who were of old, men of renown."*
>
> *Genesis 6:1-4*

There are varying views about what is being referred to in this passage. Some believe that "the sons of God" is a reference to the men in the lineage of Seth and "the daughters of men" is a reference to the women in the lineage of Cain. Others believe that "the sons of God" is a reference to fallen angelic beings who abandoned their proper abode and took upon themselves flesh and had sexual relationships with "the daughters of men" with the offspring of these unions being the giants, or "Nephilim". I personally believe the later explanation though I would certainly admit that I do not claim to understand how this would all take place. The fact that there were giants during this time and even some after the flood is well documented in Scripture. The actions of fallen angels at that time appears to be what is referred to in two New Testament passages, 2 Peter 2:4-5 and Jude 6.

> *"For if **God did not spare angels when they sinned**, but cast them into hell and committed them to pits of*

*darkness, reserved for judgment; (5) **and did not spare the ancient world**, but preserved Noah, a preacher of righteousness, with seven others, when He brought a flood upon the world of the ungodly;"*
2 Peter 2:4-5

*"And **angels who did not keep their own domain, but abandoned their proper abode**, He has kept in eternal bonds under darkness for the judgment of the great day," (7) just as Sodom and Gomorrah and the cities around them, **since they in the same way as these indulged in gross immorality and went after strange flesh**, are exhibited as an example in undergoing the punishment of eternal fire.   Jude 1:6-7*

Of course we do not know for sure if this is a correct understanding of these passages of Scripture and of "the Nephilim", but if this is what the Bible is telling us, then we might expect that the same sort of thing might happen again in the days that Jesus said will be like the days of Noah. Could it be that when wickedness and ungodliness reach certain levels among humans, doors for various types of impact from the spiritual forces of darkness are opened. If this is the case it could be a part of the great deception in the last days with many already looking for highly evolved alien lifeforms from beyond the earth. (We will look further into this search for alien lifeforms in a later chapter.) Numerous Bible teachers believe that this may be the case. Chuck Missler and Mark Eastman write about the return of the Nephilim in their book Alien Encounters.

The fact that the Bible describes deception in the last days which is so strong that even the elect would be deceived if that were possible (note - He does not say the elect will be deceived) should alert us to the very real possibility that the wickedness on the earth in the last days and the rejection of God and His Word, may open up mankind to direct influences from fallen spiritual beings that are abnormal and have not been seen before except possibly in the days of Noah. Even if this line of thinking is incorrect it is absolutely clear from Scripture that both wickedness and deception will continue to increase in the last days leading up to the 2nd coming of Christ.

Before I close this chapter I want to make reference to a recently published book by Jonathan Cahn entitled, "The Return of the Gods". Jonathan Cahn has written a number of powerful books including "The Harbinger" which deals with America, and "The Oracle" which deals with Israel. In "The Return of the Gods" Jonathan shows powerfully how America and the Western World have opened the door through blatant sinfulness to ancient gods which were worshiped in pagan cultures of the past. He shows how the moral decline in America and the practices that have been embraced line up with the behaviors encouraged and demanded by these ancient gods, which are spiritual entities that lost their hold on much of the world for centuries as Christianity was embraced, but which have now again found their place of dominance in modern western culture.

He speaks of three ancient gods in particular, Baal, Ashtoreth (also called Ishtar), and Molech. He shows how these false gods influenced and destroyed the lives of people in ancient pagan cultures and how those same influences and destructive practices are becoming more and more accepted in the modern Western World. For example, these gods required the sacrifice of innocent children and today the lives of millions of innocent children are sacrificed on the altar of convenience through abortion.

I encourage you to read this book or listen to the audio book. I believe it will help you to understand the spiritual battle that those who follow Christ are facing today.

The increase of immorality and wickedness in the world today is abundantly clear and is another sign that the 2nd coming of Jesus Christ is near!

CHAPTER 10

"The Book of Daniel and the New World Order" (Globalism)

As the title of this book suggests, one of the central topics of this book has to do with the development of a New World Order, a global system that includes government and an economic structure, in the end times leading up to the 2nd coming of Jesus Christ. The next seven chapters all deal with aspects of this key topic. I believe that only the emergence of the nation of Israel in the last days and the issues surrounding that are more significant to understanding end time Bible prophecy than the events involved in establishing a New World Order in these days.

In this chapter we will look at passages of Scripture to see how this development has been predicted in the Bible and to see why the development of a New World Order is significant within the big picture of end times Bible prophecy.

Unlike some aspects of Bible prophecy, the Bible never directly says "In the last days there will be a New World Order" or "a global government will emerge in the last days." Still, when we understand key prophetic passages, we can see that the Bible is clearly indicating that this development will come to pass in the last days.

Probably the most significant passage indicating that there will be a global system of government and economy in the last days is found in Daniel, chapter 2. This chapter tells of an event that took place while the nation of Israel was captive to the Babylonian Empire and Nebuchadnezzar was the king of Babylon. Daniel was among the Jewish captives but he had risen to a place of influence along with Shadrach, Meshach and Abednego. King Nebuchadnezzar had a dream that was very troubling to him, the type that you feel has a meaning attached to it. God revealed what the dream was and what the interpretation of the dream was to Daniel who then explained these things to the king. The dream involved a revelation of the kingdoms or empires that would arise in world history. Through the information in chapter 2 along with further information found in Daniel, chapters 7 & 8, we know that the dream predicted a Babylonian Empire, followed by a Medo-Persian Empire, followed by a Greek Empire. All of these are named specifically in the book of Daniel. A fourth empire is described as being strong and powerful, beyond the other empires, and appears to describe the Roman Empire. There are then indications of a beast empire in Daniel 2 as well as in chapters 7 & 8. The dream that King Nebuchadnezzar has in chapter 2 involves a statue of a man with a head of gold, breasts and arms of silver, loins of brass, legs of iron and feet of iron mixed with clay. Chapters 7 & 8 correspond with visions of various animals representing the same empires. The beast that corresponds to the feet of iron mixed with clay is a dreadful and terrifying beast with ten horns. The ten horns may correspond to the ten toes of the statue in chapter 2. The key part of the passage in Daniel, chapter 2 that we want to look at here is found in verses 40-45. Note that the kingdom represented by the feet and toes on the statue is actually a continuation of the 4th kingdom (probably the Roman Empire) represented by the iron legs of the statue.

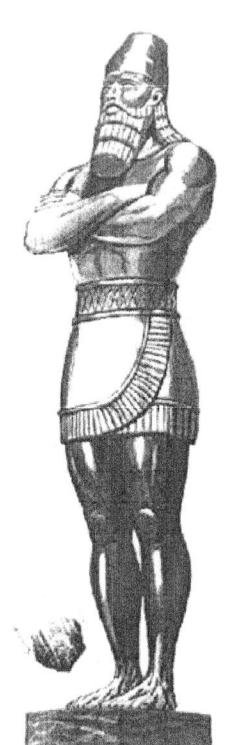

> *"Then there will be a fourth kingdom as strong as iron; inasmuch as iron crushes and shatters all things, so,*

like iron that breaks in pieces, it will crush and break all these in pieces. (41) "In that you saw the feet and toes, partly of potter's clay and partly of iron, it will be a divided kingdom; but it will have in it the toughness of iron, inasmuch as you saw the iron mixed with common clay. (42) "As the toes of the feet were partly of iron and partly of pottery, so some of the kingdom will be strong and part of it will be brittle. (43) "And in that you saw the iron mixed with common clay, they will combine with one another in the seed of men; but they will not adhere to one another, even as iron does not combine with pottery. (44) **"In the days of those kings the God of heaven will set up a kingdom which will never be destroyed, and that kingdom will not be left for another people; it will crush and put an end to all these kingdoms, but it will itself endure forever.** *(45) "Inasmuch as you saw that a stone was cut out of the mountain without hands and that it crushed the iron, the bronze, the clay, the silver and the gold, the great God has made known to the king what will take place in the future; so the dream is true and its interpretation is trustworthy." Daniel 2:40-45*

Since this prophetic passage referring to the establishment of God's Kingdom says that the God of heaven will set up a kingdom "in the days of those kings" it has been understood by many that a worldwide empire will be established and be in place at the time Jesus returns and establishes His Kingdom on earth.

Another passage that seems to indicate that a global system of government and economy will be in place in the last days is found in Revelation, chapter 13. In this chapter we are told of a beast that will arise in the last days and will exercise dominion over the whole earth. A second beast arises as well and is involved in causing people throughout the world to worship the beast. Note the indications of global dominance and influence in the following passages from Revelation 13.

> *"It was also given to him to make war with the saints and to overcome them, and **authority over every tribe and people and tongue and nation was given to him**."*   Revelation 13:7

> ***"All who dwell on the earth will worship him***, *everyone whose name has not been written from the foundation of the world in the book of life of the Lamb who has been slain."*   Revelation 13:8

> *"Then I saw another beast coming up out of the earth; and he had two horns like a lamb and he spoke as a dragon. (12) He exercises all the authority of the first beast in his presence. And **he makes the earth and those who dwell in it** to worship the first beast, whose fatal wound was healed."*   Revelation 13:11-12

> *"And **he deceives those who dwell on the earth** because of the signs which it was given him to perform in the presence of the beast, **telling those who dwell on the earth to make an image to the beast** who *had the wound of the sword and has come to life. (15) And it was given to him to give breath to the image of the beast, so that the image of the beast would even speak **and cause as many as do not worship the image of the beast to be killed**."*   Revelation 13:14-15

> *"And **he causes all, the small and the great, and the rich and the poor, and the free men and the slaves**, to be given a mark on their right hand or on their*

*forehead, (17) and he provides that **no one** will be able to buy or to sell, except the one who has the mark, either the name of the beast or the number of his name."*   *Revelation 13:16-17*

As you can see, Revelation 13 seems to indicate that the beast (or beast empire) that is given dominion for a short time in the last days will have dominion over the entire earth and over all people throughout the earth. Note especially the words in verse 7, "authority over every tribe and people and tongue and nation was given to him." This certainly would indicate a global system affecting all people. Verses 16-17 give clear indications that this global system will involve a global economy since the beast will have the ability to determine who can buy and sell throughout the earth.

Revelation 17 also refers to what appears to be a uniting of kings (or nations) in the last days, joining together to follow the beast empire.

*"The ten horns which you saw are ten kings who have not yet received a kingdom, but they receive authority as kings with the beast for one hour. (13) **"These have one purpose, and they give their power and authority to the beast.** (14) "These will wage war against the Lamb, and the Lamb will overcome them, because He is Lord of lords and King of kings, and those who are with Him are the called and chosen and faithful."*   *Revelation 17:12-14*

Revelation 19 speaks in vivid terms of the glorious return of Jesus Christ. We are told that at the time of His return He is coming to a battle with the beast and kings of the earth that have gathered to make war with Him. Note the language used to describe the ungodly army that will assemble for battle against Jesus.

*"Then I saw an angel standing in the sun, and he cried out with a loud voice, saying to all the birds which fly in midheaven, "Come, assemble for the great supper of God, (18) so that you may eat **the flesh of kings and the flesh of commanders and the flesh of mighty men** and the flesh of horses and of those who sit on them and **the flesh of all men, both free men and slaves, and small and great**." (19) And **I saw the beast and the kings of the earth and their armies assembled** to make war against Him who sat on the horse and against His army."*   Revelation 19:17-19

Nothing of the language used in any of these passages would suggest a world divided into individual nations that are each taking their own path, separate from one another. There are "kings", plural, but they are united together to follow the beast and they are united against Jesus Christ at the time of His return. Their assembly together to make war against Jesus as He returns shows the insanity of minds darkened by sin and reminds me of the words of Psalms 2:1-4 that say -

"Why are the nations in an uproar and the peoples devising a vain thing? (2) The kings of the earth take their stand and the rulers take counsel together against the LORD and against His Anointed, saying, (3) "Let us tear their fetters apart and cast away their cords from us!" (4) He who sits in the heavens laughs, The Lord scoffs at them."   Psalms 2:1-4

Another passage in the book of Daniel that appears to refer to an end time global system is found in Daniel 7:23-27. This passage gives us information concerning the fourth beast Daniel saw here in a vision. Just as the legs of iron in the statue represented a fourth kingdom (commonly believed to represent the

Roman Empire) and the legs of iron continued into the feet and toes of iron mixed with clay (commonly believed to represent an end time revived global empire), the fourth beast seen in Daniel 7 appears to both represent a fourth empire in history and its revived form in the last days. With that in mind note the text here.

> *"Thus he said: 'The fourth beast will be a fourth kingdom on the earth, which will be different from all the other kingdoms and **will devour the whole earth and tread it down and crush it.** (24) 'As for the ten horns, out of this kingdom ten kings will arise; and another will arise after them, and he will be different from the previous ones and will subdue three kings. (25) **'He will speak out against the Most High and wear down the saints of the Highest One**, and he will intend to make alterations in times and in law; and **they will be given into his hand for a time, times, and half a time.** (26) 'But the court will sit for judgment, and **his dominion will be taken away, annihilated and destroyed forever. (27) 'Then the sovereignty, the dominion and the greatness of all the kingdoms under the whole heaven will be given to the people of the saints of the Highest One**; His kingdom will be an everlasting kingdom, and all the dominions will serve and obey Him."*   Daniel 7:23-27

This beastly empire is said to devour the whole earth. The anti-God or anti-Christ heart of the beast is clear. Also, this appears to be the same empire spoken of in Revelation since authority and dominion over the saints is given to the beast for 3 ½ years, just as we see in Revelation 13.

These passages are at the heart of the belief that a one world global system will emerge at the end of time leading up to the 2nd coming of Jesus Christ.

There are other passages that would not in themselves necessarily indicate a one world global system, but fit well with this understanding of the end times. For example in Revelation 11:10-12 we read about the death of the Two Witnesses who have borne witness to the truth of God's Word for 3 ½ years. Verse 10-12 indicates that after their death inflicted upon them by the beast, "those who dwell on the earth will rejoice over them, and celebrate." It also appears that their resurrection is seen by people around the world who are watching the unfolding of these events. Verse 10 also indicates that the reason those who dwell on the earth rejoice over their death is that they had "tormented those who dwell on the earth". This is an example of a passage that in itself does not predict a one world global system but appears to fit with that understanding.

Also 2 Thessalonians 2 speaks of the coming of the lawless one (or the antiChrist) who will seat himself in the temple, declaring that he is God. The chapter goes on to speak of powerful signs and wonders and deception that will deceive all those who are perishing, and did not receive the love of the truth so as to be saved. Again, this chapter does not in itself indicate a one world global system but its contents seem to fit better with that system than a world divided into individual nations functioning separately.

In the following chapters we will look at many things in the world today pointing toward the rapid development of and movement toward a one world global system. As we look at these things it is important to keep as our backdrop, the prophetic passages of Scripture that indicate such a one world global system will be put in place in the end times.

CHAPTER 11

"The Roots of the New World Order" (1945-1948)

In Matthew 24:32 Jesus speaks of the parable of the fig tree.

"Now learn the parable from the fig tree: when its branch has already become tender and puts forth its leaves, you know that summer is near; (33) so, you too, when you see all these things, recognize that He is near, right at the door." Matthew 24:32-33

It is commonly believed that the fig tree in this parable refers to the nation of Israel. We spoke of this in chapter 2 and looked at how the Jewish people have miraculously returned to the land of Israel after over 1800 years of being scattered around the world, and how Israel became a nation on May 14, 1948. The fig tree has blossomed and by this we know that the 2nd coming of Jesus Christ is nearing.

I refer to this parable again in this chapter because of something Jesus said in Luke's record of this same Olivet Discourse that is recorded in Matthew 24-25. Luke adds just a few words here to what Matthew recorded in Luke 21:29.

*"Then He told them a parable: "Behold the fig tree **and all the trees**;"* Luke 21:29

Luke adds the words "and all the trees". When I noticed this years ago I pondered the meaning of this. If the fig tree represents the nation of Israel and the Jewish people, might "all the trees" represent the nations and peoples of the world? Assuming this may be the case I asked, "what would the nations of the world blossoming be referring to?" The answer I felt made the most sense was the development of a New World Order, a global system and society that the Bible appears to indicate will be in place when Jesus comes again.

With these things in mind I began to research the time period when Israel became a nation again in 1948. I found some very profound things to be true of the 4 year period from 1945 and the end of WWII through 1948. Many of the things that transpired during this short period of time might certainly have been a response to the horrific aspects of WW2 and the enormous amount of lost lives during the war. It is amazing to see how many key organizations and entities were put in place during this short window of time that provided the roots for the development of a New World Order. All of this at precisely the same time as Israel is becoming a nation again after nearly 2,000 years. In addition to the establishment of numerous organizations and entities, other key developments in technology and education were occurring as well at this time.

Note the following developments that all took place during the window of time between 1945 and 1948.

1) **The United Nations** is Formed **(October 24, 1945)** The United Nations is probably the most important organization in the development of the New World Order. (Main Headquarters in New York, New York and the Representative Office of the Secretary-General in Geneva, Switzerland.
2) **The European Union** began as The European Movement **(October 25, 1948)** The European Union is a major player in the movement toward a New World Order. (Parliament

buildings in Brussels, Belgium, Strasbourg, France & Luxembourg)

3) **The World Council of Churches** Formed **(August 23, 1948)** The World Council of Churches is key to the promotion of the idea that all religions can be blended together. (The World Council of Churches is headquartered in Geneva, Switzerland.)

4) **The World Trade Organization** (Began as General Agreement on Tariffs and Trade) **(January 1, 1948)** Key to the development of international trade and economy. (Note - The World Trade Organization now works in cooperation with the World Economic Forum, a major player in the movement to establish a global economic system and government, as seen by the production of their joint publication in 2022 dealing with "trade-tech".) (The World Trade Organization is headquartered in Geneva, Switzerland.)

5) **The World Federalist Movement** (which came to include the Institute for Global Policy) **(August, 1947)** This organization's mission statement is found on their website. "Our Mission is to promote global governance to address inequality, violent conflict, mass atrocities, climate change and corruption".[1] This additional statement is found on their website concerning their purpose. "As world federalists,

---

[1] https://www.wfm-igp.org/

we view the world as one society embracing all of humanity in all its diversity."² (The World Federalist Movement is registered as a non-profit organization in the U.S. and in the Netherlands.)

6) **The World Health Organization (April 7, 1948)** This organization became dominant in world affairs in 2020 in light of the COVID-19 health situation. Now, the WHO wields tremendous power and their opinions and decisions impact the lives of people worldwide.)(Their governing body, the World Health Assembly meets in Geneva, Switzerland where the headquarters of the WHO is located.

7) **The World Court or International Court of Justice (First Justices Elected in 1946)** The World Court is one of six principal organs of the United Nations and is the only international court that adjudicates general disputes between countries, with its rulings and opinions serving as primary sources of international law. (Headquartered in the Netherlands)

8) **The World Bank (Began Operations - June 25, 1946)** On their website this statement concerning their purpose and priorities is found. "Three priorities guide our work with countries to end poverty and boost prosperity for the poorest people. Helping create sustainable economic growth, investing in people and building resilience to shocks and threats that can roll back decades of progress."³ (Headquartered in Washington, D.C.)

---

² https://www.wfm-igp.org/about-us/
³ https://www.worldbank.org/en/what-we-do

9) **The International Monetary Fund (December 27, 1945)** The International Monetary Fund is a major financial agency of the United Nations. It is an international financial institution consisting of 190 nations. Its stated mission is "working to foster global monetary cooperation, secure financial stability, facilitate international trade, promote high employment and sustainable economic growth, and reduce poverty around the world." (The International Monetary Fund is headquartered in Washington, D.C.)

10) **The Computer Age - (June 21, 1948)** The first program, consisting of seventeen instructions and written by Tom Kilburn, a researcher for the University of Manchester, ran on June 21st, 1948. This was the first program to ever run on an electronic stored-program computer.[4] The development of the computer age is obviously absolutely essential for the creation of a global New World Order.

11) **Legalized Abortion (The Eugenics Protection Law in Japan - 1948)** It is hard to identify a specific beginning of legalized abortion in the world but certainly one law that can be found as a key turning point is the Eugenics Protection Law passed in Japan in 1948. The law allowed both voluntary and involuntary sterilization in keeping with Eugenics, the so-called self-direction of human evolution. Along with this it also legalized abortion in cases of rape, leprosy, hereditaryily-transmitted disease, or if the physician determined that the fetus would not be viable outside of the womb. The consent of the woman and her spouse were not necessary. The law was amended in 1949

---

[4] https://zionkerala.blogspot.com/2015/12/1948-first-computer-program-to-run-on.html

to allow abortions for economic purposes.[5] The Eugenics Protection Law made Japan one of the first countries to legalize induced abortions.[6]

12) **Cable Television in the United States (Spring of 1948)** Cable television was first made available in the United States in 1948. It is claimed that the first cable television system in the United States was created in 1948 in Mahanoy City, Pennsylvania by John Walson to provide television signals to people whose reception of television stations was poor because of tall mountains and buildings blocking tv signals.[7] The development of television and in particular cable television has obviously become extremely important to the connecting of people's ideas, thoughts and likes throughout the world.

13) **The "Big Bang Theory" (Published on April 1, 1948)** This popular evolutionary idea concerning the origin of the universe which has become the dominant view within scientific circles was published in the scientific journal "Physical Review" under the name "The Origin of Chemical Elements".[8] It was later nicknamed "The Big Bang" by Sir Fred Hoyle in 1949. It would be hard to overstate the enormous role that the teaching of the Big Bang and the Theory of Evolution, which propose a world without a Creator, have played in the direction that the world has taken in recent decades. An examination of

---

[5] https://en.wikipedia.org/wiki/Eugenics_in_Japan
[6] https://en.wikipedia.org/wiki/Abortion_in_Japan
[7] https://en.wikipedia.org/wiki/Cable_television_in_the_United_States
[8] https://www.history101.com/april-1-1948-alpher-bethe-gamow-propose-big-bang-theory

Romans 1:18-32 in light of the world we live in today is very revealing.

14) **Release Time for Religious Education Ruled Unconstitutional for the First Time (March 8, 1948)** In the landmark Supreme Court ruling McCollum v Board of Education decided in March of 1948 the court struck down a Champaign, Illinois release time educational program. At the time release time, where public schools set aside class time for religious education, was common and practiced in over 2,000 U.S. communities.[9] This shift in U.S. education was a key part of moving America forward into a secular mindset.

I believe it is noteworthy that all the global institutions and organizations listed above (numbers 1-9) are headquartered in either Europe or in the United States, with the majority residing within European countries. Europe's role in the movement toward a secular, global New World Order is significant and I will discuss this more in the next chapter.

In Luke 21 Jesus alluded to a time when "all the trees" would put forth their leaves. Exactly what Jesus was referring to is not something that we can definitively say, but it makes sense that the shift within the nations toward both a secular and global mindset would create the opportunity for a New World Order that would be primed and ready to receive an antiChrist leader described in the Bible as one who will come to power in the times leading up to the 2nd coming of Jesus Christ.

I find it amazing that so many significant things happened among the nations of the world in the same window of time that Israel was coming to life and emerging as a nation again after nearly 2,000 years. During the window of time between 1945 and 1948 it seems as though a switch was flipped and all the roots of a

---

[9] https://en.wikipedia.org/wiki/McCollum_v._Board_of_Education

developing secular, global system, a New World Order, began to take hold within the nations of the world.

In the chapters that follow we will see how these roots have now taken hold and the growth in the movement toward a New World Order has now quickened and increased dramatically.

CHAPTER 12

The European Union and The New World Order

Europe and the European Union have been at the heart of the movement to establish a global New World Order. In part European nations have already experienced the type of things that globalism will bring. They have experienced the yielding of national sovereignty. They have experienced the benefits of workers, goods, services and capital being able to cross national borders easily, producing benefits for individuals and companies at times, but the crushing of economic growth through massive amounts of regulations and laws that hinder individual nations and private companies. They have also experienced political benefits as their collective voice yields more power than any of their individual voices would, but the dangers of being pulled as individual nations into situations and conflicts apart from their own interests. They have also experienced negative results as countries cede some of the powers that sovereignty is designed to protect—national budget-making, monetary policy, and immigration and work authorization laws.

One of the probable reasons that Europe has been as interested as they have been in experimenting with moving from sovereign nations to a union of nations approach is that both WWI and WW2 were fought primarily upon their lands and involved European nations at war with one another creating devastating impacts.

As I mentioned in chapter 6, the European Union is a major proponent of the advancement of a global system and European nations lead the way in the push for a New World Order. As we saw in the last chapter, the majority of the international organizations and entities that are leading the way in the movement toward globalism are headquartered in Europe.

Identifying the spirit and motivation behind the European Union can help us understand the spirit and motivation behind the push for a global society. On the surface the goals and objectives of the European Union and its humanitarian arm The Council of Europe seem good and commendable. Though the stated goals appear upright and good there are indicators of what is really at the heart of the European Union and the push toward a unified Europe and a unified global society.

In 1563 Pieter Bruegel the Elder painted his famous painting entitled "The Great Tower of Babel" which remains to this day as the most recognizable depiction of the Tower of Babel.

The Biblical account of the Tower of Babel makes it clear that the tower did not represent a noble enterprise. It was man's attempt to build something great apart from God, not to draw closer to God and to give God glory. It appears to have been inspired not only by human pride and self-will, but by demonic influences as well. The Tower of Babel is probably the single most significant example of rebellion against God seen in the Bible. It was on account of what was taking place there at the time that God confused their languages. We see the results of that time still today as multiple languages are spoken around the world. (It is interesting that guiding principle #3 on the Georgia Guidestones is "Unite humanity with a new living language) (Spoken of in chapter 6).

A poster developed by the Council of Europe which appears to be designed to promote a unified Europe, was known as the "construction site poster". When looking at this poster it is clear that the 1563 painting by Pieter Bruegel of the Tower of Babel provides the theme for the poster. The caption "Europe, many tongues, one voice", which is seen on the poster, speaks to the intent to accomplish what the people in Genesis 11 were not able to accomplish. To see a copy of the poster, go online and do an image search for "Europe: Many Tongues One Voice". It is hard to imagine such imagery being used if a God honoring heart were at the core of the development of the European Council and European Union.

Note also the use of upside down pentagrams at the top of the poster. The circle of stars in the European flag is obviously referred to here but with a strange twist. Underneath the upside down pentagrams people are seen working, it appears, to complete the work that was not completed in Genesis 11.

From what I have been able to discover it appears that this poster was developed in the 1990s and was removed from use after protests by Christians.

Another poster that was on display at one point in the European Commission headquarters, which is the administrative arm of the European Union has the caption "Europe4All - We can all share the same star". The star is made up of many symbols representing all of the major religious beliefs in the world. It is very telling that included in these symbols are five of the hammer and sickle symbols which represent communism. This poster can also be found online by doing an image search for "Europe4ALL poster".

In Strasbourg, France stands a building which houses the parliament of the European Union and is the official seat of the

European Union Parliament. The European Union also has parliament buildings in Brussels, Belgium and Luxembourg City, Luxembourg.

The building that houses the E.U. Parliament in Strasbourg was built in the late 1990s and opened in 1999. When looking at the building it is easy to see that the European Union again chose to use the Tower of Babel as their inspiration. One might say that those leading the European Union simply see the Tower of Babel as a picture of people working together to build something good. Still, it is hard to imagine a group of leaders being ignorant of the Biblical meaning attached to the Tower of Babel. It seems much more likely that the tower was chosen purposely because of its human endeavor apart from God connotations.

Javier Solana, the European Union's former foreign policy chief made a distinction between Europe and America in a 2003 statement where he said, "We in Europe are as societies more secular . . . nobody could imagine there being a sentence on the euro which said 'In God we trust' but that's what it says on a dollar." [1]

It is probably not news to most that European nations tend to be further along the path of becoming secular than the United States, even though the United States has continued along the same path. An article by Pew Research speaks of 5 ways that Americans and Europeans are different. One of the 5 ways was in how important they view religion in their lives. The article reports that "just over half in the U.S. (53%) say religion is very important in their life, nearly double the share who hold this view in Poland, which registered the highest percentage among EU nations polled

---

[1] https://www.ph.ucla.edu/epi/bioter/warnotjustfied.html

in 2015. In France, only 14% consider religion very important."[2]

The same article revealed that Europeans tend to be much more open to Socialist forms of government as well. Those questioned were asked "What's more important in our society, that everyone be free to pursue their life's goals without the interference from the state or that the state play an active role in society so as to guarantee that nobody is in need?"[3] A chart revealing the answers of people in the U.S. and a number of European countries that are (or were) a part of the European Union shows that though more Americans are open to Socialism than in previous years, as a whole they are still less open to Socialist ideas than those who live in nations that are a part of the European Union. This survey was taken in 2011 so the numbers may very well have increased in all of the nations since Socialism continues to be promoted in both Europe and America.

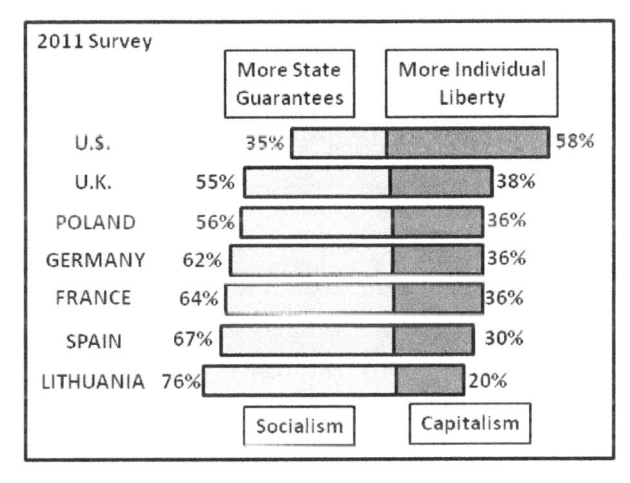

2011 Survey	More State Guarantees	More Individual Liberty
U.S.	35%	58%
U.K.	55%	38%
POLAND	56%	36%
GERMANY	62%	36%
FRANCE	64%	36%
SPAIN	67%	30%
LITHUANIA	76%	20%
	Socialism	Capitalism

In front of the European Union Parliament building in Strasbourg, France there is a statue entitled, "The Removal of Europa" which has a woman riding atop a wild bull. Though the meaning of the statue is related to Greek mythology and the union between Zeus and Europa, the statue also bears an eerie resemblance to what is described in Revelation 17, a harlot riding a great beast. Similar statues are located in other key locations

---

[2] https://www.pewresearch.org/fact-tank/2016/04/19/5-ways-americans-and-europeans-are-different/
[3] ibid

throughout Europe including in Brussels outside the Council of the European Union Headquarters and at The Hague, where the International Court of Justice, an arm of the United Nations, is located along with over 200 other international agencies. (The picture shown here is of the statue at The Hague in the Netherlands.)

From July 28 - August 8, 2022 the Commonwealth Games were held in Birmingham, England. During the opening ceremonies, which were overseen by King Charles, then Prince Charles, an elaborate story was enacted before the large crowd who were assembled there.

People from various countries were seen by video to have supposedly found light shards which fell to earth from an exploding star in the heavens. They are viewed as having been miraculously transported with the light shards to the stadium. Then a huge mechanical bull enters the stadium and is angry. The bull is tamed by the light shards and eventually participants from many nations are seen bowing before the now tamed bull, worshiping the bull. (Images of this scene can be found online both in the form of still photos and video images.) The ceremony also includes a structure that resembles the Tower of Babel. In the later portion of the ceremony the tower is seen with light streaming from it. Eventually light streams forth from the top of the Tower into the heart of the bull. At this point in the ceremony the flags of all the participating nations have been placed around the bull, encircling the bull that has been worshiped by the participating nations.

Of course other explanations are given by narrators, as to the meaning of these things, but the symbolism seems very telling. Ancient pagan cultures worshiped false gods that were represented by graven images of a bull. A thorough explanation of the symbolism seen in this ceremony can be found in the rumble video entitled

"The Commonwealth Beast of July 2022 announced the SOON Coming Antichrist KING!".[4]

With Europe's great influence toward the building of a future, global society, it would seem that a global system that is God honoring is unlikely. It appears more likely that a system that includes pagan gods and human endeavors to build a society apart from God is what globalists have in mind. Still, many gladly move toward a global system as spiritual deception abounds!

Europe - The Revived Roman Empire?

Another important aspect of the development of the European Union is the potential for this development to be a fulfillment of important Bible prophecies concerning the last days. These prophecies are found in the book of Daniel. We looked at some of these in chapter 10 but it would be good for us to look at these prophecies and ask the question, "Is the modern development of a unified Europe a rebirthing of the Roman Empire and a fulfillment of prophecies found in the book of Daniel?"

In Daniel, chapter 2 we read of the vision that King Nebuchadnezzar had of a statue that represented world empires that would arise and fall throughout world history. We read this description of the legs, feet and toes of the statue in verse 33 and the meaning of this aspect of the vision in verses 40-45.

> *"its legs of iron, its feet partly of Iron and partly of clay."*   Daniel 2:33

> *"Then there will be a fourth kingdom as strong as iron; inasmuch as iron crushes and shatters all things, so, like iron that breaks in pieces, it will crush and break all these in pieces. (41) "In that you saw the feet and*

---

[4] https://rumble.com/v2ll9lc-the-commonwealth-beast-of-july-2022-announced-the-soon-coming-antichrist-ki.html

toes, partly of potter's clay and partly of iron, it will be a divided kingdom; but it will have in it the toughness of iron, inasmuch as you saw the iron mixed with common clay. (42) "As the toes of the feet were partly of iron and partly of pottery, so some of the kingdom will be strong and part of it will be brittle. (43) "And in that you saw the iron mixed with common clay, they will combine with one another in the seed of men; but they will not adhere to one another, even as iron does not combine with pottery. (44) **"In the days of those kings** *the God of heaven will set up a kingdom which will never be destroyed, and that kingdom will not be left for another people; it will crush and put an end to all these kingdoms, but it will itself endure forever. (45) "Inasmuch as you saw that a stone was cut out of the mountain without hands and that it crushed the iron, the bronze, the clay, the silver and the gold, the great God has made known to the king what will take place in the future; so the dream is true and its interpretation is trustworthy."* Daniel 2:40-45

We should note that there appears to be a continuation of the legs into the feet and toes. The interpretation of the vision also seems to describe not a separate empire but a morphed version of the empire represented by the legs with the strength of iron. We are told that it will, in the end, (represented by the feet and toes) be a mixture of peoples with some strong and some brittle. We are told that it will be in the days of those kings (that together make up this empire) that the God of heaven will destroy the kingdoms of men and will set up His eternal Kingdom that will never be destroyed.

If the 4th kingdom within this vision, represented by the legs of iron is the Roman Empire, then the end time kingdom represented by the feet and toes would almost certainly be a revived Roman Empire of some type. If this is the case then the development of a revived Europe, where the capital of the Roman Empire was located, is of great importance. The Roman Empire was not the largest in history, but many believe it was the strongest in history and that it remained intact for the longest period of time. By 117 A.D. The Roman Empire encompassed basically all of Europe, as well as the Middle East, parts of Northern Africa and parts of Asia Minor.

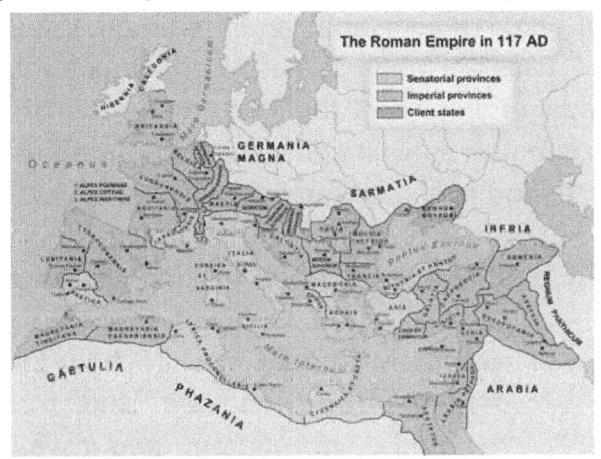

It may also be significant that the British Empire which rose to prominence from the 16th through the 20th centuries and at its height stretched across nearly one fourth of the globe and held sway over about 23% of the world's population, was also centered in Europe.

In a movie made a few years ago to encourage British people to vote in favor of Brexit, leaving the European Union, much information is given about the big government techniques, massive regulations, heavy controls, and lack of accountability of leaders, all found within the European Union.[5] This could be a preview of what type of governing will be involved if a global system emerges out of the current European model.

It is commonly believed that the fourth beast empire of Daniel 2 and Daniel 7 is a reference to the Roman Empire that followed the Babylonian, Medo-Persian and Greek Empires. For this reason many, myself included, who are looking for the fulfillment of Bible prophecy have been looking with great interest at the developments among European nations for decades now.

When we look at prophecies found in Daniel 7 we see the

---

[5] https://www.youtube.com/watch?v=UTMxfAkxfQ0&t=3727s

information of chapter 2 confirmed and additional details given within the vision that is here given to Daniel. The first three empires are confirmed but this time are represented by various beasts (head of gold = a lion) (arms and breast area of silver = a bear) (loins area of brass = a leopard). The fourth empire that was represented by the legs of iron and the feet and toes of iron mixed with clay is confirmed as well and described as a dreadful and terrifying beast with iron teeth and ten horns.

> "After this I kept looking in the night visions, and behold, **a fourth beast**, dreadful and terrifying and extremely strong; and **it had large iron teeth. It devoured and crushed and trampled down the remainder with its feet; and it was different from all the beasts that were before it, and it had ten horns.** (8) "While I was contemplating the horns, behold, another horn, a little one, came up among them, and three of the first horns were pulled out by the roots before it; and behold, this horn possessed eyes like the eyes of a man and a mouth uttering great boasts."
> Daniel 7:7-8

The little horn appears to be referring to the coming antichrist and further information of his boastful, blasphemous words and actions is given later in the chapter. Later in the chapter more is said of this fourth beast which is different from all the rest as well.

> "Then I desired to know the exact meaning of **the fourth beast, which was different from all the others, exceedingly dreadful, with its teeth of iron** and its claws of bronze, and which devoured, crushed and trampled down the remainder with its feet, (20) and the meaning of the ten horns that were on its head and the other horn which came up, and before which

three of them fell, namely, that horn which had eyes and a mouth uttering great boasts and which was larger in appearance than its associates. (21) **"I kept looking, and that horn was waging war with the saints and overpowering them (22) until the Ancient of Days came and judgment was passed in favor of the saints of the Highest One, and the time arrived when the saints took possession of the kingdom.** *(23) "Thus he said:* **'The fourth beast** *will be a fourth kingdom on the earth, which will be different from all the other kingdoms and* **will devour the whole earth and tread it down and crush it.** *(24)* **'As for the ten horns, out of this kingdom ten kings will arise; and another will arise after them, and he will be different from the previous ones and will subdue three kings. (25) 'He will speak out against the Most High and wear down the saints of the Highest One**, *and he will intend to make alterations in times and in law; and* **they will be given into his hand for a time, times, and half a time. (26) 'But the court will sit for judgment, and his dominion will be taken away, annihilated and destroyed forever. (27) 'Then the sovereignty, the dominion and the greatness of all the kingdoms under the whole heaven will be given to the people of the saints of the Highest One; His kingdom will be an everlasting kingdom, and all the dominions will serve and obey Him.'**

Daniel 7:19-27

In chapter 7 we again see that the end times kingdom or empire is not actually a separate kingdom from the fourth kingdom (which most believe to be the Roman Empire) but rather the same kingdom revived in the last days, in an altered form and consisting of multiple kings or nations. Notice in verse 23 that it will "devour the whole earth". This may very well be speaking of an end time kingdom that is global but is centered in the area of the old Roman Empire, which includes Europe.

As you can see this passage also appears to speak of the antichrist waging war against the saints for 3 ½ years and then being destroyed. Also consistent with chapter 2 is this beast empire being followed by the return of Jesus Christ to establish the eternal kingdom of God which is "given to the people of the saints of the Highest One."

The Growth of Islam in Europe

There are some who believe that the fourth beast empire of Daniel 2 and Daniel 7 actually refers to the Islamic Empire rather than the Roman Empire. If that is true the developments in Europe would still be significant, especially in light of the fact that Islam is growing greatly in strength in numerous European nations.

The cooperation of globalists and Muslims is very curious. One would think that secularists who are heavily entrenched in the globalist movement would want nothing to do with those whose religious beliefs are extremely non-secular, inflexible and are in many cases enforced with violence. One would also think that Muslim leaders would view secularists as ungodly and as people they would not want to be in collaboration with. Yet somehow secularists promoting a humanistic global system and Muslims longing for a global Islamic caliphate are often seen working together. For example the "World Government Summit 2022" was held in Dubai, United Arab Emirates with the theme "Shaping Future Governments. I believe this seemingly unthinkable cooperation is made possible because of the influence of demonic powers, guiding the world toward an end time global system.

In Europe, where so much movement toward a global system is occurring, the number of Muslims is growing substantially. According to the Pew Research Center the number of Muslims in the European region was more than 25 million by 2016 with France and Germany leading the way with nearly 6 million Muslims residing in France and nearly 5 million in Germany.[6] The same study estimated up to 75 million Muslims living in Europe by 2050.[7]

Anti Semitism On The Rise in Europe

On another front, anti semitism is on the rise in many European nations in recent years. One report in 2019 entitled "Anti Semitism Rising Sharply Across Europe, Latest Figures Show" said that there had been a 74% increase of offenses against Jews in France and a 60% surge in reports of violent attacks on Jews in Germany.[8]

Another 2019 article entitled "The Alarming Rise of Anti-Semitism in Europe" reported that a 2018 survey by the European Union's Fundamental Rights Agency found 89% of Jews living in Austria, Belgium, Denmark, Germany, France, Hungary, Italy, The Netherlands, Poland, Spain, Sweden, and the UK feel anti-Semitism has increased in their country over the past decade, while 85% believed it to be a serious problem.[9]

It may not be a coincidence that growth in antisemitism is taking place in Europe at the same time that the movement toward a global system is finding traction. Ephesians 2:2 speaks of "the spirit that is now working in the sons of disobedience." The dark spirit that will bring rise to the antichrist is already at work in the world and one of the traits of this spirit is a hatred for the Jewish people and a

---

[6] https://www.pewresearch.org/religion/2017/11/29/europes-growing-muslim-population/
[7] ibid
[8] https://www.theguardian.com/news/2019/feb/15/antisemitism-rising-sharply-across-europe-latest-figures-show
[9] https://www.hrw.org/news/2019/06/04/alarming-rise-anti-semitism-europe

hatred of true followers of Jesus Christ. Revelation 12 reveals that in the last days when Satan is cast down to the earth for a short time he will quickly begin an attempted onslaught focused on the Jewish people and those who keep the commandments of God and hold to the testimony of Jesus. (Revelation 12:13-17)

Hitler & The Altar of Zeus

It is hard to think about Europe and antisemitism without thinking of the man who instituted the horrible atrocities of the Holocaust during WW2. Adolf Hitler believed that the Jewish people were less than human and he made it his mission to rid the world of them along with others he felt polluted the Aryan race that he believed to be a superior race of people.

Hitler's words and actions both revealed his hatred of the Jewish people. He is quoted as having said, *"The Jews undoubtedly are a race, but they are not human."*[10]

He also is quoted as having said, *"Under the guidance of the Reich, Europe would speedily have become unified. Once the Jewish poison had been eradicated, unification would have been an easy matter."*[11]

Hitler believed in both Darwinian evolution and a byproduct of the theory, eugenics. Eugenics is in essence the belief that only people of superior physical and intellectual qualities should be allowed to have children, in order to build and sustain a superior race of people. Hitler's beliefs in these ideas certainly opened his mind to some of his unthinkable opinions of the Jewish people. This quote from Hitler reveals his belief in both evolution and eugenics. *"The stronger must dominate and not mate with the weaker, which would signify the sacrifice of its own higher nature. Only the born weakling can look upon this principle as cruel, and if he does so it is merely because he is of a feebler nature and narrower mind; for if*

---

[10] https://www.goodreads.com/quotes/10670444-the-jews-are-undoubtedly-a-race-but-they-are-not
[11] https://libquotes.com/adolf-hitler/quote/lbr4r2n

such a law did not direct the process of evolution then the higher development of organic life would not be conceivable at all."[12]

Deception that can come when people believe ideas that are not biblical is seen in the life of Hitler who apparently was so deceived that he actually believed that his evil acts were pleasing to God. He is quoted as saying, *"I believe today that my conduct is in accordance with the will of the Almighty."* [13]

Hitler became to many in Germany a messianic type figure. He adopted the title "Fuehrer" which means leader. Everywhere he went crowds would lift their hands toward him and say "Heil Hitler". This common gesturing and the words spoken revealed the level of reverence that was given to Hitler by much of the German population. This public reverence was often voluntary and was sometimes compulsory. "Heil Hitler" certainly appears to be a throwback to the days of the Roman Empire and the use of "Hail Caesar". The gesture used with "Heil Hitler" of the right arm and hand extended upward and outward is often referred to as "the Roman salute". [14] Benito Mussolini had also incorporated this Roman salute into Italy just prior to its common use in Germany.

After immigrating to the United States from Germany in 1937 Erika Mann wrote a book entitled, *"School for Barbarians: Education Under the Nazis".* In her book she reveals the deeper meaning behind the greeting "Heil Hitler". She says, *"Heil really means salvation, and used to be applied to relations between man and his God; one would speak of ewiges Heil (eternal salvation)".*[15] The online ReversoDictionary confirms that "ewiges heil" is German for "eternal salvation". [16] Erika Mann also revealed how German children in the 1930s would hear "Heil Hitler" constantly. She said, *"Every child says "Heil Hitler!" from 50 to 150 times a day, immeasurably*

---

[12] https://www.goodreads.com/author/quotes/30691.Adolf_Hitler?page=1
[13] https://www.goodreads.com/author/quotes/30691.Adolf_Hitler?page=2
[14] https://en.wikipedia.org/wiki/Roman_salute
[15] https://www.facinghistory.org/resource-library/heil-hitler-lessons-daily-life
[16] https://dictionary.reverso.net/german-english/ewiges+Heil

more often than the old neutral greetings. The formula is required by law; if you meet a friend on the way to school, you say it; study periods are opened and closed with "Heil Hitler!"; "Heil Hitler!" says the postman, the street-car conductor, the girl who sells you notebooks at the stationery store; and if your parents' first words when you come home for lunch are not "Heil Hitler!" they have been guilty of a punishable offense and can be denounced.[17]

Though I can not find the video any longer, I have seen a video clip of German school children singing a song in their school classroom about Hitler being their savior.

Hitler mesmerized massive crowds with his speeches. I believe that this happened for more reasons than he was simply a powerful speaker. I believe there was a spiritual, or demonic element involved. As we just referenced, he was treated as a messianic type figure. Consider the following information as well that may shed some light on what was happening at that time. I share all of this here because I believe that much of the same spiritual deception that took place in Germany in those days is influencing many in Europe again today, though obviously it looks different and it has not reached the same level publicly as of yet.

In Revelation 2:12-13 there is a reference to "Satan's throne" in Pergamum.

> "And to the angel of the church in Pergamum write: The One who has the sharp two-edged sword says this: (13) 'I know where you dwell, where Satan's throne is; and you hold fast My name, and did not deny My faith even in the days of Antipas, My witness, My faithful one, who was killed among you, where Satan dwells." Revelation 2:12-13

Pergamum was a city and region in what is now modern day

---

[17] https://www.facinghistory.org/resource-library/heil-hitler-lessons-daily-life

Turkey. Though the meaning of "Satan's throne" in Revelation 2:13 is not known as a historical fact, one view is that it is a reference to "the Altar of Zeus" which was built in Pergamum in the 2nd century B.C. Pergamum and the surrounding region was certainly known as an idolatrous place in New Testament times and "the Altar of Zeus" was a key part of that idolatry. As would be expected, this altar deteriorated over the centuries. In the late 1800s the entire site of the ancient altar was excavated and the remains were taken to Germany, where they were reconstructed and made available for viewing in what was and is called "The Pergamon Museum" in Berlin, Germany. The basic structure of the altar is easily identifiable. It has numerous pillars all across the front of the structure and has protruded sections on both the right and left sides. Since the time the remains were first reconstructed in Germany they have been replaced by reproductions of the original remains and the altar remains in the revised museum today, drawing hundreds of thousands of tourists each year.

from Wikipedia Commons

In 1934 Hitler's chief architect Albert Speers used the Altar of Zeus as his inspiration to design the massive Zeppelin Field Stadium that was then used by Adolf Hitler as a backdrop to speak at rallies to huge crowds of Germans. During nighttime rallies the magnificent structure included 150 searchlights facing upwards, producing streams of light miles up into the night skies. In September of 1935 over a million people gathered for Hitler's speech here which included his introduction of the

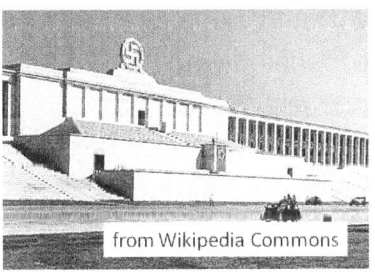

from Wikipedia Commons

Bundesarchiv, Bild 102-04062A / Georg Pahl / CC-BY-SA 3.0, CC BY-SA 3.0 DE
Via Wikipedia Commons

Nuremberg Laws, which was the formal beginning of the systematic marginalization of Jewish people from German society. It was in this speech in front of the massive replica of the Altar of Zeus that he first publicly used the term "the final solution", later realized to be a reference to the systematic killing of the Jews, now commonly referred to as the Holocaust. He said, "Bitter complaints have come in from countless places citing the provocative behavior of Jews. This law is an attempt to find a legislative solution ... if this attempt fails it will be necessary to transfer (the Jewish problem) ... to the Nationalist Socialist Party for a final solution."[18]

    I do not believe that Hitler's choice of patterning the place he would speak from after the ancient Altar of Zeus is coincidence or accidental. As he would descend the steps of the massive stadium structure to the podium prepared for him to the worship-like adoration of the massive crowds, his apparent messiah complex was on full display. It was from this podium that his words seemed to mesmerize people of all ages and his evil intentions were voiced with bold but innocuous sounding words. The connection between the spiritual realm and the natural realm is striking.

    What took place in Europe during the Holocaust was clearly satanic and demonic at its roots. It is difficult for most people to believe that massive amounts of people could have adored and followed a man who we now see as someone filled with evil. Yet this took place less than one hundred years ago.

    Not only has Europe not turned to God since those days but there are many indicators that Europe as a whole has fallen further from God in recent decades. If Europe truly is at the forefront of the movement toward a New World Order and a powerful leader should arise who appears to have the answer for the world's problems it is certainly reasonable to believe that the same sort of deception could again capture the hearts of multitudes who are trusting in their own intellect and looking for worldly solutions apart from

---

[18] https://www.youtube.com/watch?v=9r83ZRissyw

dependency upon God. The Bible says that Satan disguises himself as an angel of light.[19] Spiritual deception has continued throughout history and Bible prophecies make it clear it will only increase in the last days.

Today, there are many, a good number of them in Europe, who are proposing ideas of world domination. They speak of these things as noble and good. Many of these ideas have already been shown to be extremely destructive through previous examples within nations and even in very recent preliminary results of the push toward globalism.

For the Christian, it is critical that one keep their eyes on Jesus, the true Christ, Who is the same yesterday, today and forever! All of the current events in Europe and around the world moving us closer to globalism will at some point soon be interrupted and halted by the glorious 2nd coming of our Lord Jesus Christ!

---

[19] 2 Corinthians 11:14

CHAPTER 13

A Sustainable World and "The Great Reset"

The attempts by those who envision a New World Order are not without opposition. Many, especially those in more prosperous nations of the world, are content with a world filled with many sovereign nations that have the freedom to make their own choices and their own laws. Bringing billions of people together as one, when considering law, economy, ethics, religion, political systems, government, etc. is no small task. As a matter of fact, it appears that such a thing would never happen voluntarily without some extraordinary methods. It also appears that such a thing would never happen without large measures of compulsion.

For decades now, those who long to see a global government, economy and society have realized that they would have to have a cause to legitimize the massive changes they seek to bring upon all who live upon the earth. They would have to trumpet this cause and convince the masses that something very bad will happen, that will impact all of humanity if the change to a global system is not accomplished.

That cause has been found in what was once called "Global Warming" and is now referred to as "Climate Change". For years now doomsday scenarios of the results of global warming or climate change have been proclaimed. Massive changes are proclaimed to be absolutely essential to avoid total catastrophe. Though the narrative has been altered some, the basic message has remained the same and supposedly the narrative has been proven to be trustworthy by unquestionable scientific evidence. Scientists who have dared to express a different view and who point to scientific evidence to support their view have been minimalized and their evidence has often been ignored.

Al Gore, who has championed the Climate Change message, revealed how far those promoting this message will go in making elaborate, so-called scientific, claims. At a January 2023 WEF meeting in Davos, Switzerland, Gore went on what many called a rant. He stated *"We're still putting 162 million tons (of greenhouse gas) into it (the atmosphere) every single day,"* and *"The accumulated amount is now trapping as much extra heat as would be released by 600,000 Hiroshima-class atomic bombs exploding every single day on the earth."*[1]

Consider that 600,000 atomic bombs per day would be 219 million atomic bombs exploding on the earth each year. That's more than one per square mile. This type of extravagant claim serves to instill fear, motivating change, but appears to be completely outside the realm of reality.

I believe these claims come because those who want to see a global New World Order know that the transition to such a system, as they envision it, will involve massive changes in billions of people's lifestyles that can only be justified if they are necessary to save the entire planet. Personal sacrifice for the good of everyone is what we now hear about increasingly as those promoting this new global system become more open about what they are proposing. We are told that our lifestyles must be sustainable!

In 2020 and 2021 people throughout the world experienced how quickly lifestyles can be altered, somewhat voluntarily and in part by compulsion, when a global crisis is put in the mix. Globalists have said that the crisis that climate change presents is greater and more extensive than the crisis that Covid-19 presented. Though few know what measures globalists intend to take in the next few years,

---

[1] https://www.youtube.com/watch?v=rfAYLSQIxTI

they have openly indicated that major changes to the lifestyles of many are coming quickly.

Simple and quick internet research can reveal the fact that there are now many organizations, foundations, conferences, summits, governments and groups of individuals lending their time and energy to the movement toward a New World Order, though they may refer to it by different names. I remember researching these types of things in the 1980s and it was quite fun and intriguing. Now, the study of these things is not fun because we are feeling the impacts of the beginning phases of this movement which impacts our lives here and now. I will not attempt to identify all, or even many of the groups promoting globalism but I want to give attention to two particular leading organizations in this quest.

These two organizations are the United Nations and the World Economic Forum. In chapter 11 I listed numerous international organizations that were founded in the window of time between 1945 and 1948 which have provided the structure or skeleton for the globalist movement but among them all, it appears that the United Nations and the World Economic Forum have emerged as the leading forces in the movement.

The United Nations has long touted the dangers of global warming and climate change and measures that they believe must be taken to avoid the total destruction of the earth.

In 1992 the United Nations "Agenda 21" plan was presented and approved by the vote of 179 nations. Within the "Agenda 21" plan numerous things that are a part of Western values and lifestyles were deemed to be "unsustainable". In other words, these things can not continue as they are now without the total destruction of the environment being the inevitable result.

Rosa Koire, author of "Behind the Green Mask" has described the agenda of the United Nations in this way, ""UN Agenda 21 / Sustainable Development is the **action plan implemented worldwide to inventory and control all land, all water, all minerals, all plants, all animals, all construction, all**

means of production, all energy, all education, all information, and all human beings in the world. Inventory and Control." [2] & [3]

The United Nations and others speak a lot in terms of that which is "sustainable" and that which is "equitable". All of this is in reference to the things within the lifestyles of those who live in Western, more prosperous nations, which they have determined to be a detriment to the environment and a contributing factor to inequality between those living in poorer nations and those living in more prosperous nations. They emphasize that aspects of life that are "unsustainable" and "unequitable" must be changed or done away with.

As we will see, all of this fits with the push toward transition from democratic and capitalist forms of governments and economies to a more socialist, marxist type of government and economy. Individual freedoms and incentive toward working to make a better life for one's self and family are viewed as obstructions to an equitable and sustainable world.

In the Agenda 21 plans numerous things were identified as being **"unsustainable"**. Among these things were **"middle class lifestyles", "single family houses or dwellings", "private vehicles", "meat eating", "air conditioners", and "appliances"**. The idea is that billions of people owning their own home and car or truck, eating meat most days, running the air conditioner in their house, and using various appliances throughout the day, is unsustainable for our future here on earth.

Maurice Strong, former Under-Secretary-General of the United Nations and Executive Director of the United Nations Environment Programme spoke a lot about the unsustainable lifestyles of middle-class people in western countries.

He is quoted as saying, *"It is clear that current lifestyles and consumption patterns of the affluent middle-class involving high*

---

[2] http://integratingdarkandlight.com/agenda-21-plan-for-total-control/
[3] https://www.youtube.com/watch?v=3PrY7nFbwAY&t=41s

meat intake, consumption of large amounts of frozen and convenience foods, use of fossil fuels, appliances, home and work-place air-conditioning, and suburban housing-are not sustainable. A shift is necessary toward lifestyles less geared to environmentally damaging consumption patterns." [4]

The World Economic Forum has become a leading voice in the movement towards a New World Order as well. They have openly proclaimed that current free market capitalist systems that they refer to as "shareholder capitalism" have failed and that they must be replaced by "stakeholder capitalism". I will discuss later what "stakeholder capitalism" means.

The World Economic Forum produced a short video a few years ago that presented their "8 Predictions for the World in 2030". These 8 predictions reveal much of the same ideas that have been communicated by the United Nations' proclamations concerning a sustainable world. They also present some further aspects of their plans related to government and economic systems. In the video they make no effort to elaborate or explain each of these predictions but state them in simple, bold terms. The video is only about 90 seconds long. As of the beginning part of 2023 you can still view the video on YouTube if you type in 8 predictions for 2030 - World Economic Forum. One of the available YouTube videos has just the WEF video with no extra commentary. [5]

Here is a list of their 8 predictions shown in their video. I have shortened and altered the words of some of the predictions slightly here.

1) You'll own nothing and you'll be happy
2) The U.S. won't be the world's leading superpower
3) We won't transplant organs, we'll print new ones instead
4) You'll eat much less meat
5) A billion people will be displaced by climate change

---

[4] https://www.azquotes.com/quote/713885
[5] https://www.youtube.com/watch?v=AQqH1f_54A4

6) Taxes will be placed on Carbon Dioxide emission (Fossil Fuels will become a part of history)
7) Safe space travel will increase - Journey to find alien life?
8) Western values will be kept in check and balanced by Government

Let's look a little deeper at what is being said here. First of all, though these 8 things are referred to as "predictions", it stands to reason that they reflect what the World Economic Forum wants to see happen as they work the plans they have to create what they would refer to as a better world, with a more stable environment and with greater equity for all. I encourage you to think of these things in terms of things that globalist groups hope to bring to pass by the year 2030, which is only 7 years away.

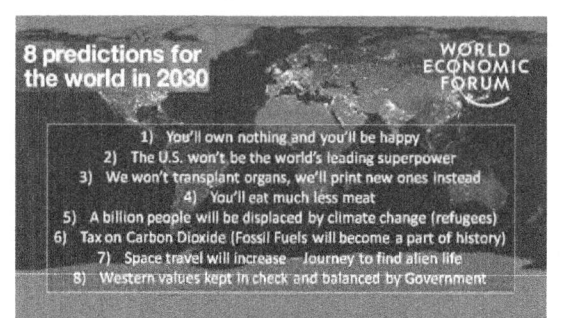

Number 1 is perhaps the most telling of the 8, at least when it comes to individual lifestyles. **"You'll own nothing and you'll be happy".** The video goes on to say "whatever you want you'll rent and it will be delivered by drone". If none of us own anything that will mean that everything is owned by the state. This involves a radical departure from the individual freedoms that Americans and many others have known throughout their lives. When they say, "and you'll be happy", we might ask how do you know that? The statement implies that the big brother government that owns everything will be kind, loving and considerate of the needs of all of their subjects who now are dependent upon the state for everything. History shows that this has never been the case anywhere that totalitarian governments have ruled over people.

It is difficult to imagine what kind of radical plans globalists may have in mind if they are predicting that none of us will own our own house, our own car, our own furnishings, etc., just seven years from now! Prior to 2020 it would have been nearly impossible to fathom radical change of this nature in such short order. Through Covid-19 lockdowns and shutdowns we have now gotten a glimpse of how quickly governments can impose major changes upon the masses.

It has been documented that foreign governments and some of the super rich have been buying up farmland and industries across America but what the World Economic Forum is predicting would involve something much more radical. I do not claim to know or understand what they may have in mind. I can only speculate that it could involve some sort of freeze on all bank accounts and/or the calling of all loans suddenly in response to some so-called crisis that supposedly justifies such measures. Time will tell.

One thing is easy to see. People owning property and personal belongings is a part of a lifestyle that globalists consider both unsustainable and inequitable. It appears that they have intentions of somehow changing the current realities in the very near future. Research into what books are most often required reading in top American universities reveals that the top two books were "The Republic" by Plato and "Leviathan" by Thomas Hobbes. Both of these books view private property and private wealth as detrimental to what they see as the best forms of government. I will speak more of this in a later chapter but for now I will just say that it is apparent that many young people in America have been being prepared for these radical changes for decades.

As Christians, we know that we ought to pray about these things. We might pray that God stops all of this and prevents the plans of the United Nations, the World Economic Forum and others from coming to pass. God is a good God and He may very well stop all of this and prevent it from happening. Then again we might need to pray that God prepares us for these changes that may very well be a part of the prophesied last days that the Bible speaks about. We may need to live with a much greater level of faith and dependency upon God. We should be comforted in the words the

Lord speaks to us in Scripture where He promises "I will never leave you nor forsake you!"[6] One thing is for sure. No plans and measures taken by globalists can take away from us the One Who is truly our provider, protector and loving Heavenly Father!

The second of the 8 predictions by the World Economic Forum gives us insight into what is taking place in the United States today and in recent years. What a bold prediction for them to make! **They boldly predict that "the U.S. won't be the world's leading superpower!"** The United States, which has been the world's leading superpower for decades, with its freedoms, its strength and its prosperity is the greatest obstacle for the development of a New World Order. The prediction is that this will no longer be the case within 7 years from now. That's bold! We could ask, is this prediction based on observations and a hunch, or is this prediction based on plans that are already in place to weaken the United States and to take away its prominence in the world?

I will not address this in any detail here. I have devoted a later chapter to this issue and will deal with this in much more detail there.

Number 4 gives another indication of the intentions of globalists to alter the lifestyles of the middle-class in many nations. When **they predict that "you'll eat much less meat"** we can again ask if they make this prediction on observation of trends or if they make this prediction based on plans to purposely impose this change of diet upon multitudes of people. I find it hard to believe, but it is true that a number of those trumpeting climate change have actually said they believe that cows are a problem for the environment because they belch while they are eating. Some have suggested that cows should have to wear masks and diapers to contain methane emissions.[7] Wow! On a lighter note, I will admit that quite often when I enjoy a steak, a chicken breast or a hamburger, I

---

[6] Hebrews 13:5
[7] https://www.foxnews.com/media/farmer-speaks-out-against-forcing-cows-wear-diapers-contain-methane-emissions-loony-town

think about their prediction for 2030 and give thanks that for today I am free to enjoy meat regularly in my diet and that God has given us meat as a gift to enjoy and be nourished by.

Number 5 deals with immigration and ties it to climate change. Again, it is suggested that radical changes are coming, and are necessary, no matter how difficult, because of the impending doom they suggest the climate change crisis is creating. Over the past decade in America, the difficulties associated with illegal Immigration of have been seen and experienced. It is estimated that around 15.5 million illegal immigrants lived in the U.S. as of 2021 and that the cost of illegal immigration to the nation had totaled over 140 billion dollars.[8] Also, in recent years millions of refugees have come to European nations and much has been written about the related difficulties associated with this migration. One 2020 BBC article said this regarding the influx of over a million refugees into Europe in 2015, "But the sudden influx of people sparked a crisis - both humanitarian and political - as Europe struggled to respond."[9] It went on to say the impact of this mass migration is still being felt today.

With this as a backdrop consider the fifth prediction of the WEF. It says, **"A billion people will be displaced by climate change."** That is 3 times the number of people now living in all of the United States. It is hard to fathom how nations would deal with this many refugees within the next 7 years. It is also hard to fathom this amount of environmental decline within the next 7 years. They go on to say "We'll have to do a better job at welcoming and integrating refugees". It would seem that these kinds of shifts in population would create a catastrophic crisis. Any difficulties experienced by the influx of refugees and immigrants into countries in the past would be dwarfed by the crisis that a billion displaced people, about

---

[8] https://www.fairus.org/issue/illegal-immigration/2021-update-how-many-illegal-aliens-live-united-states
[9] https://www.bbc.com/news/world-europe-53925209

15% of the world's population, would create.

The key ingredient in a formula for forcing major changes upon masses of people is crisis, whether brought about by circumstances beyond human control or brought about purposely with intent. People are much more accepting of change when in crisis.

I believe that these predictions give us insight into the minds and hearts of those who want to force a global system upon billions of people who live in nations all around the world today. I believe that their predictions actually reveal their intentions.

Before moving on to the 6th prediction I want to say something about the Christian's response to massive amounts of immigrants and refugees into their communities. Jesus has made it clear that His will for us is that we would be loving people and that we would treat people who come into our lives like we would treat Jesus if He moved next door (see Matthew 25:31-46). He has also made it clear that our mission in life involves using every opportunity in life to tell others about Jesus and His love. Even if situations are manufactured by globalists to create a crisis, in order to bring about an environment for change, the Christian should view massive amounts of people coming to live near them as an opportunity to love people with a Christlike love and to share the Gospel of Jesus Christ with those same people.

The 6th prediction of the WEF involves another major change in lifestyle for millions of people. They predict that **"Polluters will have to pay to emit carbon dioxide."** It then adds, **"There will be a global price on carbon. This will help make fossil fuels history."** It is hard to imagine fossil fuels being history in 7 years. This would involve another massive change for billions of people.

Natural gas, coal and oil are all examples of fossil fuels. Fossil fuels are a key part to many parts of our lives beyond the gasoline that we burn in our cars. One 2019 article entitled "75 Uses of Fossil Fuels in Daily Life" says "Do you know that fossil fuels run the world? Life as we know it would come to a standstill if we ran out of these precious compounds. Fossil fuels supplement the production of many products. Diverse items such as household items, clothes, your car, airplanes, boats, pesticides, bags, purses, and even food are preserved with a little help from fossil fuels."[10]

It is not surprising that a high percentage of commercials now for cars and trucks are advertising electric vehicles even though only 1% of passenger cars on the road in America in 2022 were electric vehicles.[11] During the 2022 Super Bowl 6 out of the 7 car commercials that aired were for electric vehicles even though only 9% of car sales were for electric cars at that time.[12]

As I write in early 2023 the latest buzz in matters related to fossil fuels is that some are suggesting that gas stoves should be banned, including the U.S. Consumer Product Safety Commission. Growing numbers of local municipalities, as well as some states are now passing legislation to prohibit any use of fossil fuels including appliances in new buildings.

The WEF may simply be predicting that use of fossil fuels will be taxed heavily by 2030 which will lead to the eventual abandonment of fossil fuel use altogether. Even if this is the case, it points to another part of the plan to use climate change as an excuse for radically changing life as we know it.

I will deal with the significance of prediction #7 concerning future space travel and the search for alien life in a later chapter. I believe that this may end up being a part of the deception that affects many in the last days.

Prediction #8 involves another very telling statement, concerning the intentions of the World Economic Forum. It says, **"Western values will have been tested to the breaking point."** It

---

[10]https://allusesof.com/energy/75-uses-of-fossil-fuels-in-daily-life/
[11]https://gearandcylinder.com/what-percentage-of-cars-are-electric-the-answer-may-surprise-you/
[12]https://www.cnbc.com/2022/02/14/evs-dominated-super-bowl-ads-but-only-9percent-of-passenger-car-sales.html

then says, **"Checks and balances that underpin our democracies must not be forgotten."** This reference to "western values" seems to clearly be pointing to the lifestyles of those in western culture, especially in the United States.

The United Nations has identified many aspects of the lifestyles of those in western nations, especially the "middle-class", as "unsustainable". Here the WEF is saying that much of what we value in life will have been tested to the breaking point. In other words, it will have been determined by powerful organizations and governments that aspects of the lifestyles of those living in prosperous countries cannot continue without checks and balances that will control people's lifestyles "for the good of the planet".

The words used in this 8th prediction could be taken as innocent indications that everyone will voluntarily choose to be more careful about certain things like recycling and using alternative energy sources when they are a good option, if it were not for the many other things stated by the United Nations, the WEF, and others which indicate clear intentions of establishing global governance to make many lifestyle changes compulsory.

"The Great Reset"

"Introducing the 'Great Reset,' world leaders' radical plan to transform the economy". This was the title of a June 2020 article, featuring a picture of Prince Charles, where I first heard about the Great Reset. [13]

The cover of Time magazine for their November 2-9, 2020 issue read "The Great Reset" by Klaus Schwab and it featured a picture of construction workers reconstructing the earth.[14]

Since its introduction in 2020 much attention has been given to the "Great Reset" both by those who are working to accomplish it

---

[13] https://thehill.com/opinion/energy-environment/504499-introducing-the-great-reset-world-leaders-radical-plan-to/

[14] https://thecsspoint.com/product/time-magazine-2nd-november-2020/

and by onlookers. Amazingly, even though much has been said publicly about this reset of the world's governmental and economic systems by those promoting it, some media outlets have begun to claim that it is a conspiracy theory. Certainly, as with any major issue, unsubstantiated claims can be found concerning the "Great Reset" but the reality of it cannot be denied without ignoring the words and actions of those openly promoting it.

In response to the Covid-19 pandemic the World Economic Forum, including numerous world leaders, began to call for a great reset of the world's economy. The World Economic Forum said this of their call for a great reset. "There is an urgent need for global stakeholders to cooperate in simultaneously managing the direct consequences of the COVID-19 crisis. To improve the state of the world, the World Economic Forum is starting The Great Reset initiative." [15]

They describe the reasoning behind this reset in a section entitled "The Context". They state, "The Covid-19 crisis, and the political, economic and social disruptions it has caused, is fundamentally changing the traditional context for decision-making. The inconsistencies, inadequacies and contradictions of multiple systems - from health and financial to energy and education - are more exposed than ever amidst a global context of concern for lives, livelihoods and the planet. Leaders find themselves at a historic crossroads, managing short-term pressures against medium- and long-term uncertainties." [16]

They explain further in a section called "The Opportunity". Here they say, "As we enter a unique window of opportunity to shape the recovery, this initiative will offer insights to help inform all those determining the future state of global relations, the direction

---

[15] https://www.weforum.org/great-reset
[16] ibid

of national economies, the priorities of societies, the nature of business models and the management of a global commons. Drawing from the vision and vast expertise of the leaders engaged across the Forum's communities, the Great Reset initiative has a set of dimensions to build a new social contract that honours the dignity of every human being."[17]

It is clear that the World Economic Forum and others have seen the Covid-19 pandemic as an opportunity. When viewed as innocent goals, this "opportunity" would refer to a chance to fix things that existed before the Covid-19 pandemic especially dealing with the planet (climate change issues) and equality (fixing an economic system that results in a widening gap between those who have and those who don't have). When viewed as goals that are more than they are presented outwardly, this "opportunity" might refer to a chance to implement a heavy handed global government and economy that will resemble Marxism much more than a system fostering freedoms for all and rewards for diligent work and effort. Either way, the opportunity they speak of clearly relates to moving from independent nations to global systems that makes the cooperation of all nations compulsory, for the sake of the planet.

In their paragraph statement under "The Context" the key phrase is, "the inconsistencies, inadequacies and contradictions of multiple systems - from health and financial to energy and education - are more exposed than ever ...". Here, our current system within the world of multiple nations, with each establishing their own laws, systems and values, is said to contain inconsistencies, inadequacies, and contradictions. It is easy to see how this sentiment leads to the thought that a global system is now needed.

Under the section called "The Opportunity" we learn that the Global Reset initiative is designed to offer insights to inform all those determining the future in a number of areas listed. A key phrase is found towards the end of the section that says, "to build a new

---

[17] ibid

social contract that honors the dignity of every human being." A contract suggests something that is binding, in this case upon all the peoples of the world.

Honoring the dignity of every human being certainly sounds good and admirable if it does not include insisting that unbiblical values espoused by some must be applauded and approved of by all in order to honor the dignity of all. We have seen in modern culture the redefining of the word "tolerance" from "choosing to treat those with whom you disagree with respect and kindness", to a new meaning of "acknowledging that the values and beliefs of those you disagree with are true and right even if they are much different than your values and beliefs and even if they are contrary to the Bible". If honoring the dignity of every human being involves this new so-called tolerance, then this would be a problem for anyone who believes in absolute truth that comes only from God, and is found in His Word the Bible. In truth, loving people and treating them with respect and dignity is not the same as agreeing with every belief and every form of lifestyle others may espouse as though all beliefs are equally true and there is no absolute truth.

"Stakeholder Capitalism vs. Shareholder Capitalism"

A key element of the "Great Reset" is to reset the world's economic system, moving from free market systems they refer to as "Shareholder Capitalism" to an altered system they call "Stakeholder Capitalism". The term "Stakeholder Capitalism" is used often by Klaus Schwab, the founder and chairman of the World Economic Forum.

When hearing a description of the differences between these two economic systems it is easy to see why the change would be suggested. "Shareholder Capitalism" is described as corporations and businesses that are run with the bottom line always being profits for the shareholders. All the management and operational decisions in this model are made with profits for the shareholders in mind. The executives know that their jobs depend upon making money for the shareholders, even if this means not doing what it is best for the laborers and the world outside of the corporation.

The proposed "Stakeholder Capitalism" model is said to be based on corporations and businesses run with many more factors in mind. In this model corporations and businesses have a stake in building a better world, along with governments, organizations and individuals around the world. As a result, business decisions are made by executives with care for the planet in mind, benefits to society in mind, care for the underprivileged in mind, as well as profits for the shareholders, who also see themselves as "stakeholders" in the global world.

There is no question that when explained in these terms the change to "Stakeholder Capitalism" seems to be the right thing for everyone. In essence it sounds like simply moving from selfishness and greed to caring and sharing.

Even Pope Francis has publicly indicated that he feels that the current capitalist economic systems have failed and that significant changes must be made.[18]

The problem with all of this is that the same human beings would be involved in both systems. There is nothing in "Shareholder Capitalism" that prevents the executives and shareholders of a corporation from choosing to consider the needs of their workers, the care of the planet and the needs of those outside their company in every business decision they make. It is that which is inside the hearts of men that causes selfishness and greed to abound, not the system itself. Even now most corporations do donate funds and products to help others. They could choose under the current system to do much, much more if they simply chose to. They could choose under the current system to make the well being of their workers a high priority. They could choose under the current system to be very conscious of their companies' impact upon the

---

[18]https://nypost.com/2020/10/04/pope-frances-says-market-capitalism-has-failed-amid-covid-19/

environment.

Under the "Stakeholder Capitalism" model, human beings, with the same hearts, would be involved. The real difference is that a different set of people would have the power to sway the decisions and practices of businesses and corporations. Rather than shareholders driving the decisions of corporate executives, a group of people enforcing agreed upon procedures and practices would be driving the decisions of corporate executives. In order for businesses and corporations to change their motives there would need to be a way to push them into changes.

ESG Scores (Rating Corporations and Individuals)

The motivation for businesses and corporations to change is already being implemented to a degree in the form of something called **"ESG scores"**. "ESG" stands for "**E**nvironmental", "**S**ocial", and "**G**overnance". Businesses and corporations are given scores based on how well they are doing in addressing environmental issues, addressing social issues, and having governance systems that are considered fair and equitable. Emitting carbon gas will lower a score while use of renewable energy sources will raise a score in the area of "environment". Being supportive of organizations and causes deemed important to the scorekeepers will raise a score, while speaking out or being supportive of organizations and causes deemed dangerous, hateful or unimportant to the scorekeepers will lower a score in the area of "social". Having the right ethnic, gender and sexual orientation balance on a board of directors will raise a score, while appearing to be narrow minded

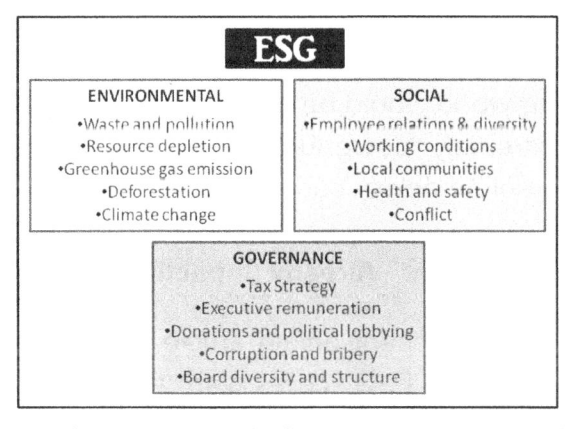

ESG

ENVIRONMENTAL	SOCIAL
•Waste and pollution	•Employee relations & diversity
•Resource depletion	•Working conditions
•Greenhouse gas emission	•Local communities
•Deforestation	•Health and safety
•Climate change	•Conflict

GOVERNANCE
•Tax Strategy
•Executive remuneration
•Donations and political lobbying
•Corruption and bribery
•Board diversity and structure

and dominated by a certain type of individuals will lower a score in the area of "governance".

You probably have already identified that whoever the scorekeepers are in ESG scores for businesses and corporations will now assume great power in shaping the world. (In other words, whoever determines how ESG scores will be calculated.) If a business or corporation scores low they can be reprimanded, shunned by investors or blackballed. The use of ESG scoring has already started but may very well become a dominant force, controlling businesses around the world if the "Stakeholder Capitalism" system is fully adopted. If this occurs, though it is technically a capitalist system, it could end up functioning more like a socialist or communist system since businesses would have to fall in line with the mandates of those creating the criteria for ESG scores in order to function and prosper or even remain solvent.

In a "Shareholder Capitalism" system if the hearts of men are Christlike, much love, caring and sharing can abound. If the hearts of men are filled with selfishness and greed the system can produce bad results. The same is true of a "Stakeholder Capitalism" system as it has been described. The system is not what will determine the outcome. The hearts of men will determine the outcome.

The added danger of the "Stakeholder Capitalism" system as it has been described is that the power to control the direction and outcomes of businesses, corporations and lives of people around the world would be placed in the hands of a few who would become extremely powerful. It has been said that "power corrupts and absolute power corrupts absolutely."

ESG Scores - Already Impacting the World

A recent online article by the Market Business News reveals how much ESG scores were already having by the beginning of this decade. The article explains, *"ESG stands for **E**nvironmental **S**ocial and **G**overnance, and refers to the three key factors when* *measuring the sustainability and ethical impact of an investment in a business or company. Most socially responsible investors check companies out using ESG criteria to screen investments."* [19]

The article later states, *"ESG standards are gradually becoming a significant part of the alternative investment world. ... Traditional investors are becoming increasingly interested in the ESG framework, and many have begun using its criteria for assessing risk in the investment decision-making process."*[20]

A 2020 Forbes article explains where ESG scores originated and shows the magnitude of impact this is having upon the world. Would you like to guess where ESG standards and scores originated? I think your guess would most likely be correct.

"ESG issues were first mentioned in the 2006 United Nations' Principles for Responsible Investments (PRI) report ... ESG criteria was, for the first time, required to be incorporated into the financial evaluations of companies. This effort was focused on further developing sustainable investments."[21]

That's not a surprise is it? ESG standards and scores originated through the United Nations. An entity dedicated to the development of this was established by the United Nations called "PRI" or "Principles for Responsible Investments". On the PRI's website they describe themselves as "supported by, but not part of, the United Nations."[22]

The magnitude of impact upon the world that this is having is also reflected in the Forbes article. The article states, "At the time (that is in 2006), 63 investment companies composed of asset owners, asset managers and service providers signed with $6.5 trillion in assets under management (AUM) incorporating ESG issues. As of June of 2019, there are 2,450 signatories representing over

---

[19] https://marketbusinessnews.com/financial-glossary/esg-definition-meaning/
[20] ibid
[21] https://www.forbes.com/sites/betsyatkins/2020/06/08/demystifying-esgits-history--current status/?sh=675a10902cdd
[22] https://www.unpri.org/about-us/about-the-pri

$80 trillion in AUM."[23] A graph on the PRI website shows that the growth of these numbers has continued at a rapid pace. The graph reveals that by 2021 there were 3,826 signatories representing over $121 trillion in Assets Under Management.[24]

I'm sure many of us are both surprised and alarmed by how deeply ESG standards and scores have already infiltrated the business world. All of this before "Stakeholder Capitalism" is put in place. Actually, what we may be seeing is the gradual implementation of "Stakeholder Capitalism" without most people even realizing that it is happening.

The story gets deeper and broader when we come to understand that these ESG standards and scores are not only designed for businesses and corporations, they are also already being used for governments and for individuals.

One of the organizations involved in monitoring ESG scores is MSCI which stands for Morgan Stanley Capital International. On their website they state that "MSCI ESG Government Ratings covers 198 countries and regions and provides ratings on more than 99 percent of outstanding sovereign debt in the marketplace."[25]

Hitting even closer to home is information related to ESG scores for individuals in the U.S. and elsewhere.

In an online article by "The Impact Investor" updated in Nov. of 2022 and entitled "How to Calculate Your Individual ESG Score", it is stated that a system of ESG scores for individuals is being implemented in the U.S. and will soon be in many other nations. [26]

The article states, *"People have credit scores that tell lenders and other parties if they can pay their debts. It is similar to a credit score when it comes to an individual ESG score, but instead of rating creditworthiness, it rates a person's ESG risk."* [27]

---

[23] https://www.forbes.com/sites/betsyatkins/2020/06/08/demystifying-esgits-history--current-status/?sh=675a10902cdd

[24] https://www.unpri.org/about-us/about-the-pri

[25] https://www.msci.com/www/research-report/msci-esg-government-ratings/03174655227

[26] https://theimpactinvestor.com/calculate-individual-esg-score/

[27] ibid

Further explanation of these new developments are also given. *"Many mainstream financial institutions are creating a new platform that is centered on ESG scores. In addition to creating this platform, their lending guidelines are also getting an update that includes new rules that will tie your individual ESG score to your ability to secure lending."*[28]

Recently, I preached on a Sunday morning at the church I had pastored for many years before stepping down to devote the rest of my life to writing, traveling and speaking on issues related to Christian apologetics. I mentioned the development of ESG scores during my message. On Tuesday morning of that week I received a text message from one of the worship leaders at the church who works at a local lending institution. The text said, "Look what was in my inbox this morning." It was a memo to employees regarding the beginning of training in the use of ESG scores.

Not surprisingly, China has already instituted their own version of ESG scores for their citizens. This is addressed in an August, 2020 online article by the South China Morning Post entitled "What Is China's Social Credit System and Why is it Controversial?"

The article begins by stating that, *"China's social credit system, by its wide definition, is a set of databases and initiatives that monitor and assess the trustworthiness of individuals, companies and government entities. Each entry is given a social credit score, with reward for those who have a high rating and punishments for those with low scores."*[29]

Although the 2020 article says that the system is still in the developmental stages, information given within the article would make it appear that the system is advancing quickly. Note the following.

"According to data from the People's Bank of China (PBOC),

---

[28] ibid
[29] https://www.scmp.com/economy/china-economy/article/3096090/what-chinas-social-credit-system-and-why-it-controversial

the nation's central bank, the social credit system already covered 1.02 billion individuals and 28.34 million companies and organizations by the end of 2019. Many of these had already been rated, and some had even been blacklisted.

The NDRC said in July 2019 that 2.56 million people had been restricted from taking flights, 90,000 people had been prevented from using high-speed rail services and 300,000 people had been deemed untrustworthy by Chinese courts." [30]

The article also mentions that China is experimenting with collecting data from video surveillance and real-time data transfers. According to a December 2017 BBC article, "China has been building what it calls 'the world's biggest camera surveillance network'. Across the country, 170 million CCTV cameras are already in place and an estimated 400 million new ones will be installed in the next three years. Many of the cameras are fitted with artificial intelligence, including facial recognition technology."[31]

In considering China's social credit system we should keep in mind that this is the country known for severely limiting the freedoms of its people. China has been aggressively suppressing Christianity and persecuting believers for decades. Yet, in a November 2022 television interview Klaus Schawb said that China is *"a role model for many nations"* and that the *"Chinese model is certainly a very attractive model."* [32]

In a later chapter we will look at developments in the area of programmable digital currency and see that combined with developments in ESG scores for businesses, governments and individuals, the makings of a "you can't buy or sell unless you comply" type of scenario are becoming more and more feasible.

---

[30] ibid
[31] https://www.bbc.com/news/av/world-asia-china-42248056
[32] https://www.breitbart.com/europe/2022/11/24/wefs-klaus-schwab-says-communist-china-is-a-role-model-in-the-systemic-transformation-of-the-world/

Many Working Together Toward a New Global System

Every year the World Economic Forum hosts a meeting of international politicians, business leaders, celebrities and journalists in Davos, Switzerland where matters concerning global interest are discussed. From these meetings many of the plans for the establishment of a global system emerge. Their meeting in 2022 centered around the theme "History at a Turning Point: Government Policies and Business Strategies.". While addressing a number of listed topics they would also be, in their terms, *"reinforcing the foundations of a stable global system."*[33]

Many other organizations and groups are on board, promoting the movement toward a global system. The "TEDConferences" organization has been sponsoring conferences each year to encourage many of the same goals as the U.N. and WEF, including an October 2020 event called "Global Launch". The "Project Management Institute" is another hosting annual "Global Summits" to teach project management professionals, rising leaders, and volunteers how to better promote U.N. sustainability goals. The **"World Governments Summit Organization"** is a global, neutral, non-profit organization dedicated to the shaping of future governments. [34] They also hold an annual summit, promoting the same ideas and plans to thought leaders, global experts and decision makers from around the world. This organization is led by His Highness Sheikh Mohammed bin Rashid Al Maktoum, Vice President and Prime Minister of the UAE, the Ruler of Dubai.[35]

The World Economic Forum website has an "Our Partners" page that includes an alphabetized list of **hundreds of partners** including many of the most known businesses and organizations in America and elsewhere. The "United Nations Global Compact" said

---

[33] https://www.weforum.org/agenda/2022/05/davos-2022-whos-coming-and-everything-else-you-need-to-know/

[34] https://www.worldgovernmentsummit.org/about

[35] ibid

to be "the world's largest corporate sustainability initiative" reports on their website that they have **21,218 participants** (as of January 2023).[36] Their website also shows that their global compact is based on **E**nvironment, **S**ocial and **G**overnance.

On the World Economic Forum's website page for "Davos 2023" they speak of the incredible group who will be attending the 5 day event in January of 2023 including many world political leaders, heads of international organizations, over 1,500 leaders of international businesses and corporations, as well as leaders of civil society.

In June of 2019 the World Economic Forum and the United Nations signed a strategic partnership framework "outlining areas of cooperation to deepen institutional engagement and jointly accelerate the implementation of the 2030 Agenda for Sustainable Development."[37]

It is clear that the movement toward a global New World Order, striving for a more "sustainable world" and looking to put a "great reset" in place is now in high gear. It would appear that there is nothing on man's part that will be able to stop this movement now with governments, the business community, financial institutions, media outlets and even some religious leaders all on board. It may very well happen very soon, putting things in place in the world that will provide the framework for the fulfillment of Bible prophecies concerning the end times.

It is also still very much a possibility that the God of heaven will say, "Not now" and if He does plans will slow or be halted, no matter how powerful the earthly forces are behind them.

Every believer must keep 3 important things in mind. God told us ahead of time that these things would happen, the God of the Bible is still in charge, and Jesus Christ, God's Son is coming again soon and He will establish His eternal, worldwide Kingdom!

---

[36] https://www.unglobalcompact.org/
[37] https://www.weforum.org/press/2019/06/world-economic-forum-and-un-sign-strategic-partnership-framework

CHAPTER 14

Globalism & The United States

In the last chapter we looked at the 8 Predictions by 2030 put forth by the World Economic Forum. **Prediction #2 says, "The U.S. won't be the World's Leading Superpower."**

That's a bold prediction! We could assume that this prediction is simply based on the observations of outsiders of what is happening within the U.S. For instance, anyone interested can easily track the amount of national debt that is being accumulated by the U.S. government and how that enormous amount of debt would look, even if it were to be divided into the amount of taxpayers throughout the country. As of the beginning part of February, 2023 the U.S. national debt was well over 31 trillion dollars.[1] If this amount is divided among all the taxpayers throughout the nation it comes to approximately a quarter of a million dollars per person, for every taxpayer in the United States! Based on this, it would not be difficult to predict that the strength of the United States could very well be diminished rapidly and very soon.

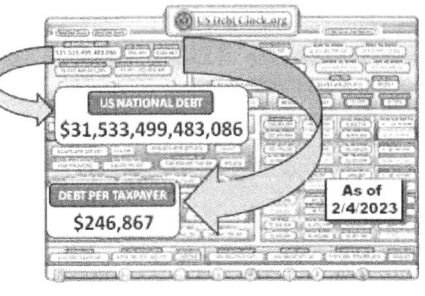

Based on many other factors we might instead assume that this bold prediction is made because there are plans already in place to ensure that the United States' status as the world's leading superpower comes to an end, allowing for a global system to

---

[1] https://www.usdebtclock.org/index.html

emerge. The WEF's prediction goes on to say of this new emerging global system, "a handful of countries will dominate."

It is not hard to see why those who believe that what is best for the world is a global, socialist system would see a strong and free capitalist superpower as a hindrance to globalists' goals.

Some of this may very well have been foreseen a few years ago when Donald Trump served as the president of the United States. During his years in office President Trump withdrew the United States from a number of international agreements and organizations, including "The Paris Climate Agreement", "The Trans-Pacific Partnership", the U.N.s culture and education body known as "UNESCO", and the "UN Human Rights Council", as his administration declared it to be "hypocritical and self-serving."[2] In July, 2020 Trump announced the U.S. was also withdrawing from the World Health Organization.

In his 2018 book "Globalization and Its Discontents - Revisited", nobel prize winner Joseph E. Stiglitz begins his introduction to the book by saying, "Donald J. Trump became president of the United States on January 20, 2017 and threw a hand grenade into the global economic order." In an interview he also said that Donald Trump is *"basically going to throw out what has been achieved over a 60 year period."*[3]

In January of 2020 Trump spoke at the World Economic Forum's meeting in Davos and said, "We're committed to conserving the majesty of God's creation, and the natural beauty of our world ... but to embrace the possibilities of tomorrow we must reject the perennial prophets of doom and their predictions of the apocalypse ... These alarmists always demand the same thing, absolute power to dominate, transform and control every aspect of our lives. We will never let radical socialists destroy our economy, wreck our country ..."[4] In these statements the president was clearly alluding to

---

[2] https://www.trtworld.com/americas/trump-s-top-five-withdrawals-from-international-agreements-18543
[3] https://www.youtube.com/watch?v=WWVf7dkys4g&t=108s
[4] https://www.youtube.com/watch?v=sb9jRqgDOJ8

alarming claims of climate change that are being used as an excuse for a massive shift toward a controlling global system that would have preeminence over independent nations and would dominate the lives of people around the world.

Two days later billionaire George Soros said during the same Davos meetings, "The 2020 U.S. election will determine the fate of the whole world."[5] Soros had said two years earlier at an earlier Davos meeting, "Clearly, I consider the Trump administration a danger to the world, but I regard It as a purely temporary phenomenon that will disappear in 2020."[6]

President Trump also addressed the United Nations General Assembly in November of 2019 and said, "Wise leaders always put the good of their own people and their own country first. The future does not belong to globalists, the future belongs to patriots."[7]

American economist Jeffery Sachs, who is the Director of the Center for Sustainable Development at Columbia University and President of the U.N. Sustainable Development Solutions Network expressed the sentiments of many globalists about the United States in 2020 as he spoke on February 5, 2020 at a conference that was a part of the "Pontifical Academy of Social Sciences". He referred to the United States as "an Imperial Power in decline". He continued by saying "and it is a dangerous country right now. It will be absolutely dangerous if Trump wins reelection."[8] Later, he referred to how the U.S. was out of step with the rest of the world as he said, "The General Assembly routinely votes 185 against the United States on almost everything right now. One after another it's the U.S. and two or three allied countries."[9]

---

[5] ibid
[6] ibid
[7] ibid
[8] https://www.youtube.com/watch?v=hs4Odu0X4Uw
[9] ibid

A strong America, determined to retain its independence, sovereignty and freedom to make its own decisions concerning the lifestyles of its people, is not a favorable thing for those who believe that a great reset of the entire world is needed. This is clear from one of the main explanations given for the so-called desperate need to have a new global deal. They speak often of the inequality between those in the west, particularly the U.S., and those in underdeveloped countries. The fact that the United States has done much to assist and lift up those in less fortunate countries does not appear to come into the equation of globalists' ideals.

Maurice Strong, former Under-Secretary-General of the United Nations and Executive Director of the United Nations Environment Programme once said, *"What if a small group of world leaders were to conclude that the principal risk to the Earth comes from the actions of the rich countries?... In order to save the planet, the group decides: Isn't the only hope for the planet that the industrialized civilizations collapse? Isn't it our responsibility to bring that about?"* [10]

As predicted by George Soros, the problems for globalists being caused by a U.S. with strong nationalist goals disappeared in November of 2020. The United States' position on U.N. initiatives, WEF initiatives and other global issues drastically shifted after that time with the insertion of a new administration. The United States' opposition to the move toward a great reset was halted and the conversation changed.

An About Face

One of the decisions I have prayerfully contemplated in the writing of this book has been what I would choose to say about what took place in the United States in November of 2020 and what words I would choose to use.

In one sense, anything I say about those events will not

---

[10] https://www.azquotes.com/author/14256-Maurice_Strong

directly impact the main focus of the book. The shaping of the world toward a biblically prophesied global government is easy to see, no matter a person's view of what has brought about the changes that have occurred in the United States in recent years. Whether the major changes in the U.S. came about legitimately or not doesn't alter the fact that the United State's opposition to those promoting a global system has been removed by in large.

On the other hand, if the means used to bring about the governmental changes in the United States were not above board and consistent with constitutional means of selecting leaders, then the seriousness of the times we now live in is further confirmed.

With this in mind I will simply say that the nation was divided over whether or not the results of the 2020 selection process were legitimate or not, with millions indicating that they believed the results were true and millions pointing to numerous pieces of evidence that they believed showed the results given were not a true reflection of the will of the people. Debate over this was fierce for a short while but was soon hindered by the censoring of the opinions of many on popular internet platforms. I experienced this to a degree myself at that time. In posting my third video on YouTube and on our ministry Facebook page which called people to pray for our nation, I used a word in the title of the video (which I have avoided using here) that resulted in Facebook not allowing us to boost ads for the next couple of years.

By now, anyone reading this book has probably made up their mind on what they believe took place. Though there are certainly still divided opinions on how we got here, one thing is clear to all. After November of 2020 the future course of America being promoted by governmental leaders shifted drastically and the resistance to the goals and plans of globalists by America's leaders turned into agreement and cooperation almost overnight.

An Infamous Day in American History

Most of the expressed concerns about the validity of the selection results were voiced in the weeks leading up to a major event that took place in the beginning of January in 2021.

Though I have chosen to say very little about November of 2020, I want to say a bit more about what took place in America in January of 2021 because I believe it may very well reveal that the elimination of the hindering influence of the United States to globalists' plans is both planned and broad in scope.

The events that took place in Washington D.C. the first week of January in 2021 changed the narrative and the mood within America drastically. Pictures and videos were seen by virtually everyone of large numbers of people battling with law enforcement officers to penetrate the United States Capitol building. According to the narrative presented, the huge crowd that had gathered in Washington to peacefully protest the selection results that were scheduled to be ratified at that time by the Congress, and to pray, had turned violent and attempts were made to take over the United States Capitol building. It was described as a dangerous and deadly insurrection that threatened our very democracy.

As a result of the events of that day, almost immediately, all opposition to the selection results were dropped and the results were ratified quickly and easily. The mood of the nation changed within hours and as a result, anyone still speaking out about their concerns with the selection results did so with the danger of being labeled an insurrectionist and even a domestic terrorist. Numerous people who were at the Capitol building that day ended up in prison for entering the building, clashing with police, or for perceived involvement of some type. As of March of 2023 numerous people who were a part of the events of that day are still being held in jail, without bail, still awaiting their day in court, after more than 2 years!

There is no question that there were some in the crowd that day who behaved in inappropriate ways and some became involved in behavior that would be considered criminal. Yet there is also much evidence that what took place that January day was not at all what was presented on the evening news and in many news publications. To what degree the events that unfolded were caused by disgruntled people, as opposed to other causes is hard to say. From what investigation I have done it appears that some of what took place was truly the result of a peaceful protest taking a wrong turn. It is also clear that there are other factors and players involved, encouraging the transition from peaceful protest to something violent, illegal and wrong. It is clear that a trap was set that numerous people, unknowingly walked into.

There are many lingering questions about what really took place that day at the Capitol building. Video footage and stories of eye witnesses present many confusing details and questions.

Why were a number of Capitol police officers told to go home early at 10:00 A.M. that day? Why was one man who is seen and heard in video footage specifically directing people to go into the Capitol building never indicted or prosecuted like so many others who had much less of a role? This man was also videotaped speaking with a young man, apparently giving him some instructions moments before the young man, and others with him, pushed through a temporary police barricade that was set up.

Why were some of the exterior and interior doors of the Capitol building undefended as protesters entered unhindered. Why did police stand by silently watching them walk by peacefully? There are numerous versions of video showing this as well.

Why was the most visibly recognizable man of the entire crowd, who wore a fur hat with viking-like horns, allowed to walk throughout the building freely, including all around the house chamber, all the while posing for photographs by professional photographers, one of which worked for Getty images? These images are still very easy to find. In March of 2023 surveillance video from inside the Capitol building was released, showing Capitol police escorting this man around the building and even helping him open doors and helping him make his way into the house chambers. Police made no attempts to stop or hinder this man though he was walking around by himself, at times in the presence of up to 9 police officers. Video footage recorded him praying a prayer of thanks to God for the police who allowed them to be in the building.

This man became the face of the "insurrection" and was sentenced to more than 3 ½ years in prison though it can be shown that he did not participate in any violent activity. Keep in mind that just months earlier mobs burned down numerous neighborhoods in American cities and most were not prosecuted. In Portland, OR. a Federal Building was set on fire in the summer of 2020 and Federal officers were physically attacked by rioters. Yet, after arrests were made, it appears that none of those who committed these crimes were prosecuted for their attacks on government buildings or officers.[11]

Why were peaceful scenes inside the Capitol shown live on national television with protesters casually walking through the rotunda as a few police officers freely allowed them to mill about?

Why is there video footage of police officers waving people toward the Capitol building on the Capitol grounds and video footage of police officers talking momentarily to a large group of protesters outside and then literally walking back from barricades, moving out of the way and allowing the group to proceed freely toward the Capitol?

Maybe the most puzzling question has to do with motive and timing. Why would people wanting to see something changed take actions that would obviously be viewed as criminal and dangerous

---

[11]https://www.dailywire.com/news/biden-admin-clears-remaining-federal-charges-against-portland-rioters-most-get-probation-community-service

minutes before congress would be talking about possibly doing the very thing the protesters wanted to see accomplished? **Their actions would cancel any chances of their desired outcome coming to pass.** Their actions would ensure that nothing would be done within congressional meetings to address concerns about the results from 2 months earlier. This should have been obvious ahead of time. Certainly, the results of the events of that day galvanized the transitional direction of the nation. If these events had occurred a day later, after a decision had been announced that was objectionable to many, it would have fit the narrative that was presented. As it is, it makes no sense that people would purposely plan and engage in behavior that negates any chance of them seeing the outcome they had gathered to pray for.

In addition to these questions it can be noted that eyewitness accounts and video footage confirm that Antifa members were interspersed within the crowd. Also, a great percentage of those on the front lines of clashes with law enforcement and those breaking down doors and windows, are seen wearing helmets and/or gas masks. Whoever these people were, and whatever their political views were, they obviously came prepared for what was then taking place.

Also, it would seem inconsistent with an attempted violent takeover of one of the most secure buildings in the world, that those involved would do so unarmed. As far as I know, no one was armed with any type of gun. Many called those in the Capitol building that day "armed" because they were carrying flag poles as they walked around in the building.

Also, on multiple occasions, groups of protesters are seen in video footage talking peacefully with police officers both outside and inside the building and then being allowed to pass by freely. In one case a group is seen having a discussion with a lone police officer in a doorway. He appears to be left alone to defend this entrance to one of the most secured buildings in the world. After a short discussion with the crowd at the door the police officer moves backward and picks up a baton laying on the floor behind him. He then continues to move backward and up a flight of stairs as a photographer or videographer is seen rushing into place to capture the entire scene as the group then chases the officer up the flight of stairs.

Certainly, there are many varying opinions as to what really took place that day at the Capitol building. One thing is for sure. It was a sad day in the history of America. Many believe that any suggestions that something was involved other than what was presented on the evening news are purely counterproductive conspiracy theories. Many others are convinced that the events of that day were designed to trap unsuspecting individuals and create a political narrative that would then create an environment where it would be difficult for anyone to openly question or challenge the government, for fear of being called an insurrectionist or domestic terrorist.

I include this information because I believe that the aftermath of the events of that January day have helped pave the way for major changes in America. These changes can now move forward without serious challenge since few desire to be linked with the sick images that remain in the minds of Americans. Ongoing government hearings serve to keep the memories of that day fresh in people's minds.

Whether or not what took place on that day was premeditated or not, and by whom, the main point of our discussion here remains. America has been wounded further by these events and any bold, strong talk about keeping America strong and independent now has to overcome the mental images of a very sad and terrible scene at our nation's Capitol building.

My greatest concern about what took place that day, and how it has been portrayed, is that it served to soil the image of Christians. It is common knowledge that a great percentage of those who went to Washington that day were Christians. They went to pray and ask God for His intervention in the nation they love and in the affairs they believed were adversely impacting that nation. They sang Amazing Grace and other songs of praise to God. They came to peacefully stand before God on behalf of the nation.

Some people in the world may automatically separate these people from the images of dangerous, violent acts witnessed that day. Some, though, now have a skewed view of peaceful, loving Christians who are now linked in their minds with violence and insurrection. I'm not saying that Christians are incapable of doing wrong or that no one involved in wrong acts that day were Christians. I am saying that the vast majority of those who gathered in Washington that day, did so with pure, godly intentions. They had no part in the ugly things that took place, no matter who instigated the violence and why it took place.

The Moral Decline of America

I have heard it said many times that the Roman empire was never conquered from without but that it crumbled from within because of its internal corruption. Many have been warning of a similar fate for America for years now.

In a previous chapter I spoke about the fulfillment of Bible prophecies concerning the increase of immorality and wickedness in the world in the last days. Much of that chapter dealt with what has been taking place in the United States in recent decades.

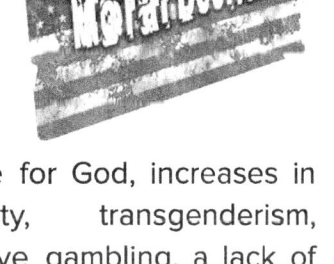

When speaking of the moral decline of America we can point to greed, sexual immorality, lying, theft, a lack of reverence for God, increases in violence, pornography, homosexuality, transgenderism, drunkenness and drug addiction, compulsive gambling, a lack of ethics, etc. The moral decline of America is seen everywhere we look. Increasingly, immoral behaviors are being legalized and protected in the United States. A few years ago when legalized gambling took hold in America, I had a sense that the legalization and taxation of marajuana would be next, and then the legalization and taxation of prostitution. Well, the legalization and taxation of marajuana is well underway now and about a year and a half ago I heard an interview with a government official running for a high profile office which included a question about their position on whether or not prostitution should be legalized. They openly replied that they didn't think the government should get involved in sexual relationships between two consenting adults. Now, in February of 2023 a San Francisco supervisor introduced a resolution to legalize prostitution in the San Francisco area.[12]

As we saw in chapter 9 dramatic impacts on morality in America after the removal of prayer and Bible reading from our public schools in 1962 and 1963 can be easily seen.

Romans 1:18-32 gives strong warning to any people group or nation who cease to honor God as creator and turn away from the worship of God and unto the worship of created things. Around 75 years ago public schools in America began to teach children that all of life came about through natural evolutionary processes apart from a living, wise and powerful creator, apart from God. Since that time America has followed the path described in Romans 1 in dramatic ways. The increase in both the practice of, and the celebration of all forms of homosexuality in America is exactly what Romans 1 warns will happen within a nation when God is no longer honored and thanked as the creator and giver of life. It would be easy to forget when looking at the United States today that this nation was once a nation devoted to Christianity and to biblical values. Today, there are even attempts to pull young children into immoral thoughts and behaviors well before they even approach puberty. I recently saw a video clip of a drag queen speaking in a school to a group of very young boys and girls. America has lost its

---

[12]https://www.nbclosangeles.com/news/national-international/san-francisco-bill-to-legalize-sex-work/3096867/

way because America has turned from God.

The moral decline in America is very much a part of the decline of America culturally, economically, politically, and the decline of American strength.

The Bible speaks prophetically of the rise of a global system in the last days. A strong America is an obstacle to the rise of such a system. The decline of American influence in the world, though prophesied, is the result of our sinfulness which causes God to lift His hand of blessing and protection from us as a nation.

A Nation In Turmoil

There are a number of other ways in which the United States is being weakened, especially in the past 3-4 years. No matter your views concerning the things I mention here, I'm confident that we would all agree on this simple fact. America has been weakened as a nation by the things we will now look at.

Jesus told us in Mark 3:24-25 that any kingdom or house divided against itself cannot stand.

> *"If a kingdom is divided against itself, that kingdom cannot stand. (25) "If a house is divided against itself, that house will not be able to stand."*   Mark 3:24-25

One of the things we have seen happening in America over the last few years is the increase of talk about racism. Many would say that this increase in talk about racism is a response to the reality of systemic racism that exists and is increasing in the United States. I do not believe that this is the case. I believe that the increase of talk about racism is another source of weakening us as a nation and is not an accurate reflection of how the vast majority of Americans actually feel toward one another.

I'm sure you are like I am in feeling that actual racism is sickening. Mistreating someone because of the color of their skin is both ridiculous and evil. I remember seeing an old movie once that included a kind, elderly black gentleman who was working on a farm for a white lady. In the film, a local KKK group attacked him one night for no reason and beat him severely. I felt my blood boiling as I watched this terrible example of human stupidity and depravity. I'm sure that just about everyone I know would have a similar reaction.

Watching the movie "Remember the Titans" about a high school football team forced to learn to function together as black and white players, I found myself moved by the loving relationships that were built among the players and coaches as the movie progressed. Yet in this movie as well I became angry during a scene when black players were told they wouldn't be served at a local restaurant, simply because of their skin color. Thankfully, today in America it would be hard to find a restaurant like that and it would be very common to find high school, college and professional sports teams that exhibit black, white, hispanic and asian players getting along quite well as brothers, fighting together for their team.

Racism is a real thing of course, but I do not believe that it is prevalent in America in the proportions many speak of. I'm in my 60s now and I have had opportunities to have many interactions with both white and black people throughout my life. My best friend in 5th grade was black and some of my best friends as an adult have been black men. I live in a pretty normal city and go to a typical Walmart on a regular basis. I see people of all different skin colors and rarely see any sign of people treating each other badly because of their skin color. Yet we are all faced now with a continual narrative that racism is rampant and that America is a racist nation. This narrative does create division and a lack of trust one with another. This narrative weakens us as a people and as a nation.

I encourage you to think of the people you know all around you and consider how the people you know treat one another. We can all do better in treating one another with respect and Christlike love but I'm confident that if you base your opinion of America on what you see around you, you will not come away thinking that America is a racist nation. The constant narrative of the news media, telling us that we don't like or respect one another paints a picture that I believe both wounds our relationships and weakens us as a nation.

To whatever extent racism exists in America it weakens us as a nation and to whatever extent the narrative that America is a racist nation fills the minds of people, it weakens us as a nation. Jesus' words are so true. Any house divided against itself cannot stand.

One of the ways that the narrative of systemic racism in America is presented is through the idea that law enforcement officers are by in large systemically racist. There is no question that there have been examples of unacceptable interactions between police officers and people of color, but to equate this with systemic racism is unfortunate. As of 2019 there were just about 1,000,000 state and local police officers in the United States.[13] If we multiply this number by 40 hours a week we come up with 40 million hours of police work and activity every week in America. In the age of cell phones and body cams a great percentage of interactions between police officers and individuals is caught on video. If these officers were systemically racist it would stand to reason that there would be hundreds, or even thousands of publicly known examples seen and heard every week. Though even one example is unfortunate, and is a reminder of the flaws in human nature, the infrequency of examples in comparison to the millions of hours of policing each week seems to point to something very different than the narrative that police officers in general are racist.

Calls to actually "defund the police" that have become pretty common in recent years may remind us of another sign of the end

---

[13] https://usafacts.org/articles/police-departments-explained/

times that Jesus spoke about in Matthew 24:12.

> *"Because lawlessness is increased, most people's love will grow cold."*   *Matthew 24:12*

It is hard to imagine what it would be like to live in a world with no law enforcement. Jesus appears to be indicating that the world will move in that direction in the end times. America is weaker today because of the lowering of trust levels in law enforcement officers, whether for valid reason or not.

Another issue weakening the United States that is related to one of the 8 Predictions of the World Economic Forum is that of illegal Immigration. Prediction number 5 by the WEF says that by 2030 a billion people will be displaced by climate change and that we will have to do a better job of welcoming and integrating refugees. Integrating numbers of people at this level is hard to even imagine.

One of the major issues over the past 10-20 years in America has been that of illegal immigration. Some of the policies enacted concerning illegal immigrants are confusing at best as many who come across the borders of the U.S. illegally are given various government benefits. In many cases, even those who commit crimes within the country are not prosecuted and are allowed to continue living freely within the nation. All of this adds another aspect of that which continues to weaken America. When a nation does not uphold its own laws it is inevitably weakened.

In this issue, as with other issues we have spoken of, Christians need to remember to follow the directives of the Bible. Though promoting legal immigration versus illegal immigration aligns with the Scriptural teaching of honoring established laws unless they violate God's laws, we should still choose to show love and kindness to those we find around us in our communities. It is not our responsibility to find out how those we meet in our community got there. We should show people the love of Jesus and we should also share the gospel of Jesus Christ with people we work with, live near or encounter within our community.

Changing the Minds of Generations of Students

It is a well known fact that one of the best ways to bring changes into a culture is through the teachings presented to students in schools. This would be true of students of all ages.

One of the fiercest battles in the United States today has to do with what will and will not be taught to young children in America's public schools.

Proponents of sex education materials that openly and aggressively promote sexual activity at early ages, homosexual lifestyles, and transgenderism seem relentless in their efforts to force these materials upon the minds of children as young as kindergarten and first grade.

A couple of years ago I spoke at a church on a Wednesday night. The church had a meeting after the service to discuss how they could respond in their community to the push within our state, and as a result in their community, to use new sex education materials within local schools at elementary grade levels. A copy of the state's proposed 3rd grade level book was made available for people to see what was being taught. When I thumbed through the book I was appalled at the contents. It truly was pornography. Lots of animated pictures of naked boys and girls in various positions. It was disgusting and it was another example of how the prophetic words of Romans 1 are being lived out in America today.

I want to touch on another example of how education is weakening America today in various ways. This example comes not from elementary grade levels but from University classrooms.

A few years ago I did some research about what is being taught in many universities across America today. During my research I discovered information on the books most often used as required reading materials in top U.S. universities. More than one list of this nature is out there depending upon which schools were a part of the survey but there is a lot of overlap in the various lists. One of the surveys dealt with many of the Ivy League schools and presented this list of the top 10 books of required reading material.[14]

1) The Republic (by Plato)
2) Leviathan (by Thomas Hobbes)
3) The Prince (by Niccolò Machiavelli)
4) The Clash of Civilizations (by Samuel Huntington)
5) The Elements of Style (by Willam Strunk)
6) Ethics (by Aristotle)
7) The Structure of Scientific Revolutions (Thomas Kuhn)
8) Democracy in America (by Alexis DeTocqueville)
9) The Communist Manifesto (by Karl Marx)
10) The Politics (by Aristotle)

With just a bit of research about the content of many of these books it is easy to see that college students in America today are basically being taught that the United States, with its current form of government and economy, is bad.

In the number 1 book, Plato's "The Republic", he undertakes to show what justice is. According to Plato, the ideal state comprises three social classes: rulers, guardians (or soldiers), and producers (e.g., farmers and craftsmen).[15]

In a Wikipedia article about "The Republic" it is stated that Mussolini admired the book and often read it for inspiration. The article goes on to explain why the book was appealing to Mussolini. "*The Republic* expounded a number of ideas that fascism promoted, such as rule by an elite promoting the state as the ultimate end,

---
[14]https://qz.com/602956/these-are-the-books-students-at-the-top-us-colleges-are-required-to-read
[15] https://www.britannica.com/topic/The-Republic

opposition to democracy, protecting the class system and promoting class collaboration, rejection of egalitarianism, promoting the militarization of a nation by creating a class of warriors, demanding that citizens perform civic duties in the interest of the state, and utilizing state intervention in education to promote the development of warriors and future rulers of the state."[16]

Plato presents "Timocracy" as a favorable form of government. Of this form of government he says, "*The accumulation of gold in the treasury of private individuals is the ruin of timocracy; they invent illegal modes of expenditure; for what do they or their wives care about the law?*" [17]

It is clear that Plato presents ideas about government and economy that are much more in line with socialism or communism than they are of our Republic form of government and free market form of economy.

Also worth noting, Plato depicts a society where efforts are undertaken to improve human beings through selective breeding. [18] This practice, now referred to as "Eugenics" gained support in the late 1800s after Francis Galton, the half cousin of Charles Darwin coined the term to refer to selective human breeding to preserve favorable traits and eliminate the rest. Galton was influenced by Darwin's theory of natural selection.

The second book on the list is "Leviathan" by Thomas Hobbes, published in 1651. The main practical conclusion of Hobbes' political theory is that state or society cannot be secure unless at the disposal of an absolute sovereign. From this follows the view that no individual can hold rights of property against the sovereign, and that the sovereign may therefore take the goods of its subjects without their consent.

Hobbes argued that the absolute power of the sovereign was ultimately justified by the consent of the governed, who agreed, in a

---

[16] https://en.wikipedia.org/wiki/Republic_(Plato)
[17] https://www.sparknotes.com/philosophy/republic/full-text/book-viii/
[18] https://www.britannica.com/science/eugenics-genetics

hypothetical social contract, to obey the sovereign in all matters in exchange for a guarantee of peace and security. [19] This makes me think of the recent words of the Secretary General of the United Nations regarding a global response following COVID-19. He said we have "An opportunity to build back a more equal and sustainable world ... based on a New Social Contract and a New Global Deal."

Hobbes also believed that religion was natural for humans, as it calmed anxieties, but that the sovereign authority should control and dictate the religious beliefs of its people to prevent conflict.[20] In *Leviathan*, Hobbes explicitly states that the sovereign has authority to assert power over matters of faith and doctrine and that if he does not do so, he invites discord.[21]

As in "The Republic" so in "Leviathan" individual freedoms and the right to own private property is not seen as something favorable. Again, systems where sovereign rulers reign over the people are presented as favorable alternatives.

Number 3 on the list is "The Prince" written by Niccolò Machiavelli in 1513. "The Prince" is a short treatise on how to acquire power, create a state, and keep it. The book represents Machiavelli's effort to provide a guide for political action based on the lessons of history and his own experience as a foreign secretary in Florence. His belief that politics has its own rules so shocked his readers that the adjectival form of his surname, Machiavellian, came to be used as a synonym for political maneuvers marked by cunning, duplicity, or bad faith.[22] The general theme of *The Prince* is to accept that the aims of princes – such as glory and survival – can justify the

---

[19] https://www.britannica.com/topic/Leviathan-by-Hobbes
[20] https://study.com/learn/lesson/leviathan-thomas-hobbes-summary-quotes-analysis.html
[21] https://en.wikipedia.org/wiki/Leviathan_(Hobbes_book)
[22] https://www.britannica.com/topic/The-Prince

use of immoral means to achieve those ends.[23]

The 4th book on the list is "The Clash of Civilizations" by Samuel Huntington written in the 1990s. He speaks of the post Cold-war world being divided into a number of "civilizations" and that adjustments must be made to understand how to function together as civilizations. He argues that the widespread Western belief in the universality of the West's values and political systems is naïve and that continued insistence on democratization and such "universal" norms will only further antagonize other civilizations.[24]

In a 1999 article entitled "The Lonely Superpower" Huntington says of the United States, ""For that reason the United States could find life as a major power in a multipolar world less demanding, less contentious and more rewarding than it was as the world's only superpower." [25] Huntington's ideas about "the West's values" remind me of the 8th prediction of the WEF which says "Western values will have been tested to the breaking point." His thoughts about the United States finding it more rewarding to be a major power in a multipolar world than being the world's only superpower sounds exactly in line with the 2nd prediction of the WEF which states, "The U.S. won't be the world's leading superpower. A handful of countries will dominate."

Looking at these top 4 books that college students are reading and studying in American universities reveals a lot about the change in thoughts and ideals, as well opinions about the United States, that are so readily seen in younger generations. That's before we mention the 9th book on the list.

The 9th book on the list of books which are most often required reading in top U.S. universities is none other than "The Communist Manifesto" by Karl Marx and Friedrich Engels. Hard to believe, but true!

---

[23] https://en.wikipedia.org/wiki/The_Prince
[24] https://en.wikipedia.org/wiki/Clash_of_Civilizations
[25] https://prezi.com/assobctvyg02/american-visions-of-the-post-cold-war-world/

Some lists show the Communist Manifesto higher than 9th. I saw one where it was listed 7th and another that had it listed 3rd. Each year millions of families sacrifice financially in order to send their children to universities across the nation. What a shame to think that many of them end up studying the Communist Manifesto and a number of other books that glorify views of government, economy and society that are contrary to the nation we live in.

Just think about it for a moment. These are books that have been read and studied by many of our current governmental leaders and that are being read and studied now by many of our future government leaders as well as our future doctors, lawyers, business leaders, clergy, etc.

This is one more thing put in place to move any U.S. hindrance out of the way of a new global government and economy.

Abortion and God's Judgment

When looking at the United States and what has been taking place within the nation to weaken it, we cannot ignore the issue of abortion.

It is staggering to realize that over 64 million innocent babies have been killed through the practice of abortion in the United States since 1973.

64,000,000+

In the Old Testament we read of harsh judgments that were pronounced upon nations or people groups who were involved in the practice of sacrificing their children to gods and idols. Even Israel, God's chosen people developed these horrible practices at times in their history and were judged because of it. In Leviticus 20:2-5 God condemned these practices and gave strong warnings to Israel concerning these practices. Yet, Israel disobeyed God and Ezekiel speaks of Israel's participation in offering up their children to false gods in Ezekiel 16:20-21.

> "Moreover, you took your sons and daughters whom you had borne to Me and sacrificed them to idols to be devoured. Were your harlotries so small a matter? (21) "You slaughtered My children and offered them up to idols by causing them to pass through the fire."
>
> Ezekiel 16:20-21

Later in the same chapter Ezekiel speaks of the judgment from God that is coming upon Israel because of these sinful practices.

> "Behold now, I have stretched out My hand against you and diminished your rations. And I delivered you up to the desire of those who hate you, the daughters of the Philistines, who are ashamed of your lewd conduct."
>
> Ezekiel 16:27

The prophet Jeremiah also speaks of judgment which came upon Israel because of their worship of false gods, and in particular their practice of offering up their innocent children to those false gods. Jeremiah 32 is an amazing chapter which speaks of Israel's terrible sins which provoked the Lord to anger, the resulting pronouncement of God's judgment, and a prophetic look at the future merciful redemption that God promised to His people. The context of the chapter is the destruction of the city of Jerusalem by Nebuchadnezzar and the Babylonian army. God says He is giving Jerusalem (and Israel) into the hands of their enemies as judgment upon their sins. Many of their provoking sins are listed but the pinnacle of this list of sins is seen in Jeremiah 32:35.

> "They built the high places of Baal that are in the valley of Ben-hinnom to cause their sons and their daughters to pass through the fire to Molech, which I had not commanded them nor had it entered My mind that they should do this abomination, to cause Judah to sin."
>
> Jeremiah 32:35

This practice of offering up their innocent children as sacrifices to false gods is something that is so sinful that the Lord says in Jeremiah 32:35, "nor had it entered My mind that they should do this abomination, to cause Judah to sin."

The practice of offering children to Molech was a practice of heathen nations that was then adopted by Israel. In 1 Kings 11:7 we are told that Solomon built a high place "for Molech, the detestable idol of the sons of Ammon." Here is a description of the detestable practice of child sacrifice to Molech. *"The ancients would heat this idol up with fire until it was glowing, then they would take their newborn babies, place them on the arms of the idol, and watch them burn to death."* [26]

We struggle to conceive how people could be involved in anything so horrendous, especially when it involved tiny innocent children. When we consider what has been happening in America through abortion over the past 50 plus years, we tend to think that these sins are not as brutal and horrendous as ancient child sacrifices to idols. In reality, not much has changed in this regard. Though not all abortions are the same there have been countless late term and partial birth abortions that are included in the more than 64 million murders of innocent babies in America over these recent decades. All abortion involves the sinful taking of an innocent life but late term (2nd and 3rd trimester) and partial birth abortions involve procedures every bit as brutal as ancient child sacrifices to false gods.

The animated 4 minute film entitled "The Procedure" shows and tells the story of an ultrasound technician who finds himself thrust into an operating room where a late term abortion is about to take place. He witnesses the horrific procedure referred to as "Dilatation and Evacuation", that involves the baby being torn apart

---

[26] https://carm.org/miscellaneous-topics/moloch-the-ancient-pagan-god-of-child-sacrifice/

in the womb limb by limb while still alive, and removed piece by piece. During the procedure the baby squirms about trying to avoid the doctor's tool of destruction but has nowhere to go to avoid the unthinkable thing that is happening in what should be the baby's safe place in the mother's womb. As of February 2023 the film can still be viewed on YouTube.[27] Though it is difficult to watch, I encourage you to do so prayerfully, allowing God to cause your heart to ache for the innocent lives being taken each day in the United States and around the world.

Another form of abortion used for 2nd and 3rd trimester abortions is called "saline amniocentesis" or "salt poisoning". In this procedure, *"a needle is inserted through the mother's abdomen and 50-250 ml (as much as a cup) of amniotic fluid is withdrawn and replaced with a solution of concentrated salt. The baby breathes in, swallowing the salt, and is poisoned. The chemical solution also causes painful burning and deterioration of the baby's skin. Usually, after about an hour, the child dies. The mother goes into labor about 33 to 35 hours after instillation and delivers a dead, burned, and shriveled baby."* [28] Just as babies were burned to death outside the womb in ancient times, they are now burned and poisoned to death inside the womb in America today. I wonder if in those days the truth of the horrible practices that people were involved in was somehow hidden away or just not talked about because it was too uncomfortable to speak of?

A third form of late term abortion, is "partial birth abortion", sometimes called an "intact D&E" abortion. Here is a description of this form of murder of innocent children. *"Guided by ultrasound, the abortionist reaches into the uterus, grabs the unborn baby's leg with forceps, and pulls the baby into the birth canal, except for the head, which is deliberately kept just inside the womb. (At this point in a partial-birth abortion, the baby is alive.) Then the abortionist*

---

[27] https://www.youtube.com/watch?v=rTlrNEkwFW4
[28] https://www.nrlc.org/abortion/medicalfacts/techniques/

jams scissors into the back of the baby's skull and spreads the tips of the scissors apart to enlarge the wound. After removing the scissors, a suction catheter is inserted into the skull and the baby's brains are sucked out. The collapsed head is then removed from the uterus."[29]

I realize that these descriptions are hard to read about or hear about. I include them so we can face the reality that America has turned so far from God and hardened its collective heart so much that these kinds of brutal, murderous procedures are not only allowed, but they are applauded and celebrated by many within the land. In January of 2019 the state of New York passed a bill to make late term abortions, like the ones described above, legal in the state, even if federal protections of such procedures should be removed. The governor held a special signing celebration meeting and multiple legislators and organizational leaders gathered, giving a standing ovation as they celebrated the signing of the bill. In news interviews that day the typical rhetoric was used to justify the action. Phrases such as "abortion is a medical procedure, it is not a crime", and "women's health matters, women's lives matter, and women's decisions matter" were used to cover up the truth about what is really at issue, as innocent babies have their choice to live removed and their lives are brutally taken from them. No rhetoric can change the truth that abortion is murder.

In September of 2022 the governor of California signed numerous new bills designed to protect, fund and promote abortion into law. He also funded a billboard campaign in 7 other states where laws restricting abortions had been passed.[30] For example, the campaign funded billboards in Texas that read, "Texas does not own your body, you do - learn more at abortion.CA.gov." In an unthinkable action that displays the level of deception that has taken over the minds of many Americans and American leaders, one

---

[29] ibid

[30] https://www.cbsnews.com/losangeles/news/come-to-california-newsom-sponsored-abortion-rights-billboards-go-up-in-7-states/

of the billboards used in these other states read, "NEED AN ABORTION? CALIFORNIA IS READY TO HELP - LEARN MORE AT ABORTION.CA.GOV" Then, underneath this was the blasphemous use of words from Jesus which were used to justify the promotion of the murder of innocent babies. The billboards read, "Love your neighbor as yourself, there is no greater commandment than these. - Mark 12:31" This blatant example of the lack of the fear of the Lord is shocking!

Judgment, now coming upon what was once a great and powerful nation, is at least in part, a result of the innocent blood being spilled out daily across the land under the guise of freedom of choice!

In his book "The Return of the Gods", author Jonathan Cahn details how much of what is being observed in declining America today is parallel to the common practices of ancient apostate Israel and ancient heathen cultures. He speaks of three false gods referred to often in the Old Testament, Baal, Ashtoreth (also referred to in other cultures as Ishtar), and Molech. He powerfully makes the case that these false gods that were so prominent in ancient times and cultures were removed from their places of power and prominence when Christianity took root and began to change the world. Still, these spiritual entities, or demonic powers, did not cease to exist and have now re-emerged into prominence and power in the world, as America and other nations have turned from God and have given themselves over to the same fleshly lusts that the ancients were given to. As a result, these false gods are gaining more and more power over cultures today and demanding sacrifices in much the same way as before, although certainly in a way that looks much different in a technological and modern society.

The Harbinger

Another book by Jonathan Cahn published in 2011 entitled "The Harbinger" reveals in amazing detail how the United States has followed the same path as ancient Israel when Israel moved toward her collapse and toward the Babylonian captivity.

The context of the book is that the northern 10 Tribes of Israel refused to repent after they were initially struck by the Assyrians. The initial strike was a warning from the Lord, giving them a chance to repent before a more severe judgment came. Instead of heeding the warning and humbling themselves in repentance, they boasted of their resolve, that they would rebuild stronger and better than before. They ignored the warning and rejected the call to return to God. They were defiant. Sadly, their defiance led to the nation's total destruction years later.

Reverend Cahn shows how the ancient prophecies spoken to Israel at that time reveal nine harbingers of coming judgment now seen in modern day America and marking America as the nation in danger of judgment. The key prophetic passage is found in Isaiah 9:8-11.

> *"The Lord sends a message against Jacob, And it falls on Israel. (9) And all the people know it, That is, Ephraim and the inhabitants of Samaria, Asserting in pride and in arrogance of heart: (10) "The bricks have fallen down, But we will rebuild with smooth stones; The sycamores have been cut down, But we will replace them with cedars." (11) Therefore the LORD raises against them adversaries from Rezin And spurs their enemies on,"*   Isaiah 9:8-11

It is easy to see that this passage is a passage that pronounces judgment upon Israel for their pride, arrogance of heart, and an unwillingness to humble themselves in repentance after their defenses were initially breached by the Assyrians. It is important to note however that if verse 10 is viewed apart from its context it appears to be a great faith-filled declaration of victory, determination and triumph over hardship. Verse 9 though clearly reveals that the bold statements made in verse 10 came forth from pride and arrogance, and brought further judgment from the hand of God.

Ancient Israel did not repent during the years after the initial breach of their defenses. During this time God was offering them the opportunity to do so, and to thereby avoid a much worse defeat than the initial breach of their defenses.

Jonathan Cahn equates these things to what took place in America on 9/11/2001 and afterwards. America's defenses were breached on 9/11 by enemies in a sobering way. The book reveals that in the aftermath of 9/11 America's responses brought about a fulfillment of all of the 9 harbingers of future judgment as revealed in Isaiah 9:8-11. I encourage you to get the book and read it if you haven't. The details found throughout the book are stunning. I will not attempt to give a great amount of detail here but will give a short summary of what is covered in the book. The nine harbingers are listed here.

1) The Breach
2) The Terrorists
3) The Fallen Bricks
4) The Tower
5) The Gazit Stone
6) The Sycamore
7) The Erez Tree
8) The Utterance
9) The Prophecy

The details of the 9/11 attacks and the words and actions of various American leaders that came in the wake of the attacks revealed a clear indication that though God was calling us to repentance, America chose to respond in the same ways that ancient Israel did over 2,500 years ago. Let me give you just two examples and again encourage you to read "The Harbinger" if you have not already done so.

The day after the 9/11 attacks Senator Tom Daschel, who was serving as the Senate Majority Leader at the time, addressed the U.S. Senate. During his remarks he quoted a passage from the Bible. He said, "But there is a passage in the Bible from Isaiah that I think speaks to all of us at times like this. 'The bricks have fallen down, but we will rebuild with dressed stone. The fig trees have been felled, but we will replace them with cedars.'" He then added, "that is what we will do. We will rebuild and we will recover." Amazingly, he quoted Isaiah 9:10, the very words that Isaiah said Israel said in pride and arrogance of heart, in response to a humbling breach of their defenses.

Then on September 11, 2004, Senator John Edwards, who was a vice-presidential candidate at the time, spoke at a prayer breakfast. As he spoke of all the nation had been through since the 9/11 attacks he also quoted Isaiah 9:10 and applied it to America's resolve to rebuild and recover.

Certainly neither man quoted Isaiah 9:10 in an attempt to repeat the responses of Israel over 2,500 years ago. As mentioned earlier, when verse 10 is viewed by itself, out of context, it seems like a great verse to use to respond to an attack like that which took place on 9/11. Yet, viewed in context, this verse is definitely not the response we needed. God has consistently looked for His people to humble themselves in repentance toward Him during times of shaking. Bold, self-confident resolve is not the proper response.

In addition to these two examples, all of the other 7 harbingers drawn from the Isaiah passage were seen in striking detail on 9/11 and in the months and years that followed.

Amazingly, the One Year Bible and the One Year Bible Online

reading plan assigns Isaiah 8:1-9:21, which includes Isaiah 9:10 as a part of the reading plan for September 11th each year!

Since the initial breach seen in the attacks of 9/11 America has not turned to God in humble repentance. Rather, America has in large part turned further from God and leaned more into self dependence and arrogance of heart. Jonathan Cahn wrote a sequel to his book "The Harbinger" entitled "The Harbinger 2" in 2020. Unfortunately, it reveals again in stunning detail how America has moved forward down the path toward judgment in the last two decades.

There have been many throughout the land who have with repentant hearts turned to the Lord in greater dependency. The humbling of some throughout the land brings hope that the Lord will stay His hand of judgment upon the nation, or provide protection for His people during times of judgment.

The prediction of the World Economic Forum that the United States will no longer be the world's superpower by 2030 is probably spoken out of a desire on the part of globalists to remove the hindrance to their dreams and plans. Still, if their prediction comes to pass, it may very well be because God's hand of judgment comes upon America today, much in the same way that His hand of judgment came upon Israel in the days of Isaiah 9:8-11. God's response to Israel's pride and arrogance at that time is seen in verse 11 where He says, *"Therefore the LORD raises against them adversaries from Rezin And spurs their enemies on."*

Noone desiring to see America moved from her role of world superpower could accomplish this task if God's protective hand is covering America. Though this is true, if God's protective hand is removed from America and if He "raises against them adversaries" and "spurs their enemies on", the United States will cease to be the strongest nation on the earth.

It could be that when God inspired writers of various passages of Scripture to speak of an end time global system, He did so based on His foreknowledge of America's turning away from God, bringing His judgment upon the once invincible nation.

World Heritage Sites

A quick note about an example of the deepening relationship between the United Nations and the individual nations of the world is seen through the World Heritage Sites.

A World Heritage Site is a landmark or area with legal protection by an international convention administered by the United Nations Educational, Scientific and Cultural Organization (UNESCO). [31]

There are over 1,100 world heritage sites worldwide. There are now 24 World Heritage Sites in the United States including Yellowstone National Park, The Everglades National Park, the Statue of Liberty, Grand Canyon National Park, Redwood National and State Parks, and the Great Smoky Mountains National Park.

What Should We Then Do?

Many of us have probably contemplated over the past few years, asking what we can do to help save America from judgment and from continuing to move toward destruction. I certainly have. I thank God for those who are getting involved in local, state and federal levels to attempt to bring Christian values back into our policies, laws and into our culture. All of us should pray and ask the Lord what our part should be.

One thing is clear that we should all be doing. We should all be praying for our nation! We need revival and spiritual awakening in a great way! Pray in your home and pray corporately with other believers for our nation and our world! Pray for God's grace and mercy! Pray for revival and spiritual awakening! Pray for the lost to come to know Christ! Pray for our leaders! Pray for an outpouring of God's Spirit! Pray for God's kingdom to come and be established here on earth, even as it is in heaven! Pray for God's will to be done in our lives, in His church, in this nation, and in the world! Pray!

---

[31] https://en.wikipedia.org/wiki/World_Heritage_Site

CHAPTER 15

Globalism and The Pandemic

For most of us I'm sure it is hard to comprehend all that has taken place in the world we live in since the spring of 2020 when suddenly, the world was shut down almost overnight. We sat at home, watching news of the continuing spread of the coronavirus throughout the world, and communicating with loved ones mostly by phone. We worked on projects around the house. Sports events were canceled. Businesses were closed. Hospitals were full. Schools were closed and children stayed home with their parents who were working from home or not working at all. Church services were canceled or steamed online with just a handful of people at the church singing, preaching, etc. Facial masks were seen everywhere. It all seemed surreal!

In chapter 13 we touched on the fact that organizations seeking to implement a new global system saw the COVID-19 pandemic as an opportunity. In this chapter we will further look at this and related issues.

In July of 2020 United Nations Secretary-General Antonio Guterres delivered the 18th Nelson Mandela Annual Lecture in New York City. During this address he said,

> *"Dear friends,*
> *COVID-19 is a human tragedy. But it has also created* **a generational opportunity**. **An opportunity to build back a more equal and sustainable world.** *The response to the pandemic, and to the widespread discontent that preceded it, must be* **based on a New**

Social Contract and a New Global Deal *that create equal opportunities for all, and respect the rights and freedoms of all."* [1]

Mr. Guterres further explained, *"**The New Social Contract** between governments, peoples, civil society, businesses and more must integrate employment, sustainable development and social protection, based on equal rights and opportunities for all."* [2]

Leaving no doubt as to the type of global system that he was proposing with this New Social Contract, he stated, *"A changing world requires a new generation of social protection policies with new safety nets, including **Universal Health Coverage** and the possibility of a **Universal Basic Income**. ... **Taxation and redistribution** policies also have a role in the New Social Contract."* [3]

In the last chapter we looked at the books most used for required reading in top U.S. universities. The 2nd book on the list was "Leviathan" by Thomas Hobbes. In Encyclopedia Britannica's explanation of this book it is stated, "Hobbes argued that the **absolute power of the sovereign** was ultimately justified by the consent of the governed, who agreed, in a hypothetical **social contract**, to obey the sovereign in all matters in exchange for a guarantee of peace and security. [4]

I cannot say whether or not the Social Contract that Mr. Guterres referred to, is inspired by the Social Contract spoken of by Thomas Hobbes, but there certainly are a lot of similarities in what appears to be described. University students in America have been being prepped for years for the use of this kind of language.

---

[1] https://www.nelsonmandela.org/news/entry/annual-lecture-2020-secretary-general-guterress-full-speech
[2] ibid
[3] ibid
[4] https://www.britannica.com/topic/Leviathan-by-Hobbes

Mr. Guterres was not alone in his assessment of the opportunity that COVID-19 was presenting.

Jennifer Morgan, the Executive Director of Greenpeace International said, *"**COVID-19 gives us the chance** to step back and rethink the world we would like to live in"* [5]

Sharan Burrow, General Secretary of the International Trade Union Confederation said, *"I can see how we could use this **opportunity** to design a better world."* [6]

Prince Charles (now King Charles) said in 2020, *"There is a **golden opportunity** to seize something good from this crisis...global crises know no borders, and highlight how interdependent we are as one people sharing one planet."* [7]

Justin Trudeau, the Prime Minister of Canada appeared as a part of a United Nations video conference in September of 2020 and spoke about Canada's response to the COVID-19 pandemic. In his remarks he said, *"This pandemic has provided **an opportunity for a reset**. This is our chance to accelerate our pre-pandemic efforts to reimagine economic systems that actually address global challenges like extreme poverty, inequality and climate change."* [8]

Klaus Schwab, the founder and president of the World Economic Forum said of the COVID-19 crisis, *"The pandemic represents a rare but narrow window of **opportunity** to reflect, reimagine, and **reset our world**."* [9] He has also said, *"The COVID-19 crisis has shown us that our old systems are not fit any more for the 21st century. **In short, we need a great reset**."* [10]

A video produced by the World Economic Forum compares

---

[5] https://www.weforum.org/agenda/2020/06/covid19-great-reset-gita-gopinath-jennifer-morgan-sharan-burrow-climate/

[6] ibid

[7] https://www.weforum.org/agenda/2020/06/great-reset-launch-prince-charles-guterres-georgieva-burrow

[8] https://www.youtube.com/watch?v=n2fp0Jeyjvw

[9] https://www.weforum.org/focus/the-great-reset

[10] https://www.weforum.org/agenda/2020/06/the-great-reset-this-weeks-world-vs-virus-podcast/

the COVID-19 crisis to the Climate Change crisis and speaks of what they believe we should have learned from 2020 and the COVID-19 crisis. The video states, *"and with climate change set to dwarf the damage caused by the pandemic, the message from 2020 should be abundantly clear.* **Capitalism as we know it is dead!** *This obsession that we have had with maximizing profits for shareholders alone has led to incredible inequality and a planetary emergency."*[11] It would seem to be quite a leap from a health pandemic to the need for scrapping an entire economic system, but that appears to be the conclusion that the WEF has arrived at.

As stated in chapter 13 the World Economic Forum has described what this Great Reset initiative involves. *"As we enter a unique* **window of opportunity** *to shape the recovery, this initiative will offer insights to help inform all those determining* (1) *the future state of global relations,* (2) *the direction of national economies,* (3) *the priorities of societies,* (4) *the nature of business models and* (5) *the management of a global commons. Drawing from the vision and vast expertise of the leaders engaged across the Forum's communities, the Great Reset initiative has a set of dimensions to build* **a new social contract** *that honours the dignity of every human being."* [12] (Note - the numbers in parentheses above were added to highlight the scope of this initiative.)

Please note three things in particular from the description of the Great Reset initiative as described on the World Economic Forum's website. First of all, note that we see reference again to **"a New Social Contract."** Isn't that interesting? This is the same term used by Thomas Hobbes in "Leviathan" and by the United Nations' Secretary-General in his description of the opportunity COVID-19 has brought about.

---

[11] https://www.youtube.com/watch?v=uPYx12xJFUQ&t=5s
[12] https://www.weforum.org/great-reset/

Secondly, note that the word **"opportunity"** is used here again. This certainly appears to be the mantra of all those involved in these international organizations promoting a new global system.

Thirdly, note the scope of the 5 things they list as what will be done by those they intend to inform as a part of the Great Reset initiative. I am separating them out into a list here so it is easier to look at them collectively.

1) Determining the state of global relationships
2) Determining the direction of national economies
3) Determining the priorities of societies
4) Determining the nature of business models
5) Determining the management of global commons

I think you would agree that anyone involved in determining all of these things has taken power to control the world's future!

Interesting Timeline

It is clear from the quotes above that a common theme among governmental, organizational and business leaders is that the COVID-19 pandemic is an opportunity for a "great reset".

Leading up to the pandemic there were some interesting things that transpired that could begin to raise questions about the relationship between the COVID-19 pandemic and the move toward a "great reset" of the world's government and economy.

I should probably give a "conspiracy theory" alert here. If you are of the opinion that there are no such things as conspiracies you will probably want to just focus on the main point of this chapter, being that the COVID-19 pandemic has moved the world closer to the establishing of a global reset. This much is obvious and can be clearly seen in the quotes above by world leaders. If you are of the opinion that there are sometimes unrevealed plans by people who desire change, you will probably find the following information to be confirmation that something more was going on throughout the pandemic than what was spoken of openly.

First of all, it should be noted that Klaus Schwab was calling for a "great reset" well before 2020, well before the COVID-19 pandemic. In the 2014 World Economic Forum annual meeting in Davos, Switzerland, Schwab said, "What we want to do in Davos this year in this respect is to push the reset button."[13] He went on to talk about looking at the world's future in a much more strategic and constructive way. The WEF's published meeting agenda for that year was entitled, "*The Reshaping of the World: Consequences for Society, Politics and Business.*" Then in 2015 they published an article entitled, *"We Need to Press Restart On The Global Economy".* In 2016 they held a panel called, *"How to Reboot the Global Economy"*, and in 2017 they published an article entitled, *"Our World Needs a Reset in How We Operate."* [14]

"Event201" - October 18, 2019

In May of 2018 the John Hopkins Center for Health Security hosted the "CladeX" pandemic exercise to simulate responses to a global pandemic.

On October 18, 2019 the John Hopkins Center for Health Security partnered with the World Economic Forum and the Bill and Melinda Gates Foundation to host "Event201", a pandemic simulation in New York City. The event's purpose statement says that there are about 200 epidemics around the world each year. With that in mind the purpose statement says, "*Experts agree that it is only a matter of time before one of these epidemics becomes global—a pandemic with potentially catastrophic consequences. A severe pandemic, which becomes "Event 201," would require reliable cooperation among several industries, national*

---

[13] https://www.youtube.com/watch?v=RAjYAXYGPuI&t=6s
[14]
https://sociable.co/government-and-policy/timeline-great-reset-agenda-event-201-pandemic-2020/amp/

governments, and key international institutions." [15]

Some reports reveal that the first cases of the COVID-19 virus became apparent in the Wuhan, China region in November of 2019, just a few weeks after the Event201 simulation. Since then, many of the aspects of the simulations have now played out in reality throughout the world including things like -

- Governments implementing lockdowns worldwide
- The Collapse of Many Industries
- Growing Mistrust Between Governments and Citizens
- A Greater Adoption of Biometric Surveillance Technologies
- Social Media Censorship in the Name of Combating "Misinformation"
- The Desire to Flood Communication Channels with "Authoritative" Sources
- A Global Lack of Personal Protective Equipment (E.G. Masks)
- The Breakdown of International Supply Chains
- Mass Unemployment
- Rioting In The Streets
- Public/Private Partnerships Responding to Crisis

As you might guess there has been much speculation about the timing of "Event201" as related to the COVID-19 outbreak. Of course the organizations involved have assured the public that they had no prior knowledge of the pandemic that followed the event. That may or may not be true but the timing of the event and the involvement of the World Economic Forum in the event raises questions for many, especially in light of the World Economic Forum's quick and bold response to declare the pandemic as an opportunity to move forward with the goals they had already been promoting for years.

Whether or not the timing of these things is coincidence or not, it is clear that the pandemic served as a means to walk out

---

[15] https://www.centerforhealthsecurity.org/our-work/exercises/event201/about

many of the plans covered in the simulation, which happen to be part of the plans the WEF and others have expressed in their ongoing global strategies.

This is especially seen in a part of the simulation plans found in a section entitled "Public-private cooperation for pandemic preparedness and response". In this section the following statements are found.

"The next severe pandemic will not only cause great illness and loss of life but could also trigger major cascading economic and societal consequences that could contribute greatly to global impact and suffering. Efforts to prevent such consequences or respond to them as they unfold will require **unprecedented levels of collaboration between governments, international organizations, and the private sector.**"[16] The instructions go on to give a number of details of how governmental entities, international organizations and private corporations need to partner together. These partnerships certainly make sense and produce benefits.

This happens to be a part of the WEFs model for the Great Reset with "Stakeholder Capitalism" at its core. In stakeholder capitalism, unelected leaders of corporations and international organizations have a seat at the table with governmental leaders as "stakeholders" and have a voice in making decisions that affect people around the world.

Another part of the response plans is found on this same page. It says, *"Governments and the private sector should assign a greater priority to developing methods to combat mis- and disinformation prior to the next pandemic response. Governments will need to partner with traditional and social media companies to research and develop nimble approaches to countering misinformation."* [17]

Wow, I think we would all agree that they put that one in

---

[16]https://www.centerforhealthsecurity.org/our-work/exercises/event201/recommendations.html
[17] ibid

practice pretty aggressively. This is another statement that sounds good on the surface. The problem is that the people determining what is information and what is misinformation gain tremendous power and can effectively promote whatever ideas they choose to, whether or not the "information" they act upon is accurate.

When governments and powerful big tech, social media companies partner together to promote information, true or false, they have great power to influence multitudes, especially when mainstream news outlets agree to promote the same information. Speaking of mainstream media outlets, the response plans go on to say, *"For their part, media companies should commit to ensuring that authoritative messages are prioritized and that false messages are suppressed including though (sic) the use of technology."*[18]

I find it very interesting that the phenomenon of censorship on social media platforms that we began to see in great measure in 2020 and beyond was specifically placed in response plans of the October 2019 "Event201" pandemic simulation event.

The Military World Games (October 18-27, 2019) (Wuhan, China)

On the same day that "Event201" took place in New York, another, 10 day long event began in Wuhan, China. The Military World Games took place from October 18th through October 27th in 2019 in the very location where the COVID-19 virus originated. Over 9,000 athletes who serve in the military of 110 different countries around the world gathered for this 10 day sporting event which is much like the Olympics, only all the athletes are a part of the military.

---
[18] ibid

Originally, there was much debate concerning the origin of the COVID-19 virus but in late February, 2023 the Wall Street Journal and multiple news outlets reported that the United States Department of Energy had now concluded that the COVID pandemic most likely arose from a laboratory leak at a Bio Lab in Wuhan, China.[19] Think of this, by chance or by plan, a virus was leaked out of a biolab in Wuhan, China at the same time that over 9,000 athletes from 110 countries were competing in Wuhan, China!

Many athletes from various countries later reported that they became ill while in Wuhan, while returning home, or just after they returned home. This included a number of U.S. athletes who returned to various military bases across the country. One report said, "... an investigation of COVID-19 cases in the military from official and public source materials shows that a strong correlation exists in COVID-19 cases reported at U.S. military facilities that are home bases of members of the U.S. team that went to Wuhan. Before March 31, when the Pentagon restricted the release of information about COVID-19 cases at installations for security reasons, infections occurred at a minimum of 63 military facilities where team members returned after the Wuhan games."[20]

I'm not aware of any proof that there was any plan involved in a release of the virus at the very time and place of the Military World Games in Wuhan. If it is just an unfortunate coincidence it still has significance since ultimately everything that happens in the natural realm has a spiritual aspect to it. Even if there was no human involvement in the strange timing of these things, demonic spirits, who hate people, may very well have been at work to release pain and destruction upon many across the world in this way. If there was human involvement in creating this strange timeline then obviously the COVID-19 pandemic was not merely accidental and was designed to accomplish some purpose.

---

[19] https://www.wsj.com/articles/covid-origin-china-lab-leak-807b7b0a
[20] https://prospect.org/coronavirus/did-the-military-world-games-spread-covid-19/

The Pandemic Takes Hold

At the beginning of the pandemic there was a combination of fear, anxiety and hope that experts would quickly and efficiently lead us through this terrible time successfully. Governmental lockdowns and enormous infringements of personal freedoms were for the most part accepted by everyone. It was assumed that the measures being taken would be short lived and were all in our best interest.

As time went on two very different views began to emerge to all that was taking place in the world.

One view was based on a complete trust in the information being given about each detail of the COVID-19 crisis and about each suggested (or mandated) response that was needed to combat the pandemic. These details and responses included the severity of the crisis, numbers of deaths from COVID-19, the need for masks, lockdowns, business closures, school closures, church closures, the need for isolation, avoiding home treatment plans, specific hospital protocols, and the need for all to be vaccinated multiple times by vaccines that experts said were very safe and very effective. For those holding this view any information brought forward that was contrary to the information being presented by authoritative international and national health agencies, government and media outlets, was considered dangerous misinformation or disinformation.

The other view that emerged and grew stronger as time went on was based on a lack of trust in the information being given about each detail of the COVID-19 crisis and about each suggested (or mandated) response that was said to be needed to combat the pandemic. Those holding this view began to see inconsistencies in information being presented by authoritative international and national health organizations, governments and media outlets. Those holding this view increasingly felt that aspects of the severity of the pandemic and the numbers of deaths caused by COVID-19 were skewed. As time went on they became increasingly uncomfortable with mandates for masks, isolation, lockdowns, and eventually with vaccine mandates. They were uncomfortable with the restrictions placed upon the free access to home treatment medications that were being suggested by some members of the medical field and by the attempts to silence those who suggested these treatments. As time went on those with these views became more and more convinced that many in authority did not have the best interests in mind for the average person trying to both deal with COVID-19 and continue effectively with their life. For those of this view, they became increasingly confident that much of what was being censored and/or labeled as misinformation was actually true.

The chasm between those holding these two views grew wider as more issues became a part of all that was involved in the COVID-19 crisis and the responses to the crisis. The division that grew, even within families, was unfortunate.

Globalism and the Pandemic

Before speaking about some of the specific troubling aspects of the pandemic I want to pause to state again the basic point of this chapter. The COVID-19 pandemic has moved the world further toward the "great reset" that many of those desiring a new global system seek to establish. As shown earlier in this chapter those promoting a "great reset" have openly and frequently referred to COVID-19 as an opportunity to establish the "great reset". Aspects of COVID-19 responses served as practice for ongoing use of these practices which include the partnerships of governments, international organizations and private corporations and the use of coordinated efforts to prevent information declared to be "misinformation" from spreading. As we now look in more detail at various aspects of questionable things that have taken place since the fall of 2019 please keep in mind that the main point of this chapter is true even if other questionable things that are covered here prove to be simply "conspiracy theories." Plans for a global reset are being promoted and advanced more than ever because of the global pandemic.

Confusing Policies

For those who looked beyond the major media outlets for answers to questions related to the illness itself and to the sometimes confusing measures taken in response to the disease, information began to surface that seemed to contradict aspects of the narrative being presented by the mainstream media and acknowledged health organizations.

Some funeral directors and hospital medical personnel began to speak out about questionable practices which skewed COVID-19 death tolls. In some cases hospital personnel and funeral directors were told to just mark COVID-19 as cause of death without even testing the individual. Hospitals were given government financial kickbacks for COVID-19 diagnosis and additional amounts for every patient that was put on a ventilator. The panic over COVID-19 that was stirring in much of the public was in part based on the death tolls that were updated daily. As time went on more and more people began to question what the real numbers were. I should add here that I'm not aware of anyone who questioned whether or not COVID-19 was real and that COVID deaths were occuring. The questions related to whether or not a true picture of the magnitude of the crisis was being portrayed.

I believe the most difficult question to answer about the responses to the COVID-19 pandemic is why home treatment of the disease was aggressively resisted by health agencies, governments and media outlets. From the start, something seemed very odd about this response to me. All of our lives we have been told to take certain medications to help treat various illnesses. I'm not aware of any other instance where medical professionals encouraged patients who contracted a disease to go home and wait until they get better or until they get bad enough to be checked into a hospital.

The exception to this lack of treatment was the eventual use of monoclonal antibodies in some cases for high-risk patients. Other than the use of monoclonal antibodies patients were told to just treat the symptoms and rest.

Beyond the scope of the international and governmental health agencies, various individual doctors did begin immediately to pursue potential treatments for non-hospitalized patients. Some of these doctors began to treat hundreds of patients with various treatment plans that were primarily developed with repurposed drugs that had been effective in treating other diseases and had been proven through prior use to be safe. These doctors saw wonderful results as they treated patients of all ages. Independent health organizations such as the "World Council For Health", the "Citizen's Council For Health Freedom", the "Association of American Physicians and Surgeons" (this group has been around since 1943) and the "Front Line COVID-19 Critical Care Alliance" developed home treatment plans and published them online for people to access free of charge. These efforts helped multitudes of people who were searching for help in treating the virus.

Instead of being applauded for their groundbreaking work in a time of crisis, many of these doctors were criticized, mocked and in some cases threatened by those who continued to insist that there were no safe treatments available for millions of non-hospitalized patients.

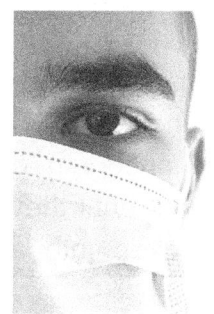

Part of the treatment plans that were offered by these doctors was the strengthening of people's immune system by taking vitamins, especially vitamin D, vitamin C and Zinc, which had shown great promise in helping people avoid COVID or do better in fighting it when they did contract it. How could something so benign be controversial? Yet, it was, and for every study showing the effectiveness of vitamin D and other natural immune strengthening ingredients, other studies or expert opinions would be sighted so as to nullify any move toward encouraging people to take these actions. All the while, those who did treat patients in these ways saw substantial positive results. It is hard to imagine any downside of encouraging people to, at a minimum, take more vitamins.

Of greater controversy was the use of two special repurposed drugs that were both inexpensive and proven to be safe after decades of use for treatment of other illnesses. Ivermectin and Hydroxychloroquine were both used by a number of doctors as part of the treatment plan for COVID-19. They consistently reported positive results in the patients they treated. At one point after the then president of the United States was treated by one of these doctors for COVID-19 he publicly spoke of the effectiveness of Hydroxychloroquine spawning hope in many that there were ways to treat the viral disease.

Again, it would seem natural that independent health organizations and the doctors, many of whom were highly respected in their fields, who explored these kinds of treatments and reported tremendous success in treating patients, would be applauded and appreciated. Instead, they were consistently contradicted, criticized and mocked. In some cases their jobs were threatened. The message was very clear! Stop talking about these treatment plans! Fortunately, many of them did not stop talking. They courageously continued to spread the word that treatments for this viral disease were available.

To illustrate my statement that many of these doctors, who were now being maligned for their promotion of home treatment plans for COVID-19, were previously highly respected, let me draw your attention to three examples.

Dr. Peter McCullough, M.D., M.P.H.
(Masters in Public Health)

Dr. McCullough is a Cardiologist, Internist and Epidemiologist. He has served as the Vice Chief of Internal Medicine at Baylor University Medical Center and as a professor at Texas A&M University. Earlier in his career He was a cardiovascular fellow at William Beaumont Hospital in the Detroit metropolitan area. Dr. McCullough has broadly published on a range of topics in medicine with over 1,000 publications and 660 citations in the National Library of Medicine. Dr. McCullough received the International Vicenza Award for Critical Care Nephrology for his outstanding work and contribution in the area of cardio-renal syndromes. He has been an invited lecturer at the New York Academy of Sciences, the National Institutes of Health, the U.S. Food and Drug Administration (FDA), the European Medicines Agency, and the U.S. Congressional Oversight Panel.

Dr. Pierre Kory, M.D., M.P.A. (Masters in Public Administration)

He has served as the medical director for the Trauma and Life Support Center at UW Health, the Academic Medical Center of the University of Wisconsin and the Critical Care Service Chief at the UW Health University Hospital. He is an expert in Critical Care Ultrasonography. He and his 2 co-editors won the British Medical Association's 2015 President's Choice award in medical textbooks for their work on Point of Care Ultrasound. He is currently the President of the Front Line COVID-19 Critical Care Alliance

Dr. Paul Marik (M.D., FCCM (Fellow of Critical Care Medicine) FCCP (Fellow of College of Chest Physicians)

Dr. Marik has served as a Professor of Medicine and Chief of Pulmonary and Critical Care Medicine at Eastern Virginia Medical School in Norfolk, Virginia. He is the Former Director at the Division Pulmonary and Critical Care at Jefferson Medical College (JMC) and Thomas Jefferson

University Hospital in Philadelphia. In 2017, Dr. Marik won the American College of Physicians (ACP) award for outstanding educator of residents and fellows. He has written more than 400 peer-reviewed journal articles, 50 book chapters, and four books about critical care, and has developed a new treatment for sepsis. He currently serves as the Chairman and Chief Scientific Officer for the Front Line COVID-19 Critical Care Alliance.

As you can see from the resumes of these three doctors, they all have great credentials, have served roles of leadership at major medical institutions, and have garnered great respect among their peers throughout their medical careers. All of them have been involved in treating patients with early treatment plans for COVID-19 and speaking out about the effectiveness of early treatment plans that include the use of ivermectin. As a result of this they have faced ridicule and backlash. Note some of the descriptions used within each of their wikipedia pages.

For Dr. McCullough - *"During the COVID-19 pandemic, McCullough has **promoted misinformation** about COVID-19, its treatments, and mRNA vaccines."*

For Dr. Kory - *"During his testimony in December 2020, Kory **erroneously claimed** that the antiparasitic medication ivermectin was a "wonder drug" with "miraculous effectiveness" against COVID-19."*

For Dr. Marik - *"He is a co-leader of the Front Line COVID-19 Critical Care Alliance (FLCCC), which has **misleadingly advocated for** the anti-parasitic drug ivermectin to treat COVID-19 against the advice of leading health agencies."*

Wikipedia's arbitrary use of phrases like *"promoted misinformation"*, *"erroneously claimed"*, and *"misleadingly advocated for"* reveals the fulfillment of strategies that were discussed in the "Event201" pandemic simulation in October of 2019 that we discussed earlier. Remember they said, *"Governments will need to partner with traditional and social media companies to research and develop nimble approaches to countering misinformation."*

Whatever your view is concerning which doctors and which studies and trials were (are) correct about treating COVID-19, it should be clear that the power of information in the hands of a select group of powerful people, determining what is "information" and what is "misinformation" for the world, is a scary proposition.

These are just examples of many highly trained and respected medical professionals who have experienced the same types of pushback for daring to stand against those who have determined the narrative that should be promoted.

What we have been witnessing in regards to doctors and the treatment of the COVID-19 virus reminds me of something else that I have become very familiar with for years through my study of scientific evidence confirming that God is creator of all life. Though there are many scientists who have come to the conclusion that science confirms that all life has an intelligent designer and though the overwhelming evidence a creator, including the language of DNA, continues to grow, those who control the public narrative continue to discount every piece of evidence that is presented and dogmatically proclaim that darwinian evolution is scientifically proven to be true. Those who do not espouse evolution are often accused of being involved in "pseudo-science".

Another correlation between these two scenarios is seen in the fact that even though evolution has been taught basically as scientific fact in public schools and universities for decades, a great percentage of people still believe that God created all of life. A 2019 Gallup poll found that 40% of Americans still believe that God created mankind in roughly the same form as we see today within the past 10,000 years, while only 22% believe that God had no role in human origins or evolution.[21] Similarly, though government representatives, international health organizations and powerful

---

[21] https://news.gallup.com/poll/261680/americans-believe-creationism.aspx

media outlets continued to disregard any validity to COVID-19 home treatment plans, a great percentage of people in numerous countries sought out these treatments, and continue to do so.

Another example of a doctor who faced persecution for treating patients with hydroxychloroquine and ivermectin was Dr. Meryl Nass who practices in the state of Maine. Dr. Nass is a long term internal medicine physician. She has expertise in anthrax and in bioterrorism. She has provided testimony to seven Congressional committees and her work has been mentioned in 25 books.[22] She testified before the Government Reform Committee on the medical response to bioterrorism a month after the anthrax letters event.[23] She received her medical training at MIT.

After decades as a respected physician whose opinion was sought out by writers and even by the U.S. government, Dr. Nass faced open humiliation and backlash in January of 2022 because she treated patients for COVID-19 with hydroxychloroquine and ivermectin, spoke out about some of the suppression of information about treatments, and spoke out about some of the dangers of the vaccines being used. In January of 2022 Maine's Board of Licensure in Medicine voted to suspend Dr. Nass' medical license for 30 days and ordered that she undergo psychiatric evaluation for spreading misinformation and because she supposedly "constitutes an immediate jeopardy to the health and physical safety of the public who might receive her medical services" [24]

In a 2022 interview Dr. Nass expressed concerns about the lack of early treatment for COVID-19 much like what I expressed earlier in this chapter, albeit from a much more informed perspective as a physician of 40 years. She criticized the *"dreadful guidelines"* directing medical professionals to tell patients to *"go home, don't do anything except Tylenol and ibuprofen until your lips are blue and*

---

[22] https://ahrp.org/meryl-nass-m-d/
[23] ibid
[24] https://summit.news/2022/01/18/mit-educated-doctor-ordered-to-undergo-psych-evaluation-after-prescribing-ivermectin/

then show up in the ER, and then we'll admit you and give you oxygen and maybe remdesivir." [25]

I personally experienced what Dr. Nass is speaking about in this interview. When I contracted COVID the first of two times, I had phone conversations with my doctor's office, my family doctor of over 30 years. In those conversations, no home treatments were recommended and I remember that at the end of the last conversation the doctor's assistant told me, "Well, get some rest." That was the extent of the home treatment plan.

Hydroxychloroquine and Ivermectin

I believe it is important to spend some time on issues related to Hydroxychloroquine and Ivermectin because these issues seem to reveal that something more than the public's best interest was involved when aggressive measures to suppress the use of these medications to treat COVID-19 were used.

First of all, as I stated earlier, both of these medications are very inexpensive (especially before they became hard to get because of governments and health organizations) and both have a record of decades of safe uses in humans to treat other illnesses.

Secondly, many seasoned physicians and independent medical organizations used these medications to successfully treat COVID.

I'll speak mostly about Ivermectin but want to note that Hydroxychloroquine was developed in 1955 and has been used for decades to successfully treat malaria, lupus and other autoimmune diseases. Like any drug it has potential side effects, especially when used continuously over multiple years, but has been known as a relatively safe drug for decades. A 2018 article from the Cleveland Clinic Journal of Medicine entitled "Hydroxychloroquine, An Old Drug With New Relevance" speaks of numerous effective uses of

---

[25] https://childrenshealthdefense.org/defender/rfk-jr-defender-meryl-nass-suspended-misinformation/

the medication.[26]

An article published in January of 2017 in the Journal of Antibiotics was entitled, "Ivermectin: enigmatic multifaceted 'wonder' drug continues to surprise and exceed expectations."[27]

The article speaks very highly of ivermectin and confirms that the medication was first used as a deworming medication in animals. It says that the human version of the medication began to be used in 1987. We have often heard ivermectin described as "the horse deworming medication" over the past couple of years. Whenever you read an article or hear a newscast that refers to ivermectin as a "horse deworming medication" or "the drug used to deworm livestock", you know they are either ignorant or more likely just being dishonest! I have seen both the horse version and the human version and they look nothing alike.

The fact that a medication has a version that is used for veterinary purposes certainly does not mean that the human version is not helpful for humans. There are numerous medicines used in both animals and humans for pain relief, to treat bacterial infections, to treat inflammation, to treat allergies, etc.

The article says, *"Over the past decade, the global scientific community have begun to recognize the unmatched value of an extraordinary drug, ivermectin. ... Today, ivermectin is continuing to surprise and excite scientists, offering more and more promise to help improve global public health by treating a diverse range of diseases, with its unexpected potential as an antibacterial, antiviral and anti-cancer agent being particularly extraordinary."*

In addition the article says, *"Today, ivermectin remains a relatively unknown drug, although few, if any, other drugs can rival ivermectin for **its beneficial impact on human health and welfare."***

Though ivermectin has primarily been used since its introduction in the 1980s to treat parasitic diseases, the article

---

[26] https://www.ccjm.org/content/85/6/459
[27] https://www.nature.com/articles/ja201711

addresses its potential benefits as an antiviral medication. It states, *"Recent research has confounded the belief, held for most of the past 40 years, that ivermectin was devoid of any antiviral characteristics. Ivermectin has been found to potently inhibit replication of the yellow fever virus ... Ivermectin inhibits dengue viruses and **interrupts virus replication, bestowing protection against infection with all distinct virus serotypes,** and has unexplored potential as a dengue antiviral."*

As I mentioned earlier, this article was published before the pandemic. Therefore, none of the praise given to ivermectin by the Journal of Antibiotics here is directly related to any ability it has to combat COVID. What we do see here is that it has been used in humans safely and effectively for decades. We also see that evidence was beginning to surface that the medication may be effective in interrupting virus replication.

Another 2011 medical report from the National Library of Medicine, was entitled, "Ivermectin, Wonder Drug from Japan: The Human Use Perspective". It said, *"There are few drugs that can seriously lay claim to the title of 'Wonder drug', penicillin and aspirin being two that have perhaps had greatest beneficial impact on the health and wellbeing of Mankind. But ivermectin can also be considered alongside those worthy contenders, based on its **versatility**, **safety** and the **beneficial impact** that it has had, and continues to have, worldwide."* [28]

The impact of ivermectin in treating malaria and other parasitic diseases in both animals and humans resulted in those who discovered and developed the medication to win a Nobel prize in 2015. [29]

With this kind of background knowledge available it would seem that in the midst of a crisis when seasoned doctors began to successfully use ivermectin and hydroxychloroquine to treat COVID,

---

[28] https://www.ncbi.nlm.nih.gov/pmc/articles/PMC3043740/
[29] https://www.nobelprize.org/prizes/medicine/2015/press-release/

there would be great optimism and interest. Instead, negative reactions abounded and many doctors had to choose to stop treating people for COVID or risk facing repercussions.

Unfortunately, we have been faced with the unpleasant task of having to choose which set of research trials to believe when one group points to positive trial results and another group points to negative trial results.

There are a number of positive examples of use of ivermectin to treat COVID in various locations around the world that were reported.

The first example was seen in Uttar Pradesh, the largest state of India. In May of 2021, as COVID cases were skyrocketing in India, officials in Uttar Pradesh ordered the distribution of home "COVID Insulation Kits" to the residents of the state, which includes 240 million people. The kits contained ivermectin, along with other vitamins and supplements. Residents were encouraged to use the medications and vitamins to treat COVID at home and in some cases as a preventative measure. The results were very telling. One report stated, *"On August 25, 2021, the Indian media noticed the discrepancy between Uttar Pradesh's massive success and other states, like Kerala's, comparative failure. Although Uttar Pradesh was only 5% vaccinated to Kerala's 20%, Uttar Pradesh had (only) 22 new COVID cases, while Kerala was overwhelmed with 31,445 in one day. So it became apparent that whatever was contained in those treatment kits must have been pretty effective."* [30]

Another example was found in Peru. This report from the fall of 2020 speaks of the effectiveness of ivermectin in eight Peruvian states. *"In these eight Peruvian State analyses, Ivermectin distributions preceded sound reductions in excess deaths and case fatality rate (CFR). The variation in the number of detected cases nor the vulnerable population decrease can explain this reduction.*

---

[30] https://www.thedesertreview.com/opinion/columnists/indias-ivermectin-blackout---part-v-the-secret-revealed/article_9a37d9a8-1fb2-11ec-a94b-47343582647b.html

Other possible explanations, such as cross-immunity with dengue, or mere causality, have been discarded due to their lack of consistency in this study. Treatment with ivermectin is the most reasonable explanation for the decrease in number of deaths and fatality rate in Peru. Its implementation in public policies is a highly effective measure to reduce the excess deaths and IFR of COVID-19." [31]

Another powerful example was seen in African countries where COVID cases and deaths were remarkably low, despite very low vaccination rates in many of those same countries.

In 19 African countries ongoing use of Ivermectin had been taking place for some time by great percentages of the population in treatment for, and prevention of Onchocerciasis, or "River Blindness". These countries became known as "APOC", "African Programme for Onchocerciasis Control".

A December 2020 report in the National Library of Medicine entitled, "COVID-19: Ivermectin, the African Enigma" reported the following. *"Conclusions: The incidence in mortality rates and number of cases is significantly lower among the APOC countries compared to non-APOC countries. That a mass public health preventive campaign against COVID-19 may have taken place, inadvertently, in some African countries with massive community ivermectin use is an attractive hypothesis. Additional studies are needed to confirm it."* [32]

On their website, The Front Line COVID-19 Critical Care Alliance cites results from 90 studies in 27 different countries

**90 studies from 963 scientists
133,842 patients in 27 countries**
Statistically significant improvement for mortality, ventilation, ICU, hospitalization, recovery, cases, and viral clearance.

---

[31] https://www.researchgate.net/publication/344469305_Real-World_Evidence_The_Case_of_Peru_Causality_between_Ivermectin_and_COVID-19_Infection_Fatality_Rate
[32] https://pubmed.ncbi.nlm.nih.gov/33795896/

that show positive results in the use of ivermectin for COVID-19.

Other examples indicating similar positive results came from Mexico City and from Japan. Of course all of these examples involved statistics showing the positive impact of ivermectin and, of course, "fact checkers" and other reports, sometimes from "official" agencies, that denied the validity of the results. In some cases those who denied the validity of the results just fell back upon the "there is no conclusive proof that the reductions in cases or deaths were a result of ivermectin."

During my research I ran across a classic example of the propaganda used to steer people away from the use of ivermectin to treat COVID 19. On a government website, that I will choose to leave nameless, there is a bold statement that ivermectin *"has not been properly tested for humans."* We have looked at plenty of information about the history of ivermectin to know that this statement is not only false, it is purposely misleading. It fits with the "horse deworming" propaganda.

In all of this it seems hard to understand why these issues became so polarizing and divisive within the medical community and beyond. If ivermectin is not helpful and is bad for people, what is the motive of the thousands of doctors around the world insisting that this inexpensive medication is helpful, even though they are often maligned because of their stance? If ivermectin is helpful in treating people for COVID-19 and can save lives, what is the motive for such strong opposition to its use by many governments, health organizations and media outlets?

Unprecedented Control

I began this chapter by referring to how quickly life changed in the United States, and around the world in the spring of 2020. Though much has gradually gone back to what was normal prior to 2020 in the past 18 months or so, some things are still much different than they were, as a result of the economic and business impacts that the pandemic and the responses to the pandemic made. Just today I drove by one of the most popular restaurants in my community in the late afternoon. It was closed and one car was in the parking lot that is so often jammed. It looked so strange but I remembered that they close every day at 4:00 p.m. now because they cannot get workers to cover an evening shift. Many businesses did not recover and driving down the street after 8:00 p.m. looks much different still, than it did before COVID.

The comments I will make here about COVID-19 and unprecedented government control in America and beyond do not need to be taken in a negative light. The main point is simply that we experienced how quickly our government could shut down life as we know it and how willing the majority of the public is willing to accept government control and mandates if the right circumstances bring those things about. Many have questioned if at some point in the future Martial Law would be imposed for some crisis and what would that be like. Though Martial Law was never imposed during the pandemic, citizens experienced much of what that might be like.

For those in authority, 2020 and 2021 could easily serve as a practice for future situations that could arise. Those promoting the great reset have openly proposed that the climate change crisis is worse than the COVID crisis. Thoughts of possible future control measures to "save the planet" are not out of the question.

At first, most of the control measures that were put in place seemed reasonable to most, given all that we were hearing about this new pandemic and the potential of millions of lives being lost. As time went on the nation grew increasingly wary of the ongoing intrusions into private lives and activities.

Some of the control measures did not make sense. I remember hearing that in my state it was legal for a family of 5 or 6 to travel together by car to a lake pulling their boat behind the car, but it was illegal for them to get into the boat together and take a ride on the lake once they got there. At one point churches were closed and not considered essential while liquor stores remained open and were considered essential.

Control measures involved how many people could gather in a room together, what times of day businesses could be open for business, mandates for wearing masks in public places, school closures, church closures, etc.

Once vaccinations came into the equation mandates became common for those in the military and for many others in multiple businesses. For many wanting to travel, vaccination became a mandatory requirement. Some nations began to legislate mandatory vaccination to be in public places. Talks of vaccine passports were very concerning to many, fearing that their liberties would be taken away.

As has already been discussed, more and more opinions about issues related to COVID-19 were censored and people became accustomed to having to carefully watch what they were saying, and where they said it or posted it.

Though numerous riots took place in the summer of 2020, with thousands of unmasked protesters filling the streets, no attempts to enforce mask ordinances were made. Yet, in September of 2020 in a small town in Idaho 3 people were arrested for not wearing a mask during an outdoor church praise gathering. As of that September date in Latah County Idaho, where the arrests were made, only 346 cases of COVID-19 had been reported, with zero hospitalizations and zero deaths reported.

Two mandates stood out as particularly intrusive and difficult. In 2020 and 2021 a number of individuals went into the hospital with COVID-19 and died before they would ever return home. Many of these spent the last days or even weeks of their lives with no visible contact with their loved ones, who were forbidden from being with them. The reasoning for this was understandable, to prevent the spread of the virus. Yet, with no alternative safety measures being offered, families were left with the horrible thought of never seeing their loved one again, and patients were left to face death alone, apart from the ones they loved and cared for.

In schools across America and in other countries small children were forced to wear masks all day long during school for months, even though more and more information became available that indicated the masks were not effective in stopping the spread of the virus. Information was also abundant that COVID-19 was of very little threat to children. Still, mandates remained intact and small children had to learn to function with a mask. Some children had been in school for months and had never seen their teacher's face. I remember seeing a video of a classroom of small children when it was announced to them that they would now be able to take off their masks. They began to celebrate and rejoice openly.

Most would agree that in certain situations, where crisis is involved, a temporary relinquishing of some personal freedoms is appropriate, as long as that relinquishing of personal freedoms is not misused and not prolonged. A simple illustration of this would be having to be detained on a roadway, even rerouted, in order to allow medical and emergency responders to deal with victims and vehicles at a large, horrible crash site.

In the case of the COVID-19 crisis many began to question whether all of the mandates and intrusions into their personal freedoms were justified. Open talk of the pandemic being an "opportunity" to reset the world and establish a new global, social contract did not help to settle those questions for many.

Safe and Effective?

Late in 2020 optimism rose as talk of vaccines being readied that would potentially end the pandemic crisis. There had been much debate about masks, lockdowns and what treatments were appropriate, etc., but most were in agreement that the prospect of vaccines was a great thing.

As the new vaccines became available in December of 2020 excitement was high with the first three million doses being distributed to all 50 states across the United States. Initial aims were to vaccinate 100 million people in the U.S. by April of 2021. Optimism was fueled by reports that the initial vaccines were up to 95% effective in preventing the COVID-19 virus.[33]

By August of 2022 over 260 million people in the U.S., representing 79% of the population, had received at least one dose of the vaccines.[34] By February of 2023 over 670 million doses of COVID vaccines had been administered in the United States.[35] As of February 13, 2023 over 69% of the world's population, or about 5.5 billion people, had received at least one dose of a COVID-19 vaccine and over 13.25 billion doses had been administered worldwide in total.[36]

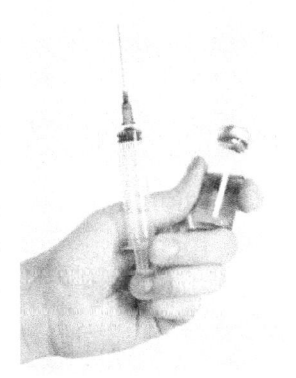

What began as an endeavor that saw people united and optimistic quickly became something that saw people increasingly divided. Many became increasingly concerned about the safety and efficacy of the new vaccines and became reluctant to receive them. Many others became increasingly agitated with those who did not get vaccinated, believing that they were hindering the stop of the pandemic and selfishly endangering the lives of those around them.

Many doctors began to speak out about their concerns regarding the safety issues that were emerging. As more information came out and more voices of concern were raised, the same type of responses that had occurred regarding early treatments began to appear again. Those who voice concerns were labeled "anti-vaxxers" and "spreaders of misinformation". One thing that was clear. Information that was highlighted regarding safety issues did little, if any, to slow the process of vaccinating billions of people around the world.

---

[33] https://www.bbc.com/news/world-us-canada-55305720
[34] https://usafacts.org/visualizations/covid-vaccine-tracker-states
[35] https://www.cdc.gov/coronavirus/2019-ncov/covid-data/covidview/index.html
[36] https://ourworldindata.org/covid-vaccinations

VAERS Numbers

Maybe the most important data regarding how vaccines are affecting people is found in a government website called "Vaccine Adverse Event Reporting System" or (VAERS) which was established in 1990 and has been in operation since. This reporting system makes it possible to report any adverse effects to any type of vaccine so that warning signs can be seen and addressed by physicians and medical organizations.

On the Center for Disease Control (CDC) website an explanation of VAERS is included. In part it reads, "As of August 2022, there are four COVID-19 vaccines approved or authorized for use in the United States to protect against COVID-19 disease. These vaccines are monitored by VAERS and several other vaccine safety monitoring systems as part of the most intensive vaccine safety monitoring effort in U.S. history. This continuous, robust safety monitoring helps keep COVID-19 vaccines safe and helps ensure the benefits of vaccination continue to outweigh any risks." [37]

A disclaimer is included on the VAERS website. It begins as follows.

"VAERS accepts reports of adverse events that occur following vaccination. Anyone, including Healthcare providers, vaccine manufacturers, and the public can submit reports to the system. While very important in monitoring vaccine safety, VAERS reports alone cannot be used to determine if a vaccine caused or contributed to an adverse event or illness. Vaccine providers are encouraged to report any clinically significant health problem following vaccination to VAERS even if they are not sure if the vaccine was the cause. In some situations, reporting to VAERS is required of healthcare providers and vaccine manufacturers.

VAERS reports may contain information that is incomplete, inaccurate, coincidental, or unverifiable. Reports to VAERS can also be biased. As a result, there are limitations on how the data can be

---

[37] https://www.cdc.gov/vaccinesafety/ensuringsafety/monitoring/vaers/index.html

used scientifically. Data from VAERS reports should always be interpreted with these limitations in mind." [38]

A website called "OpenVAERS" has been established to present the data from the VAERS website in summarized formats, to help the general public understand the data found in VAERS. On the homepage of the "OpenVAERS" website this notice appears.

"VAERS is the Vaccine Adverse Event Reporting System put in place in 1990. It is a voluntary reporting system that has been estimated to account for only 1% (read more about underreporting in VAERS) of vaccine injuries. OpenVAERS is built from the HHS data available for download at vaers.hhs.gov.

The OpenVAERS Project allows browsing and searching of the reports without the need to compose an advanced search (more advanced searches can be done at medalerts.org or vaers.hhs.gov. [39]

The above statement that only an estimated 1% of adverse events being accounted for in VAERS data due to underreporting is confirmed on the official VAERS website. Within a section entitled "VAERS Data Limitations" this statement is included. *"Underreporting" is one of the main limitations of passive surveillance systems, including VAERS. The term, underreporting refers to the fact that VAERS receives reports for only a small fraction of actual adverse events.*

With this in mind consider the following data from the OpenVAERS website. Under a tab called "COVID Vaccine Data" a dropdown tab appears entitled "Red Box" Summaries. On this page various summaries of VAERS data is made available related to the Adverse Events reported since the COVID-19 vaccines began to be administered. As of March 3, 2023 the following statistics appear.

---

[38] https://vaers.hhs.gov/data.html
[39] https://openvaers.com/

Deaths - 34,653
Hospitalizations - 193,913
Permanently Disabled - 64,038 [40]

Of this number of reported deaths, 22,255 of them were reported in 2021, the year when the most COVID vaccination occurred. Another 12,467 were reported in 2022. A graph is also available on the same page which shows how many deaths were reported to VAERS in each of the years between 1990 and 2021. The largest number ever reported in one year prior to 2021 was 602 in 2019.

Certainly, the fact that billions of doses of the vaccines were given accounts for much of the increase of these numbers. Still, when we factor in the fact that only "1%" or "a small fraction" of total adverse events are reported, it appears quite alarming. With this in mind it is possible that the 34,653 reported deaths could actually represent over 3 million. Of course, that cannot be known for sure, but the numbers seen by VAERS have been a part of what has caused great concern on the part of many physicians and people in the general public.

As you would expect, numerous "fact checking" articles were produced regarding this information. Not surprisingly, at least some of them, if not most of them, came to the general conclusion that any concerns that came out of this information were unfounded. The general conclusion continued to be that the vaccines were safe and effective.

One of those fact checking articles was produced by USA Today in January of 2022. The article was titled: "Fact Check: Reports of Adverse Events Due to COVID-19 Vaccines Are Unverifiable". [41]

The article comes to the conclusion that claims of 1 million

---

[40] https://openvaers.com/covid-data

[41] https://www.usatoday.com/story/news/factcheck/2022/01/05/fact-check-1-million-covid-19-vaccine-adverse-events-unverified/9103381002/

COVID-19 vaccine related injuries have been reported to a CDC database, are false.

Within the article though is this statement.

*"As evidence, WorldNetDaily cites OpenVAERS, a website that "posts publicly available CDC/FDA data of injuries reported post-vaccination." A USA TODAY analysis of VAERS data **confirms those numbers**, (emphasis added) which include adverse event reports for all COVID-19 vaccines in any location worldwide."* [42]

The article goes on to distinguish the numbers of worldwide reports from those just within the U.S. Even within a "fact-checking" article that in essence, denies the concerns about these numbers, the numbers reported to VAERS are confirmed. It would seem to me that these numbers constitute at least a need to look deeper into the safety of the vaccines. It certainly would appear that consistent claims that the vaccines are very safe may be overstated.

Dominating the Discussion

One of the most outspoken critics of the vaccinations has been Robert Kennedy Jr., the son of former Senator Robert Kennedy and the nephew of former President John F. Kennedy. As you might guess, Robert Kennedy Jr. has been aligned most often throughout his lifetime with what we might call "liberals". Also, he has borne one of the most respected political family names in U.S. history, particularly within liberal, or progressive circles. He helped found the non-profit environmental group "Waterkeeper Alliance" in 1999 and has served as the president of its board. From 1986 until 2017, Kennedy was a senior attorney for the Natural Resources Defense Council (NRDC), a non-profit environmental organization.

Robert Kennedy Jr. though, has raised concerns about vaccinations in general, since he founded the non-profit organization "Children's Health Defense" in 2005. He serves as the chairman of the organization. He has become very outspoken about the COVID

---

[42] ibid

vaccines in the past 3 years. He has actually written 3 books about COVID and the related vaccines. They include "The Real Anthony Fauci: Bill Gates, Big Pharma and the Global War on Democracy and Public Health", "A Letter to Liberals: Censorship and COVID: An Attack on Science and American Ideals", and "The Wuhan Cover-Up: How U.S. Health Officials Conspired with the Chinese Military to Hide the Origins of COVID-19".

Not surprisingly, Robert Kennedy Jr. has now been maligned by many in the media, and social media. A Wikipedia page dedicated to him uses the following phrases in the beginning of the article that describes him.

"known for promoting anti-vaccine **propaganda and conspiracy theories**",

"he has promoted the **scientifically discredited** link between vaccines and autism". [43]

Later, under a section labeled "COVID-19" the following words and phrases appear related to Kennedy.

"Kennedy promoted **multiple conspiracy theories** related to COVID-19"

"he touted a number of **incorrect and misleading claims** about vaccines and public health measures related to the COVID-19"

"Kennedy has **promoted misinformation** about the COVID-19 vaccine"

"In February 2021 his **Instagram account was blocked** for "repeatedly sharing **debunked claims** about the coronavirus or vaccines"

"The book repeats several **discredited myths** about the COVID-19 pandemic, notably about the effectiveness of ivermectin"

"**His YouTube account was removed** in late September 2021 for breaking the company's new policies on vaccine

---

[43] https://en.wikipedia.org/wiki/Robert_F._Kennedy_Jr.

misinformation". [44]

Two things I would like to point out here that I believe are revealed from this information that is supposed to be biographical information about a person.

First of all, notice that Wikipedia is an example of what is now common among so many online and social media sources. Rather than say "what some call propaganda and conspiracy theories" or "what some claim to be discredited myths" or "what some have called misinformation", all of these accusations, along with others, are presented as absolute facts about the person being spoken of. Certainly he doesn't claim that the information he shares is "debunked", "discredited myths", "conspiracy theories", and "misinformation", and neither do many other experts and people within the general public. Yet, Wikipedia feels the liberty to be judge and jury on these matters. This is an example of the discrediting of all those who openly speak out with opinions that do not match the politically correct narrative. Remember that in "Event201" one of the things that was laid out within the plans was how government, traditional media and social media sources must control the information (or misinformation) being disseminated.

Secondly, notice two statements that confirm what we just said. his Instagram account was blocked and his YouTube account was removed.

It is not hard to see that those who truly believe all of the current narratives regarding COVID-19 from governments and health organizations are correct, might feel as though it is appropriate for opposing views to be censored, in order to avoid dangerous confusion. On the United Nations' UNESCO website they have even coined a new word related to combating what they call misinformation. On their site

---

[44] ibid

they say that we are facing a "Disinfodemic". [45]

On the other hand, it is easy to see that those who have questions about the narratives and policies being promoted by governments and health organizations, would find the censoring of opposing views alarming and dangerous for numerous reasons. They would most definitely prefer that information, data and opinions be heard from health professionals on both sides of the arguments, unhindered, allowing the listeners to decide what they believe to be true, and what actions they should take regarding the health and well-being of themselves and their families. The censoring of opinions and information that does not fit a government narrative is not a favorable thing in the eyes of many.

Concerns Grow

The term "Sudden Adult Death Syndrome" has been around for decades but was little known until it was commonly spoken of in 2021 and 2022. Many reports of healthy, young adults, many of them athletes, suddenly collapsing to their deaths, have been seen and heard. In numerous cases, these sudden deaths were captured on video.

Excess Mortality Rates is a term used to indicate numbers of deaths in a nation or area beyond the expected, average amounts based on previous years. These excess deaths were expected in 2020 due to the COVID-19 pandemic. What has been surprising and confusing to many has been that these excess deaths have continued through 2021 and 2022. One recent article on this in the online entity, "Health Feedback" was entitled "What Can Explain the Excess Mortality in the U.S. and Europe in 2022?" The article features numerous graphs showing the excess mortality that has occurred. The article also states the following.

"However, COVID-19 deaths gradually decreased throughout 2022. With the threat of the disease appearing to diminish,

---

[45] https://www.unesco.org/en/covid-19/communication-and-information-response

COVID-19 stopped hitting the headlines and most countries lifted their restrictions on daily life. But this gradual return to normalcy belies the fact that excess mortality has continued to persist in many countries well into 2022. This observation has surprised many commentators and journalists. The trend has also become fodder for COVID-19 vaccine skepticism." [46]

As this article states, this became another point of concern for those who are wary of the safety and efficacy of COVID vaccines.

A Rasmussen report in January of 2023 reported, *"The latest Rasmussen Reports national telephone and online survey finds that (49%) of American Adults believe it is likely that side effects of COVID 19 vaccines have caused a significant number of unexplained deaths.* [47] It also reported that, *"Twenty eight percent (28%) of adults say they personally know someone whose death they think may have been caused by side effects of COVID-19 vaccines."* [48]

In his book "Cause Unknown", Ed Dowd writes about the epidemic of sudden deaths among younger populations in 2021 and 2022. He details connections between the increase of unexplained sudden deaths with the increase of COVID-19 vaccinations.[49]

Along with safety concerns, growing concerns about efficacy have emerged as well. As populations reached higher and higher levels of vaccination, it became apparent that the original hopes of near 100% efficiency in blocking virus infection were not coming true and expectations continued to be lowered. In many cases the narrative changed from "prevent infection by the virus" to "keep the infection at a lower level of severity."

One example of this was seen in Israel. By summer of 2021 Israel was one of the most vaccinated countries in the world. Still,

---

[46] https://healthfeedback.org/what-can-explain-the-excess-mortality-in-the-u-s-and-europe-in-2022/
[47] https://www.rasmussenreports.com/public_content/politics/public_surveys/died_suddenly_more_than_1_in_4_think_someone_they_know_died_from_covid_19_vaccines
[48] ibid
[49] https://www.amazon.ca/Cause-Epidemic-Sudden-Deaths-2021/dp/1510776397

the country was experiencing massive infection rates by August of 2021. One article discussing the problem stated, *"Fully vaccinated people with weakened immune systems appeared particularly vulnerable to the aggressive Delta variant."* [50]

It went on to say -

"Asked what has brought Israel to peak transmission even as the country has already provided third doses of vaccines to 1.5 million citizens, Rahav, who has become one of the best known faces of Israel's public health messaging, sighed, saying, "I think we're dealing with a very nasty virus. This is the main problem—and we're learning it the hard way." [51]

Even Bill Gates has acknowledged that the COVID vaccines have not proved to be as effective as originally thought. In a recent interview he stated, *"We also need to fix the three problems with vaccines. The current vaccines are not infection blocking, they're not broad, so when new variants come up you lose protection, and they have very short duration."* [52]

Another source of information that has proven to be alarming to many has been the testimony of some who work as embalmers. These embalmers have said openly that starting in 2021 they began to see strange white, fibrous blood clots within many of the people they were trying to embalm. These clots would have to be removed in order to get the embalming fluid to freely travel throughout the body. Of course, there would be no way of proving that these clots were caused by vaccines, but the timing of this new reality seemed to many, to be very telling.

At least three different documentary movies have been produced which deal in different ways with the safety and efficacy concerns related to the COVID vaccines. "Died Suddenly" deals especially with the alarming reality of these strange synthetic type blood clots. "Uninformed Consent" and "Safe and Effective: A

---

[50] https://news.yahoo.com/ultra-vaxxed-israel-debacle-dire-073840050.html
[51] ibid
[52] https://www.youtube.com/watch?v=kGctGh3vvJg&t=21s

Second Opinion" also deal with issues related to the vaccines.

The documentary "Safe and Effective: A Second Opinion" includes the testimony of Dr. Aseem Malhotra.

Dr. Malhotra is a highly esteemed, award-winning consultant cardiologist based at the ROC Private Clinic, London. He is a globally regarded specialist when it comes to diagnosing, preventing, and managing heart disease.[53] He was listed as one of The Sunday Times (a British newspaper) 500 most influential people in 2016 and was twice recognized as one of the top 50 black and minority ethnic community member pioneers in the UK's National Health Service by the Health Service Journal.[54]

In the film Dr. Malhotra states the following.

"Having been double jabbed and being one of the first to take the Pfizer vaccine, I have after several months critically appraising the data, speaking to eminent scientists, in Oxford, Stanford and Harvard, speaking to two investigative medical journalists and being contacted by two Pfizer whistleblowers, reluctantly concluded that this vaccine is not completely safe, and has unprecedented harms, which leads me to conclude that it needs to be suspended until all the raw data has been released for independent analysis."

These are samples of some of the sources of concerns that have emerged in the past couple of years. The fact that safety concerns have grown is not the most confusing and troubling thing in my opinion. The most confusing and troubling thing has been the doubling down by those who continue to insist that everyone should be vaccinated and that the vaccines are safe and effective. Voices that deviate from this narrative continue to be accused of spreading

---

[53] https://draseemmalhotra.co.uk/
[54] https://en.wikipedia.org/wiki/Aseem_Malhotra

misinformation and conspiracy theories. Even well respected doctors who express concerns and give data to explain why they have these concerns, are often maligned and simply referred to as "anti-vaxxers".

Instead of taking a step back and releasing the raw data for independent analysis as Dr. Malhotra and others have suggested, government health agencies continue to push forward with determination to vaccinate even younger and younger children who have extremely low risk of being harmed by COVID. It is confusing and perplexing.

Just a few days before I write here in February of 2023 the CDC has come out with new guidelines that include a new measure. They now will include COVID-19 vaccinations as a part of the regularly scheduled vaccinations for children **6 months and older**. [55] Though for now these scheduled vaccinations are not mandatory, it is another step toward mandating vaccinations for small children. An MSN article about the new CDC recommendations states, *"This move could give states the authority to make the COVID-19 vaccine mandatory for school attendance. However, some states have laws in place that prevent mandatory COVID-19 vaccinations for children. It remains to be seen how the new CDC rule will affect children living in these states."* [56]

Concerning to many is the combination of a lack of willingness to acknowledge safety concerns, the aggressive promotion of more and more boosters, the aggressive push toward vaccinating younger and younger children, and the greater levels of government controls involved in these issues. All of this continues, despite the fact that decisive evidence has now been revealed from numerous sources showing that the vaccines are not effective in preventing infection by the COVID-19 virus or the transmission of the virus.

---

[55] https://www.cdc.gov/mmwr/volumes/72/wr/mm7206a1.htm?s_cid=mm7206a1_w
[56] https://www.msn.com/en-us/health/health-news/cdc-recommends-adding-covid-19-vaccine-to-schedule-of-shots-needed-for-children/ar-AA17mapt

By the end of 2021 numerous governments were implementing or considering mandatory vaccination policies which would greatly limit unvaccinated people from living public lives. A December 2021 BBC article stated, *"Covid vaccinations are already a requirement for public life in many parts of the world. If you are a French doctor, a New Zealand teacher or a Canadian government employee, getting your shots is essential to go to work. Indonesia can deny benefits to people who refuse jabs. Greece is making them compulsory for the over 60s. Austria is set to go further still, with a plan to introduce mandatory vaccinations for all by February. This would not mean Austrians being forcibly injected. There will be medical and religious exemptions. But the bulk of the remaining unvaccinated population face fines for not getting their shots. With Germany planning a similar move it is not a debate that is going away."* [57]

Talks of COVID vaccine passports became common during the same time period. These passports would have potentially made it almost impossible for unvaccinated people to travel or to function in society. Since COVID cases diminished in 2022 the push for mandatory vaccination and vaccine passports subsided but the initiatives are all still on the table should there be a resurgence of the virus. These kinds of big brother controls of life are of great concern to many. When added to all that we have discussed earlier regarding the movement toward an all encompassing global system, it certainly appears that the framework for many of the things spoken of in the Bible, in Revelation 13 and elsewhere, may be coming together at this time.

---

[57] https://www.bbc.com/news/world-59506339

CHAPTER 16

The Mark of the Beast, 666 & Current Developments

Probably the most well known passage in the Bible related to the end times and the 2nd coming of Jesus Christ is found in Revelation 13:16-18, where the Bible refers to "the mark of the beast."

> *"And he causes all, the small and the great, and the rich and the poor, and the free men and the slaves, to be given a mark on their right hand or on their forehead, (17) and he provides that no one will be able to buy or to sell, except the one who has the mark, either the name of the beast or the number of his name. (18) Here is wisdom. Let him who has understanding calculate the number of the beast, for the number is that of a man; and his number is six hundred and sixty-six."*   Revelation 13:16-18

In this passage we see one of the biblical indications that there will be global government and economic systems in place in the last days. Verse 16 says "And he causes **all**, the small and the great, and the rich and the poor, and the free men and the slaves to be given a mark." This seems inclusive of people all around the world, rather than in just one nation or area. Verse 17 adds, "he provides that **no one** will be able to buy or to sell, except the one who has the mark ..." Again, this seems inclusive of people all around the world.

The context of this passage confirms this to be true. Revelation 13:3 says "and **the whole earth** was amazed and followed after the beast." Revelation 13:7 adds, "**authority over every tribe and people and tongue and nation was given to him**." Then in Revelation 13:8 we read this.

> *"**All who dwell on the earth** will worship him, everyone whose name has not been written from the foundation of the world in the book of life of the Lamb who has been slain."*

Again, we see that the entire world is involved in this acceptance and worship of the beast, except true Christians, whose names are written in the Lamb's book of life.

It is easy to see why Revelation 13 is one of the passages of Scripture that has led the overwhelming majority of those studying Bible prophecy to believe that there will be a global government and economic system in existence in the last days. It would appear that in order to enforce the "mark of the beast" mandate that is spoken of in verse 16-18 a government that has global authority, along with an economic system that extends globally must be in place.

Many have speculated as to what this "mark of the beast" would actually be. Would it be a literal mark, like a tattoo, placed on the forehead or hand of people? Would it be an embedded computer chip under the skin? Would it involve an actual number? Recently, some have remarked that the suggested vaccine passports could be the precursor to the mark of the beast.

One thing is certain. The mark of the beast spoken of in Revelation 13 is not a reality at this time.

In this chapter we will look at 6 indicators showing that the technology is in place now for the establishing of the mark of the beast and the needed global system appears to be emerging quickly at this time. We will also look at the spiritual aspect of the described "mark of the beast" seen in Revelation 13, seeing that it involves much more than just an economic system.

6 Indicators That the Mark of the Beast May Be Imminent

Universal Product Code (UPC Code)

The Universal Product Code (UPC), or barcode system that is used on all the products we buy, is used to scan the product quickly and calculate the price of the product. As might be expected, the UPC code on a product actually gives much more information about the product beyond the price of the product, including information about the manufacturing of the product.

Commercial use of Universal Product Codes began in retail stores in the mid-1970s with the first product being scanned on June 26, 1974 at a supermarket in Troy, Ohio. The product was a 10-pack of Wrigley's Juicy Fruit chewing gum.[1]

The scanning technology and the use of UPC codes moved the world much closer to a global system of economy and to a digital, cashless society. For these reasons alone, the use of UPC scanning of products was a development noticed by many who studied Bible prophecy.

In 1982 Dr. Mary Stewart Relfe published a book entitled, "The New Money System" that helped reveal something much more specific about the UPC codes that raised the awareness of the significance of this technological advancement to a new level. I remember learning about this in the 1980s and being taken back by the obvious connection between the UPC codes and the prophecy found in Revelation 13:16-18.

In Dr. Relfe's book, she reveals that the number 666 is embedded in the UPC code as an overarching number within the code assigned to each product worldwide!

---

[1] https://en.wikipedia.org/wiki/Universal_Product_Code

She explains how the code is structured. There is a standard version, sometimes referred to as UPC-A that is used on the vast majority of retail products, and alternative versions used in specific applications. There are 3 sets of digit bar codes used to make up the versions of the UPC codes. The standard UPC-A code uses just sets 1 & 2 while some alternate versions also draw from the 3rd set. All versions of the UPC code include the overarching number 666 but attempting to show that would get very involved so I will stick with the standard UPC-A version while attempting to explain how 666 is involved.

If you go to your kitchen cabinet or kitchen pantry and pull out numerous products you will find that the first two lines of the UPC code on the product, the middle two lines, and the last two lines are always the same. They are also the same as each other. They are longer than the other lines and do not have a number listed under them like the other lines do. These lines represent a "6". When we understand this it is easy to see that "666" is marked on each product that we buy.

The diagram above illustrates this point. From this diagram you can also see that whenever a "6" is involved on the right side of the code it will be represented by these same lines as that are used for the first, middle and last lines of the code. If you find a "6" in the digits listed on the left side of the code it will be represented by a different pair of lines. This is because a different set of digit codes is used for the numbers on the left side of the code.

I am including a second illustration here that shows something else you may discover on your products. Sometimes there will be an extra pair of longer lines just after the first set of two lines and just

256

before the last set of two lines. The number that these lines represent will usually be shown to the outside of the code but not always. They do not change the truth about the first, middle and last two lines of the code that represent a "6".

Though Dr. Relfe's book gives a much better explanation of all of this, some explanation is available on the Wikipedia page for "Universal Product Code". [2]

Let me make it clear that I am not saying the Universal Product Code is the mark of the beast. It is not. However, it is quite interesting that the overarching number used within the Universal Product Code, marked on every product we buy is "666", the very number that Revelation 13:16-18 specifies.

I think what this tells us is that when the Universal system includes an identifying number or mark for every individual who will buy or sell, the overarching number that will be included in everyone's identification number or mark, will be "666". According to Revelation 13, when that time comes it will involve more than just an economic identification. It will also involve an pledged allegiance to a world leader who has emerged, and who is claiming to be god.

Chip Implants

Another technological development that may very well have brought the world closer to the fulfillment of Revelation 13:16-18 is that of computer chip implants. The first experiments with a radio-frequency identification implant (RFID) were carried out in 1998. Since that time the technology has advanced and microchips are now commonly used to identify and locate pets. Experiments with using chip implants in humans have also advanced for various purposes.

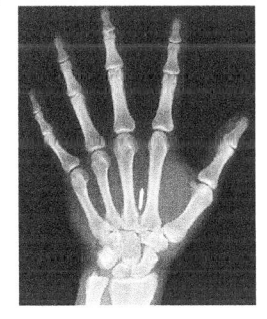

The Wikipedia article entitled "Microchip Implant (Human)"

---

[2] https://en.wikipedia.org/wiki/Universal_Product_Code

includes this description of chip implants.

"A human microchip implant is any electronic device implanted subcutaneously (subdermally) usually via an injection. Examples include an identifying integrated circuit RFID device encased in silicate glass which is implanted in the body of a human being. This type of subdermal implant usually contains a unique ID number that can be linked to information contained in an external database, such as identity document, criminal record, medical history, medications, address book, and other potential uses." [3]

The article goes on to list a number of potential uses for chip implants including Cryptocurrency Wallet, Keycards, Medical History/Medical records, Medical Identification Tag, Payment Cards and Travel Cards. [4] Note in particular that financial purposes are listed here including "Cryptocurrency Wallets" and "Payment Cards". The technology to make all financial transactions digitally controlled through embedded microchips in humans is now available, or at least in the developmental stages.

With the development of artificial intelligence, work is also being done through companies like Neuralink to implant microchips into human brains, allowing human intelligence and artificial intelligence to work together. This may play into the last days in another way, increasing the potential for a greater level of deception.

The potential for GPS tracking of humans, like that of pets, is also on the table for future uses of microchip implants.

Every potential use for these kinds of technologies can be used to accomplish wonderful things for mankind. On the other hand, these technologies can be used to accomplish unprecedented levels of control over the human population.

---

[3] https://en.wikipedia.org/wiki/Microchip_implant_(human)
[4] ibid

Programmable Digital Currencies

The use of digital currencies or "cryptocurrencies" like "Bitcoin" has paved the way for the development of government sponsored versions of digital currencies such as Bitcoin.

Bitcoin was made available for use in January of 2009. Its success has been remarkable. In September of 2010 a bitcoin was valued at $.06. By November of 2021 the value of a bitcoin peaked at over $65,000. As of February of 2023 it is valued at just over $24,000.[5] Numerous people have become rich by investing in Bitcoin.

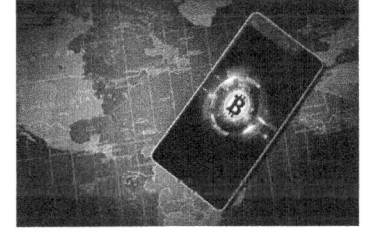

Bitcoin is decentralized and therefore has no central authority. The success of cryptocurrencies like Bitcoin has made the idea of centralized, government backed digital currencies appealing to many. Talk of government backed digital currency through a central bank has been increasing for some time now.

China already has their own version of such a digital currency, the digital Yuan. In a December of 2020 article on "Investopedia" this explanation of China's digital currency is given.

"Among the world's biggest economies, China has become the frontrunner in developing a Central Bank Digital Currency (CBDC). The Asian giant completed a trial of the DC/EP, as its digital currency is known, in September and is currently rolling it out on major e-commerce platforms within the country. Here is a brief primer on the digital currency.

What Is DC/EP?

The Digital Currency Electronic Payment (DC/EP) is a digital version of the yuan – China's national currency. The DC/EP is backed by yuan deposits held by China's central bank and has

---

[5] https://buybitcoinworldwide.com/price/

been under development for slightly more than five years. Under the current arrangement, banks are required to convert a part of their yuan holdings into digital form and distribute them to businesses and citizens via mobile technology." [6]

China's digital currency is still in its infancy stage but according to a November 2022 "Wired" article, *"The People's Bank of China reported that its official eCNY app had 261 million users at the end of 2021, and that by August 31 more than 100 billion yuan (about $14 billion) had changed hands across 360 million transactions."* [7] It seems clear that the Chinese government is committed to seeing their digital currency replace their traditional currency in the near future.

Other governments including India, Brazil, the European Union, and the United States are already considering centralized digital currencies.

In September of 2022 an article appeared on the White House website entitled "Technical Possibilities for a U.S. Central Bank Digital Currency". It stated the following. *"A United States central bank digital currency (CBDC) would be a digital form of the U.S. dollar. While the U.S. has not yet decided whether it will pursue a CBDC, the U.S. has been closely examining the implications of, and options for, issuing a CBDC."* [8]

The article goes on to explain Executive Order 14067 that directed the Office of Science and Technology Policy (OSTP), in consultation with other Federal departments and agencies, to submit to the President a technical evaluation for a potential U.S. CBDC system.[9]

For now it appears that the development of centralized digital currencies is on a nation to nation basis, rather than a centralized

---

[6] https://www.investopedia.com/understanding-chinas-digital-yuan-5090699
[7] https://www.wired.com/story/chinas-digital-yuan-ecny-works-just-like-cash-surveillance/
[8] https://www.whitehouse.gov/ostp/news-updates/2022/09/16/technical-possibilities-for-a-u-s-central-bank-digital-currency/
[9] ibid

global basis. Of course, this is all developing at the same time the United Nations, the World Economic Forum, and many others are calling for a global "Great Reset".

It is easy to see how digital currency could be another key development toward "no one will be able to buy or sell, except the one who has the mark", which is spoken of in Revelation 13:16-18. The additional characteristic of centralized digital currency that makes it sound even more like what is spoken of in Revelation 13 is that it can become programmable. In other words, employers or governments can program the digital currency in such a way that it will only work in the ways which the issuer (or controller) has programmed it to be used. Also, every transaction will be able to be directly recorded and monitored in real time.

A June 23, 2021 article on the Federal Reserve website, entitled "What is Programmable Money?" gives this description of programmable digital currency.

*"Two natural components of the definition are **a digital form of money** and **a mechanism for specifying the automated behavior of that money** through a computer program (this mechanism is termed **"programmability"** in this note)."* [10]

Again, all of these technological advances can be used for wonderful purposes. In the hands of the wrong people they can be used to control people all over the world in unprecedented ways.

ESG Scores

In chapter 13 we examined a new reality in the world today that would appear to be another potential development toward the mark of the beast spoken of in Revelation 13:16-18.

As we discussed in chapter 13, "ESG" stands for **E**nvironmental, **S**ocial and **G**overnance. Since the United Nations initiated the assigning of ESG scores for corporations and businesses around the world in 2006, the growth of ESG scores has

---

[10] https://www.federalreserve.gov/econres/notes/feds-notes/what-is-programmable-money-20210623.html

been staggering. By 2021 over 120 trillion dollars of assets were under management by the ESG initiative. Corporations and businesses are being scored for things like, how much they help or harm the environment, how they respond to social issues like LGBTQ issues, race issues, and abortion issues, and how diverse their governing boards are. A bad ESG score could prevent a corporation from doing business with other major corporations.

ESG scores are now being produced for individuals as well. In the near future a person's ability to do business with a local bank or other businesses could depend upon their ESG score.

As we discussed in chapter 13, China already has a rating system in place that rates Chinese citizens in a very similar way. Those who do not score well have in some cases been punished in tangible ways like travel restrictions and slower internet speeds in their homes.

Putting These 5 Developments Together

Before we go on I would like for you to take a moment and consider these 5 developments together that are now realities in our world.

1) UPC Codes that include "666"
2) Computer Chip Implant Technology
3) Programmable Digital Currency
4) ESG Scores for Corporations and Individuals
5) The Push for the Global Reset (Global Socialist System)

Add these 5 developments together and it is easy to see that the stage is being set for the beast of Revelation 13, (the antichrist), to demand allegiance and worship through "the mark of the beast" in order for people to be able to buy or sell. I am certainly not saying that the fulfillment of Revelation 13:16-18 has now happened. I am saying that it is clear that many different things are coming together which appear to indicate that the fulfillment of Revelation 13 is near.

Smart Cities and Video Surveillance

Another development that could certainly play into the future "mark of the beast" reality that Revelation 13:16-18 speaks about is that of "smart cities" and high tech facial recognition video surveillance.

In chapter 13 I spoke about China's development of a Social Credit System which gives individuals and businesses social scores and rewards or punishes them based on their scores. I mentioned then that one of the ways China is experimenting with collecting data is through an enormous surveillance system involving hundreds of millions of video surveillance cameras. Many of these cameras include facial recognition technology.

As would be expected, China is not the only country increasing surveillance of its citizens. Allied Market Research predicts, *"U.S. Video Surveillance Market to Hit $23.60 Billion by 2027"* [11] A January, 2023 article by "The Star" says *"In Scotland, video surveillance and a multitude of sensors will be used to make this city (Edinburgh) smarter".*[12] A January 2020, USA Today article says that as of the beginning of 2020 there were, **"1,000 smart city projects that are currently being built worldwide."** [13] Interestingly, it also states that of those 1,000 smart city projects, *"China is home to half of them."*[14] (Remember that Klaus Schawb has said that China is a role model for nations as the WEF pushes for "The Great Reset".)

So what are "smart cities"? In an article on smart cities,

---

[11]https://www.globenewswire.com/en/news-release/2021/04/26/2216972/0/en/U-S-Video-Surveillance-Market-to-Hit-23-60-Billion-by-2027-Allied-Market-Research.html
[12]https://www.thestar.com.my/tech/tech-news/2023/01/03/in-scotland-video-surveillance-and-a-multitude-of-sensors-will-be-used-to-make-this-city-smarter
[13]https://www.usnews.com/news/cities/articles/2020-01-31/are-chinas-smart-cities-really-surveillance-cities
[14] ibid

nationalgeographic.org describes them this way. *"A smart city, then, is a city in which a suite of sensors (typically hundreds or thousands) is deployed to collect electronic data from and about people and infrastructure so as to improve efficiency and quality of life."* [15]

A 2021 article on securityinformed.com entitled "Safety In Smart Cities: How Video Surveillance Keeps Security Front And Center" gives more explanation on how the data is collected and made available in a smart city. It speaks of the use of *"innovative surveillance cameras with integrated IoT and cloud technologies".* [16] It also explains that, *"The main foundations that underpin smart cities are 5G, Artificial Intelligence (AI), and the Internet of Things (IoT) and the Cloud."* [17]

If you are not familiar with what "the Internet of Things" (IoT) is, here is a description from Oracle.com. *"The Internet of Things (IoT) describes the network of physical objects—"things"—that are embedded with sensors, software, and other technologies for the purpose of connecting and exchanging data with other devices and systems over the internet. These devices range from ordinary household objects to sophisticated industrial tools."* [18] The article goes on to say that it is expected that there will be 22 billion devices connected to the IoT by 2025. Wow, I think we have all jokingly talked about whether or not our home could be monitored by our TV or some other device. I think this answers that question. If not now, it is clear that in the near future technology will allow us to be monitored even within our own homes. This real time data technology is a key part of smart cities.

---

[15] https://education.nationalgeographic.org/resource/smart-cities/
[16] https://www.securityinformed.com/insights/safety-smart-cities-video-surveillance-security-co-12058-ga.1610712054.html
[17] ibid
[18] https://www.oracle.com/internet-of-things/what-is-iot/

With facial recognition technology and the development of smart cities, gathering data in real time and relaying that information to a monitored system, it is easy to see how this will also be a part of the technology involved in what Revelation 13:16-18 speaks about.

Vaccine Passports

Another indicator of the world moving closer to Revelation 13s "mark of the beast" is the push in 2021-2022 for vaccine passports. Though the subsiding of COVID-19 allowed for the issues surrounding vaccine passports to fade into the background, at least for now, we witnessed what it might look like for people to be severely limited in what they can do and where they can go if they choose not to go along with the direction chosen for them be governments and international organizations. At one point European nations, some African nations, the United States and others were looking seriously at implementing vaccine passports which would have greatly limited those who were unvaccinated.

Whether or not the talk of vaccine passports will fade as a memory of the past or reemerge with even greater concentration is too early to tell.

One thing is for certain, we witnessed how quickly government mandates could turn into life altering requirements and monitoring systems.

More Than Economics!

A word of reminder about what the Bible teaches about the mark of the beast is in order here. The phrase "no one will be able to buy or sell, except for him who has the mark" is what gives us the understanding that this mark will be a part of a worldwide economic system. Much of what we have discussed in this chapter deals with this fact. We must be careful that in our focus on this aspect of the mark of the beast, we miss the more important aspect of what the passage in Revelation 13:16-18 is telling us.

Revelation 13:11-12 and Revelation 13:15 tell us -

*"Then I saw another beast coming up out of the earth; and he had two horns like a lamb and he spoke as a dragon. (12) He exercises all the authority of the first beast in his presence. And **he makes the earth and those who dwell in it to worship the first beast**, whose fatal wound was healed."* Revelation 13:11-12

*"And it was given to him to give breath to the image of the beast, so that the image of the beast would even speak **and cause as many as do not worship the image of the beast to be killed."*** Revelation 13:15

We have seen that the technology to monitor and control people, give them an identifying mark, cause them to not be able to participate in the economy, etc. is all coming into place. We have also seen that a movement to create a global system of government that these technologies could work in has reached a fever pitch. Yet, all of this falls short of truly understanding what the "mark of the beast" is all about.

The "mark of the beast" is all about worship of a leader who sets himself up to be god on the earth! The mark is a pledge of allegiance to this world leader and to the system he rules over.

I am convinced that when the mark of the beast actually comes into play people will know that they are doing more than participating in a global economic system by taking the mark. They will know that they are choosing to worship the antichrist and his beastly kingdom as god. They will know that they are faced with a choice. A choice to worship God and face the consequences of not being able to buy or sell, or worship the antichrist, thereby turning away from, and denying God.

The seriousness of this decision is emphasized in Revelation

14:9-11 where we read -

> "... If anyone worships the beast and his image, and receives a mark on his forehead or on his hand, (10) he also will drink of the wine of the wrath of God, which is mixed in full strength in the cup of His anger; and he will be tormented with fire and brimstone in the presence of the holy angels and in the presence of the Lamb. (11) "And the smoke of their torment goes up forever and ever; they have no rest day and night, those who worship the beast and his image, and whoever receives the mark of his name."
> Revelation 14:9-11

The perseverance of those who choose to not receive the mark of the beast, and the rewards they will receive is spoken of in the next two verses.

> "Here is the perseverance of the saints who keep the commandments of God and their faith in Jesus. (13) And I heard a voice from heaven, saying, "Write, 'Blessed are the dead who die in the Lord from now on!'" "Yes," says the Spirit, "so that they may rest from their labors, for their deeds follow with them."
> Revelation 14:12-13

The future rewards for those who do not take the mark of the beast is also referred to in Revelation 20.

> "Then I saw thrones, and they sat on them, and judgment was given to them. And I saw the souls of those who had been beheaded because of their testimony of Jesus and because of the word of God, and those who had not worshiped the beast or his image, and had not received the mark on their

forehead and on their hand; and they came to life and reigned with Christ for a thousand years."
Revelation 20:4

The antichrist (also known as "the lawless one" or "the man of lawlessness") will perform many signs and wonders and will deceive the whole world. Jesus said in Matthew 24:24 that the false signs and wonders that come in those days to deceive the world will be so convincing that if it were possible even the elect would be deceived. Through deception, false promises and through the threat of not being able to buy or sell, many will be convinced to willingly accept the mark of the beast in that day.

I believe that each of us should set our heart to follow Jesus Christ to the very end, whether that end be our death before these things come about, our being raptured at some point before these things come about, or our facing this critical moment and choosing to stay true to Jesus, no matter the cost, firm until the end!

We will discuss in more detail in a later chapter something related to all of this that I want to mention briefly here. God has proven throughout history that He is more than capable of protecting, and providing supernaturally for, His people in times of great need! In both the Old and New Testaments we read of God's miraculous protection and provisions! If you and/or I face the time of the mark of the beast, I am absolutely convinced that our God, Who never leaves us nor forsakes us (Hebrews 13:5), will provide for us as needed. He will also give us the grace to have the courage, wisdom, power and strength we need in those moments!

CHAPTER 17

Gog and Magog (Ezekiel 38-39)

One of the most detailed prophecies concerning the last days is found in Ezekiel 38 & 39. These prophecies deal with something typically referred to as the War of Gog and Magog.

Much speculation surrounds many of the details of this future war. A few things seem clear. There will be a group of countries that will invade Israel, attempting to conquer Israel in "the latter years". God will intervene on behalf of Israel and the invading armies will be slaughtered.

Some of the details concerning this war found in Ezekiel 38 would appear to fit with the "Battle of Armageddon", causing some to believe that the two are one in the same. Others contend that they are separate wars with the war of Gog and Magog coming before many other end time events, while the battle of Armageddon takes place at the time of Christ's 2nd coming. Which of these understandings of this war is correct continues to be debated in Christian circles.

Some of the similarities between the two battles are the great earthquake that accompanies both, the downpour of hailstones that kill multitudes, the location of the battles, and the supernatural protection of Israel bringing victory over the invaders. There are also apparent differences between the two battles. Ezekiel sees a specific group of nations led by "Gog, prince of Rosh" while in Revelation, John sees the armies of the nations of the world gathered, led by the antichrist, or "the beast". Ezekiel says that the invaders come to take spoil from the land while Revelation says the invaders come to make war against the Lamb of God.

Whether or not the war of Gog and Magog described in Ezekiel 38 & 39 is the same as the battle of Armageddon, the apparent preparations for this battle that can be seen in the world today, remind us that the 2nd coming of Christ is drawing near.

Ezekiel 38:1-8 explains who is involved in this invasion and the timeframe of when they will come upon Israel.

> *"And the word of the LORD came to me saying, (2) "Son of man, set your face toward **Gog of the land of Magog, the prince of Rosh, Meshech and Tubal**, and prophesy against him (3) and say, 'Thus says the Lord GOD, "Behold, I am against you, **O Gog, prince of Rosh, Meshech and Tubal.** (4) "I will turn you about and put hooks into your jaws, and I will bring you out, and all your army, horses and horsemen, all of them splendidly attired, a great company with buckler and shield, all of them wielding swords; (5) **Persia, Ethiopia and Put** with them, all of them with shield and helmet; (6) **Gomer with all its troops; Beth-togarmah from the remote parts of the north with all its troops--many peoples with you.** (7) "Be prepared, and prepare yourself, you and all your companies that are assembled about you, and be a guard for them. (8) "After many days you will be summoned; **in the latter years you will come into the land that is restored from the sword, whose inhabitants have been gathered from many nations to the mountains of Israel** which had been a continual waste; but its people were brought out from the nations, and they are living securely, all of them."*
>
> *Ezekiel 38:1-8*

The participants are listed as "Gog, of the land of Magog, prince of Rosh", "Meshech", "Tubal", "Persia", "Ethiopia", "Put",

"Gomer", "Beth-Togarmah", "many peoples with you". Verse says they come from the remotest parts of the north. Many of the names that are listed here are also listed in Genesis 10 as a part of what is commonly known as "the table of nations".

> *"The sons of Japheth were **Gomer** and **Magog** and Madai and Javan and **Tubal** and **Meshech** and Tiras. (3) The sons of Gomer were Ashkenaz and Riphath and **Togarmah**."*   Genesis 10:2-3

Here we see five of the eight lands or countries listed in Ezekiel 38. These five are listed as descendants of Japheth which comprised most of the area of Europe, Asia Minor and parts of Asia, including Russia. In particular the Russian people are believed to be

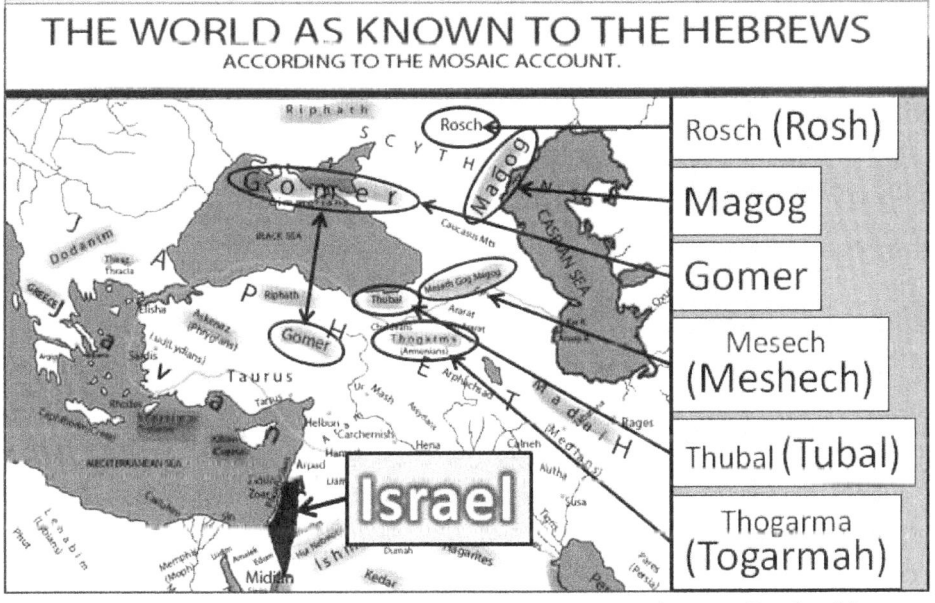

THE WORLD AS KNOWN TO THE HEBREWS
ACCORDING TO THE MOSAIC ACCOUNT.

- Rosch (Rosh)
- Magog
- Gomer
- Mesech (Meshech)
- Thubal (Tubal)
- Thogarma (Togarmah)

the descendants of Magog. The map above shows Rosh, Magog, Gomer, Meshech, Tubal and Togarmah to all be descendants of Japeth who settled north of Israel in what is now Turkey, Afghanistan, Georgia, Russia, and parts of Europe.

The other three lands or countries listed are Persia, (which includes modern day Iran and to a lesser extent Iraq), Put (which is modern day Libya - listed as one of the sons of Ham in Genesis 10:6), and Ethiopia.

Based on this and other information, many believe that Ezekiel 38-39 is describing a cohort of attacking nations which includes Russia, Turkey, Iran and Libya, along with "many peoples".

There is debate about the term "Rosh" and whether or not it is a reference to Russia. The term means "head" or "chief" and is not found in the King James Version. Even without the word though, "Gog", who appears to be the chief or head of this attack, is said to be "of the land of Magog" which includes Russia. It is interesting that Moscow is pretty much due north of Jerusalem.

"In The Latter Years"

Ezekiel 38 says that this group of attacking nations will come upon Israel **"in the latter years"**. This is another reason why those who study Bible prophecy consider the apparent development toward this invasion as a sign that the end is near. Ezekiel 38:16 also says, *"It shall come about **in the last days** that I will bring you against My land, ..."*

It should be noted that twice in Ezekiel 38 there is reference to the Jewish people who are living in the land of Israel at the time of this prophesied war, being brought back to Israel from the nations. Verse 8 says, *"you will come into the land that is restored from the sword, whose inhabitants have been gathered from many nations to the mountains of Israel"*. Verse 12 says, *"against the people who are gathered from the nations, who have acquired cattle and goods, who live at the center of the world."* In what appears as a follow-up summary of this war, in Ezekiel 39:27-28, the Lord speaks two more times of this bringing of the Jews back to Israel from the nations of the world. It seems as though this supernatural victory over attacking forces is a part of God's redemptive plan for Israel and the Jewish people.

> *"When I bring them back from the peoples and gather them from the lands of their enemies, then I shall be sanctified through them in the sight of the many nations. (28) "Then they will know that I am the LORD their God because I made them go into exile among the nations, and then gathered them again to their own land; and I will leave none of them there any longer."*   *Ezekiel 39:27-28*

Interesting side note. Ezekiel 38:12 speaks of the Jewish people being brought back to the land of Israel and says that they "live at the center of the world". This phrase could be taken figuratively to simply refer to them being at the center of world attention. This in itself would have prophetic significance since any reference to Israel being at the center of world attention, written 2,500 years ago would be quite profound. It appears that in addition to the figurative sense in which this was spoken, there is a literal sense in which it was spoken as well. Amazingly, if you take a world map, squeeze the land masses together, and then mark where the city of Jerusalem is located, you will see that Ezekiel 38:12 is accurate literally as well. Zechariah 12 and Zechariah 14 indicate that Jerusalem will be the focus of world attention in the last days. This is certainly the case today! Amazingly, it can be seen that when God created the earth, and placed His people in a specific location, He located them right in the center of the world!

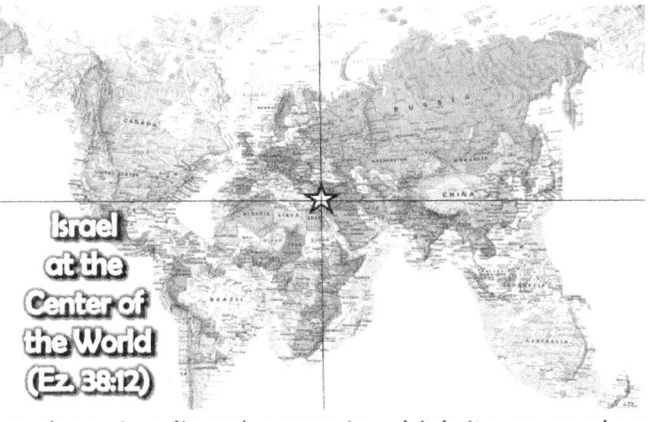

Russia, Turkey and Iran Today

Little need be said about Iran's willingness to participate in an effort to destroy the Jewish people and pilfer the land of Israel. It has been common for Iranian leaders to call openly for the absolute destruction of the nation of Israel. In an address to the "World Without Zionism" conference in Tehran, former Iranian President Mahmoud Ahmadinejad said on October 26, 2005, *"Our dear Imam, (Khomeini) ordered that this Jerusalem-occupying regime, (Israel) must be erased from the page of time. This was a very wise statement."*[1]

In a televised sermon on December 15, 2000 the Iranian Supreme Leader, Ayatollah Ali Khamenei stated, *"Iran's position, which was first expressed by the Imam (Khomeini) and stated several times by those responsible, is that the cancerous tumor called Israel must be uprooted from the region."*[2]

These are samples of statements by Iranian leaders that make it clear that Iran would not hesitate to take advantage of an opportunity to be a part of a major attack upon Israel.

Turkey's relationship with Israel has been much more friendly, but it certainly was strained by the 2010 "Flotilla Incident". Then in 2020 Turkish President Erdogan said something that was very puzzling and caused many to wonder about his future intentions. He vowed to "liberate" the Al-Aqsa mosque on Jerusalem's Temple Mount. Since the Al-Aqsa mosque was not under any adverse possession some questioned if Erdogan spoke out of his desire to see the Ottoman Empire control of the city of Jerusalem restored. He has said and done numerous things to indicate his desire to see the expansion of Turkish power, as in the days of the Ottoman Empire.

Russia has been known for decades to have been a supplier of military equipment to groups hostile toward Israel including the

---

[1] https://jcpa.org/wp-content/uploads/2012/05/IransIntent2012b.pdf
[2] ibid

Palestine Liberation Organization and Hezbollah. In 1982, when Israel invaded Lebanon it was reported that they discovered and captured large amounts of Russian military equipment and ammunition. After the 1982 invasion the Washington Post reported that Prime Minister Menachem Begin charged that *"Israeli forces in southern Lebanon captured "10 times more Russian weapons than were previously reported by our intelligence."* [3] The article also reported that Begin said that *"as of July 3, the Israeli Army had taken 4,000 tons of ammunition, 144 armored vehicles including tanks, 12,500 pieces of small arms, 515 heavy weapons, 359 sophisticated communications devices and 795 "optical instruments," among them field glasses and range finders as well as Starlight scopes for night firing."* [4]

Russia, Turkey and Iran have shown increasing friendly cooperation over the past couple of decades. In 2011 Iran began to operate a new nuclear plant with the help of Russia and Turkey, Then in 2016 started construction on a second nuclear plant with the assistance of Russia.[5]

In 2021, the volume of bilateral trade between Russia and Iran increased by 81% from the previous year, rising to $3.3 billion and in July of 2022, Russia announced that it would invest $40 billion in Iran's oil industry. [6]

A March 2021 Jerusalem Post article entitled, "Iran, Russia and Turkey Signal Growing Alliance" speaks of various indications that the three countries' growing tendency to work together. [7] Numerous 2022 articles spoke of Russia working together with Iran and Turkey in dealing with the situation in Syria.

---

[3] https://www.washingtonpost.com/archive/politics/1982/07/07/begin-describes-soviet-arms-cache/011726c2-9661-43f4-bce6-1292d5ef1974/
[4] ibid
[5] https://www.dw.com/en/iran-begins-work-on-russia-supported-nuclear-plant/a-19542191
[6] https://www.gatestoneInstitute.org/18903/iran-russia-alliance
[7] https://www.jpost.com/middle-east/iran-russia-and-turkey-signal-growing-alliance 662601

The stage may be being set for the fulfillment of the Ezekiel 38-39 passage at some point in the near future.

Hooks Into Your Jaws

In Ezekiel 38:4, God says to the nations involved in the war of Gog and Magog, *"I will ... put hooks into your jaws and I will bring you out ..."* Later in verse 12 the prophecy goes on to say that these nations will come *"to capture spoil and to seize plunder, to turn your hand against the waste places which are now inhabited, and against the people who are gathered from the nations, who have acquired cattle and goods, who live at the center of the world."*

The development and prosperity of the nation of Israel since its establishment in 1948 is nothing short of astounding and would seem to fit with the motivations in the hearts and minds of those who will attack Israel according to Ezekiel 38. The "hooks in their jaws" may be simply a spiritual motivation from God to bring judgment upon these nations. Then again these hooks may be a reference to tangible prosperity in Israel. Two things in particular come to mind.

In the past two decades Israel has gone from being an energy dependent nation to an energy independent nation and an energy exporting nation. In 2000 Israel discovered Natural Gas fields offshore in the Mediterranean. In 2009 the Tamar field was discovered with its 8 trillion cubic feet of natural gas. It began production in 2013 and began to meet Israel's growing need for energy. In 2019 the Leviathan field began production of its **21 trillion cubic feet of natural gas** supply, launching Israel forward to an unprecedented place in energy resources.

Israel has become a major energy player in a very short time with the discovery and development of these natural gas fields. In 2022 Israel's natural gas and oil revenues hit record highs as they now are exporting energy to other countries.

In addition to these natural gas discoveries, there have been oil discoveries in Israel based on 3,500 year old prophetic passages of Scripture found in Genesis 49 and Deuteronomy 33. See chapter 2 for the details on these amazing prophecies and how they have led a U.S. based oil company to drill for oil in Israel. Though tests have revealed great amounts of oil in Israel, Zion Oil Company has not yet been able to tap into the oil that is buried very deep in the ground in Israel. I believe that it is very possible that they will not be able to tap into this oil until the time is right for the war of Gog and Magog spoken of in Ezekiel 38-39 because an oil rich Israel might be what prompts the Gog and Magog nations to attack.

Ezekiel 38:13 confirms that the motive for the Gog and Magog attack is to seize plunder. Verse 13 says, "Have you come to capture spoil? Have you assembled your company to seize plunder, to carry away silver and gold, to take away cattle and goods, to capture great spoil?"

God's Wrath Poured Out Upon Gog and Magog

Ezekiel 38:18-23 speaks of God's judgment against, and victory over, the attacking nations. Verses 18-19 speaks of God's fury, His anger, and His blazing wrath being poured out upon these armies. His judgment against them will include a great earthquake, pestilence, torrential rains, hailstones, fire and brimstones. Ezekiel 39 speaks of the aftermath of war with bodies being buried by the Jewish people for seven months after the war.

The Burning of Weapons

Ezekiel 39:9-10 speaks of the people of Israel burning the weapons of the destroyed, invading armies. This has appeared to be a problem until recently with the development of 3D printed guns. Now the idea of weapons that can be burned is not only a possibility, but the use of 3D printing for military equipment is already moving forward. In an article dated June 11, 2021 in the National Defense Business and Technology Magazine plans to move ahead with 3D printed military equipment were revealed. The article was entitled "Military Looks for Novel Ways to Employ 3D Printing".[8] The article states, *"In April, the Army signed a contract for its "Jointless Hull Project," which has an ambitious goal of developing a 3D metal printer so large that it can create a military truck exterior in one giant piece."* [9] It was interesting for me personally to find out that the Army built its own 3D printing hub at Rock Island Arsenal, Illinois, where the project will kick off. The Rock Island Arsenal is about 2 miles from my home in Moline, Illinois.

In addition to 3D printed military equipment, others have said that Russia has used a wooden material called "lignostone" in military equipment that could be burned. Still others have suggested that the burning of weapons could refer to nuclear weapons that are converted for peaceful energy production.

Predatory Birds

> "You will fall on the mountains of Israel, you and all your troops and the peoples who are with you; I will give you as food to every kind of predatory bird and beast of the field."   Ezekiel 39:4

> "As for you, son of man, thus says the Lord GOD,

---

[8] https://www.nationaldefensemagazine.org/articles/2021/6/11/military-looks-for-novel-ways-to-employ-3d-printing
[9] ibid

'Speak to every kind of bird and to every beast of the field, "Assemble and come, gather from every side to My sacrifice which I am going to sacrifice for you, as a great sacrifice on the mountains of Israel, that you may eat flesh and drink blood. (18) "You will eat the flesh of mighty men and drink the blood of the princes of the earth, as though they were rams, lambs, goats and bulls, all of them fatlings of Bashan."

Ezekiel 39:17-18

In both of these passages we see references to predatory birds being summoned to come to the location where God destroys the armies of the Gog and Magog nations. It appears similar to Jesus' words in Matthew 24:27-28 where He speaks of His 2nd coming and adds the words, "wherever the corpse is, there the vultures will be gathered." This is obviously a reference to His coming to the battle of Armageddon as seen in Revelation 19 and in Zechariah 14.

It has been reported for some time that the numbers of migratory birds that pass through Israel while migrating from central Africa to Europe, many of which are predatory birds, is astounding. A 2014 CNN article entitled, "A modern day wonder in the Sea of Galilee, Israel's hotspot for migratory birds" speaks of this. It says of Israel, *"It is akin to a superhighway of bird migration routes, creating thermal currents that raptors and other birds can ride from central Africa to Europe."*[10] It goes on to explain, *"Israel is at a bottleneck on the migratory birds' flight path where an*

---

[10] https://www.cnn.com/travel/article/israel-bird-migrations-sea-galilee/index.html

estimated 540 species converge." [11] The Jewish Virtual Library reports, *"Studies over the past decade show that about 500 million birds cross Israel's narrow airspace twice every year in the course of their migrations."*[12]

It Could Happen Soon

It is hard to know for sure if the war of Gog and Magog is another description for the battle of Armageddon, or a completely separate war, at a separate time. We can clearly see that things are in place in the world today to bring about this war of Gog and Magog. This is another indication that we are living in the last days and fast approaching the time of Jesus Christ's 2nd Coming!

Ezekiel 38-39 says that when this war occurs God will exalt Himself before the nations as He brings about His supernatural victory, and He will show Israel again that He is the Lord their God!

---

[11] ibid
[12] https://www.jewishvirtuallibrary.org/bird-migration-in-israel

CHAPTER 18

The Antichrist & The Mystery of Lawlessness

In previous chapters we have already looked at the prevalence of false christs, false prophets, and deceptive teachings and ideas, in the world today. This fulfills Jesus' prophetic warnings about the last days as well as other prophetic descriptions of the world in the last days seen throughout the New Testament.

In this chapter I want to look at what the Scriptures teach about the antichrist and about the mystery of lawlessness.

Actually the term "antichrist" is not used frequently in the Bible. Also, it is not used in most of the passages we think about when we think of the antichrist. The terms "antichrist" or "antichrists" are only used 5 times in the Bible, in just 4 verses.

> "Children, it is the last hour; and just as you heard that antichrist is coming, even now many antichrists have appeared; from this we know that it is the last hour."
> 1 John 2:18

> "Who is the liar but the one who denies that Jesus is the Christ? This is the antichrist, the one who denies the Father and the Son."   1 John 2:22

> "and every spirit that does not confess Jesus is not from God; this is the spirit of the antichrist, of which you have heard that it is coming, and now it is already in the world."   1 John 4:3

> *"For many deceivers have gone out into the world, those who do not acknowledge Jesus Christ as coming in the flesh. This is the deceiver and the antichrist."* 2 John 1:7

We learn numerous things about "antichrist" from these verses even though none of these passages are the ones that people usually think about related to the antichrist.

1) There have been many antichrists (1 John 2:18) (2 John 1:7)
2) The appearances of antichrists confirm it is the last hour (1 John 2:18) (Note - It has been "the last hour" ever since the 1st century A.D.)
3) Antichrist denies Jesus is the Christ (1 John 2:22)
4) Antichrist denies the Father and the Son (1 John 2:22)
5) Antichrist is a spirit (1 John 4:3)
6) Antichrist spirit does not confess Jesus (1 John 4:3)
7) Antichrist spirit has been in the world since at least the 1st century A.D. (1 John 4:3)
8) Antichrist is a deceiver (2 John 1:7)
9) Antichrist does not acknowledge Jesus Christ as coming in the flesh (2 John 1:7)

Note that "antichrist" is a spirit. The spirit of antichrist is identified by 5 things mentioned in these verses. It denies that Jesus is the Christ, it denies the Father and the Son, it does not confess Jesus, it is a deceiver, and it does not acknowledge that Jesus Christ has come in the flesh. The lie that Jesus was a man who possessed the "Christ spirit" just like we can possess the "Christ spirit" is clearly an antichrist deception, denying that Jesus **is** the Christ and that as the Christ He came in the flesh to save the world.

Many AntiChrists Have Come

Note also that there have been, and are many antichrists that have been in the world throughout history. When we speak of antichrist we need to understand that this term does not just apply to one individual who is yet to come in the future and who will rise to power during the last days. Many antichrists have appeared in history and 1 John 4:3 clearly states that **the spirit of the antichrist is active in the world today**. There will be an ultimate antichrist in the last days but the term is not limited in the Bible to that person.

Three men in history particularly stand out as antichrist figures. They include Antiochus Epiphanes, Nero and Adolf Hitler. Others could be included but these three stand out.

Antiochus Epiphanes was a Greek king who reigned over Syria from 175 B.C. - 164 B.C. He was Antiochus IV but took upon himself the title "Epiphanes" which means "Illustrious one" or "god manifest".[1] It is hard to pinpoint the exact timing of some of his actions but according to Encyclopedia Britannica online he took Jerusalem by storm in 167 B.C.[2] In an attempt to Hellenize the region and do away with Jewish religious practices he set up an altar to Zeus in the Jewish Temple and he offered swine as a pagan sacrifice on the altar. This appears to be an initial fulfillment of Biblical prophecies of the "abomination of desolation". According to Encyclopedia Britannica, Judas Maccabeus and those with him were able to defeat Antiochus and tear down the altar of Zeus and reconsecrate the Temple in December of 164 B.C.[3] Interestingly, this means that this initial fulfillment of an "abomination of desolation" by Antiochus lasted for what appears to be 3 ½ years. In many ways Antiochus Epiphanes served as a type of the antichrist who will appear in the last days. It should be noted that the book of Daniel prophesied concerning Antiochus Epiphanes in detail hundreds of years before he was born.

This is an example of dual fulfillment of prophecy since

---

[1] https://www.gotquestions.org/Antiochus-Epiphanes.html
[2] https://www.britannica.com/biography/Antiochus-IV-Epiphanes
[3] ibid

Antiochus is an initial fulfillment of prophecies in the book of Daniel with a second and ultimate fulfillment coming in the last days.

Nero Claudius Caesar Augustus Germanicus, better known just as Nero was the Roman emperor from 54 A.D. - 68 A.D. In July of 64 A.D. the Great Fire of Rome destroyed much of the city. As rumors blaming Nero as the cause of the fire circulated, Nero sought to shift the focus of blame elsewhere so he placed the blame on Christians who lived in the city. After this he launched a horrific persecution upon all Christians, not only those who lived inside the city. He had many Christians viciously murdered, some being thrown to the lions for public entertainment and some being used as human torches to light pathways during the night. Nero continued to aggressively persecute Christians until sometime before the time of his death in June of 68 A.D. His focus shifted the last few months of his life to those who had risen up in rebellion against him, eventually leading to his defeat and suicidal death. It is interesting that it appears his aggressive persecution of Christian lasted for approximately 3 ½ years.

Some have suggested that the numeric value for Nero's name equals 666, pointing to this as another indicator that he was an antichrist who has come.

Finally, when we look at Adolf Hitler there are many indicators, showing him to have been an antichrist. We have already looked at many of these indicators in an earlier chapter. Obviously, Hitler's hatred of the Jewish people and decision to murder millions of them fits with the image of an antichrist. When reading historical records concerning the Holocaust we find that though the persecution of Jews began in the 1930s, it was after Germany attacked the Soviet Union in June of 1941 that the systematic killing of Jews began ("The Final Solution") [4] Some were killed in the later part of the summer and in the fall of 1941 German officials began the

---

[4] https://encyclopedia.ushmm.org/content/en/article/the-final-solution

process of deporting tens of thousands Jews from western and central Europe to the Lodz Ghetto. The systematic killing of over 6 million Jewish men, women and children continued until 1945. The last of the death camps were liberated in early May of 1945. Again, it is interesting that this reveals that this systematic extermination of the Jewish people took place for just over 3 ½ years. Adolf Hitler certainly appears to be another example of a person consumed with the spirit of antichrist, disguising his evil intentions with what appeared to many for a time to be noble intent.

Names or Titles of the Coming Antichrist

As we have seen, the passages of Scripture that use the term antichrist are not the primary passages that are used to speak of the coming antichrist that we think of when we think of the last days. The main passages that describe the coming antichrist and explain what he will do, use different names and titles for this one who will come.

"The Man of Lawlessness" and "The Son of Destruction"

One of the most recognized end times passage that refers to the coming antichrist is found in 2 Thessalonians 2. It begins -

> *"Now we request you, brethren, with regard to the coming of our Lord Jesus Christ and our gathering together to Him, (2) that you not be quickly shaken from your composure or be disturbed either by a spirit or a message or a letter as if from us, to the effect that the day of the Lord has come. (3) Let no one in any way deceive you, for it will not come unless the apostasy comes first, and **the man of lawlessness** is*

> *revealed,* **the son of destruction**, *(4) who opposes and exalts himself above every so-called god or object of worship, so that he takes his seat in the temple of God, displaying himself as being God."*
> 2 Thessalonians 2:1-4

The coming antichrist is here called **"the man of lawlessness"** and **"the son of destruction"**. The KJV calls him **"the man of sin"** and **"the son of perdition"**. We learn here that he will be revealed before "the coming of our Lord Jesus Christ and our gathering together to Him." We also learn that he will oppose and exalt himself above every so-called god or object of worship. Finally, we learn that he will take his seat in the temple of God, displaying himself as being God.

The fact that he "takes his seat in the temple of God" is key to the understanding that the Jewish Temple will be rebuilt in the end times.

"That Lawless One"

Later in this same chapter the coming antichrist is described as **"that lawless one"**. We are told here that he will come in accord with the activity of Satan, with power and signs and false wonders.

> *"Then* **that lawless one** *will be revealed whom the Lord will slay with the breath of His mouth and bring to an end by the appearance of His coming; (9) that is, the one whose coming is in accord with the activity of Satan, with all power and signs and false wonders,"*
> 2 Thessalonians 2:8-9

"The Little Horn"

Much of the descriptions found in Daniel 7 parallel many of the things described in Revelation 13 which speaks of "the beast" being given authority for 3 ½ years. In Daniel 7 it appears that the coming antichrist is referenced and is called **"the little horn"**. Daniel 7:7 speaks of the end times "beast" and 10 horns seen on the head of the beast. Then verse 8 refers to the coming "little horn".

> *"While I was contemplating the horns, behold, **another horn, a little one**, came up among them, and three of the first horns were pulled out by the roots before it; and behold, this horn possessed eyes like the eyes of a man and a mouth uttering great boasts."*
>
> *Daniel 7:8*

Further information about this little horn seen on the head of the beast is given in verse 11 and verses 21-26.

> *"Then I kept looking because of the sound of the boastful words which the horn was speaking; I kept looking until the beast was slain, and its body was destroyed and given to the burning fire."*
> *Daniel 7:11*

> *"I kept looking, and that horn was waging war with the saints and overpowering them (22) until the Ancient of Days came and judgment was passed in favor of the saints of the Highest One, and the time arrived when the saints took possession of the kingdom. (23) "Thus he said: 'The fourth beast will be a fourth kingdom on the earth, which will be different from all the other kingdoms and will devour the whole earth and tread it down and crush it. (24) 'As for the ten horns, out of this kingdom ten kings will arise; and another will arise after them, and he will be different from the previous ones and will subdue three kings. (25) 'He will speak out against the Most High and wear down the saints of the Highest One, and he will intend to make alterations in times and in law; and they will be given into his hand for a time, times, and*

> *half a time. (26) 'But the court will sit for judgment, and his dominion will be taken away, annihilated and destroyed forever."*
>
> *Daniel 7:21-26*

From these passages we learn that the coming antichrist, or "the little horn", will be a part of the end times beast empire that will "devour the whole earth". He will speak boastful words and speak out against the Most High, he will subdue other parts of the beast empire, he will seek to make alterations in times and in law, and he will wage war against the saints of God, wearing them down. They will be given into his hand for 3 ½ years. Then he will be judged and destroyed!

"The Prince Who Is To Come"

> *"Then after the sixty-two weeks the Messiah will be cut off and have nothing, and the people of **the prince who is to come** will destroy the city and the sanctuary. And its end will come with a flood; even to the end there will be war; desolations are determined. (27) "And **he will make a firm covenant with the many for one week**, but in the middle of the week he will put a stop to sacrifice and grain offering; and on the wing of abominations will come one who makes desolate, even until a complete destruction, one that is decreed, is poured out on the one who makes desolate."*
>
> *Daniel 9:26-27*

In this passage out of Daniel 9 which is typically referred to as the seventy weeks of Daniel (v. 24-27), another title for the coming antichrist is used, "the prince who is to come". We learn here that the people of the prince who is to come will destroy the temple and the city of Jerusalem. This was accomplished in 70 A.D. by the Romans and those who stood with them. Then we are told that the prince who is to come will establish a 7 year (one week) covenant, or treaty between many people. In the middle of that 7 year period, or 3 ½ years into it, he will desecrate the temple of God and set up "the abomination of desolation". This will bring destruction by the hand of God. This is related to his title "the son of destruction" in 2 Thessalonians 2:3.

Jesus spoke of this "abomination of desolation" in Matthew 24:15 and indicated that this event in the middle of this 7 year treaty will be followed by the great tribulation period. (see Matthew 24:15-22) Thus the great tribulation period is described in the Bible as a 3 ½ year period rather than a commonly taught 7 year period.

"The Beast"

We saw in Daniel 7 that "the little horn" was on the head of the dreadful beast and was thus a part of the beast. Many of the details of Daniel 7 are parallel to the details given in Revelation 13. With this in mind, I believe that we can recognize that "the beast" seen in Revelation 13 does not just refer to an end time world empire, but also to the person who is leading that empire. The beast of Revelation 13 is personified in numerous ways.

> *"And the dragon stood on the sand of the seashore. Then I saw a beast coming up out of the sea, having ten horns and seven heads, and on his horns were ten diadems, and on his heads were blasphemous names. (2) And the beast which I saw was like a leopard, and his feet were like those of a bear, and his mouth like the mouth of a lion. And the dragon gave him his power and his throne and great authority."*
>
> *Revelation 13:1-2*

> *"There was given to him a mouth speaking arrogant words and blasphemies, and authority to act for forty-two months was given to him. (6) And he opened his mouth in blasphemies against God, to*

blaspheme His name and His tabernacle, that is, those who dwell in heaven. (7) It was also given to him to make war with the saints and to overcome them, and authority over every tribe and people and tongue and nation was given to him."

Revelation 13:5-7

This chapter gives us many details about "the beast", the coming antichrist and his worldwide empire or kingdom. He will rise up out of the masses of people on the earth (the sea), he will be given power and authority directly from Satan (the dragon), he will speak arrogant words and blasphemies against God, His Name and His tabernacle, and he will be given authority for 3 ½ years to make war with the saints and to overcome them. He will also be given authority over every tribe and people and tongue and nation.

Later in the chapter we also see a second beast rising to deceive the world and direct the world to worship the first beast, or the antichrist. At the end of the chapter we read about "the mark of the beast" that we spoke about in detail in chapter 16.

Another detail of what the beast, or the antichrist, will do is seen in Revelation 17 and Revelation 19. The beast will lead the kings of the earth who have been deceived and now follow him, to wage war against Jesus Christ, the Lamb of God, as He returns to earth to the battle of Armageddon.

"These have one purpose, and they give their power and authority to the beast. (14) "These will wage war against the Lamb, and the Lamb will overcome them, because He is Lord of lords and King of kings, and those who are with Him are the called and chosen and faithful." *Revelation 17:13-14*

"And I saw the beast and the kings of the earth and their armies assembled to make war against Him who

sat on the horse and against His army. (20) And the beast was seized, and with him the false prophet who performed the signs in his presence, by which he deceived those who had received the mark of the beast and those who worshiped his image; these two were thrown alive into the lake of fire which burns with brimstone. (21) And the rest were killed with the sword which came from the mouth of Him who sat on the horse, and all the birds were filled with their flesh."
Revelation 19:19-21

One more detail that should be noted about the coming antichrist that is mentioned in numerous passages of Scripture. I will show the passages here and then make comments.

*"**I saw one of his heads as if it had been slain, and his fatal wound was healed.** And the whole earth was amazed and followed after the beast;" Revelation 13:3*

*"He exercises all the authority of the first beast in his presence. And he makes the earth and those who dwell in it to worship the first beast, **whose fatal wound was healed.**"*   *Revelation 13:12*

*"And he deceives those who dwell on the earth because of the signs which it was given him to perform in the presence of the beast, telling those who dwell on the earth to make an image to **the beast who *had the wound of the sword and has come to life.**"*
Revelation 13:14

*"**The beast that you saw was, and is not, and is about to come up out of the abyss** and go to destruction. And those who dwell on the earth, whose*

*name has not been written in the book of life from the foundation of **the world, will wonder when they see the beast, that he was and is not and will come.**"*
Revelation 17:8

*"**The beast which was and is not, is himself also an eighth** and is one of the seven, and he goes to destruction."*
Revelation 17:11

In five different passages we see a consistent description of the coming antichrist or beast. He will have a fatal wound and be dead for an unspecified period of time. He will then be miraculously healed and the world will wonder at this. As a result the world will be willing to worship the beast and follow the beast. Revelation 17:8 adds an important detail to all of this. It says that he will "come up out of the abyss." The abyss is also referred to as "the bottomless pit" and is considered to be the abode of the dead and demons.

The exact meaning of all of this is difficult to discern but what we can know is that when the antichrist rises to power, he will be recognized as someone who has been brought back from the dead. Isn't it interesting that the devil would attempt to imitate the resurrection of Jesus Christ in order to draw the world to his antichrist.

Destruction and Victory Contrasted

It should also be noted that many of the passages we have looked at speak of the destruction of the coming antichrist. His authority will be short-lived. He and his kingdom will be destroyed by the coming of Jesus Christ. Daniel 7:11 says, "the beast was slain, and its body was destroyed and given to the burning fire." Daniel 7:26 says, "the court will sit for judgment, and his dominion will be taken away, annihilated and destroyed forever." Daniel 9:27 says, "the wing of abominations will come one who makes desolate, even until a complete destruction, one that is decreed, is poured out on the one who makes desolate." 2 Thessalonians 2:3 calls him "the son of destruction" and 2 Thessalonians 2:8 says that the lawless one is the one "whom the Lord will slay with the breath of His mouth and bring to an end by the appearance of His coming." Revelation 17:11 says that the beast "goes to destruction". Revelation 19:20 says that the beast will be "thrown alive into the lake of fire which burns with brimstone."

In contrast, these passages remind us numerous times that Jesus Christ is coming back to establish an everlasting kingdom and that we will reign with Him in His kingdom. Daniel 7:14 says, "And to Him was given dominion, Glory and a kingdom, That all the peoples, nations and men of every language Might serve Him. His dominion is an everlasting dominion Which will not pass away; And His kingdom is one Which will not be destroyed." Daniel 7:18 says "But the saints of the Highest One will receive the kingdom and possess the kingdom forever, for all ages to come." Daniel 7:22 says that, "judgment was passed in favor of the saints of the Highest One, and the time arrived when the saints took possession of the kingdom." Daniel 7:27 says "Then the sovereignty, the dominion and the greatness of all the kingdoms under the whole heaven will be given to the people of the saints of the Highest One; His kingdom will be an everlasting kingdom, and all the dominions will serve and obey Him."

Revelation 11:15 proclaims at the blowing of the seventh trumpet, "The kingdom of the world has become the kingdom of our Lord and of His Christ; and He will reign forever and ever." Revelation 19:6 says, "Hallelujah! For the Lord our God, the Almighty, reigns." Revelation 20 speaks of the coming 1,000 year reign of Jesus Christ here on earth along with His saints and Revelation 21-22 speaks of the New Jerusalem and the eternal, peaceful and glorious reign of God, as He dwells with His people!

The Mystery of Lawlessness is Already at Work!

Just as the Bible states clearly that many antichrists have already come and that the spirit of antichrist is already in the world, the Bible also clearly states in 2 Thessalonians 2:7 that the mystery of lawlessness is already at work.

> *"For the mystery of lawlessness is already at work; only he who now restrains will do so until he is taken out of the way."*   2 Thessalonians 2:7

Who or what the restraining force is in this verse is a subject of much debate. Some say it is the church or the Holy Spirit working through the church. I believe this interpretation does not fit the context of the verse seen in the first six verses of the chapter. Some say it is human government and some say it is an angelic entity such as Michael the archangel. Whoever or whatever the restraining force is, it will be removed at the time the antichrist is revealed.

Until then the mystery of lawlessness is already at work. The spirit of antichrist is already in the world. We can easily see this all around us! It is easy to identify many things happening in the world today that are preparing the way for the revealing of the lawless one, or the antichrist!

CHAPTER 19

As In The Days of Noah
(Nephilim & UFOs)

Jesus said that the days leading up to His 2nd coming will be like the days of Noah.

> *"For the coming of the Son of Man will be just like the days of Noah. (38) "For as in those days before the flood they were eating and drinking, marrying and giving in marriage, until the day that Noah entered the ark, (39) and they did not understand until the flood came and took them all away; so will the coming of the Son of Man be."*   Matthew 24:37-39

People will be going about the business of everyday life right up until the day that Jesus returns, just as they continued in their everyday affairs until the day Noah entered the Ark and the flood suddenly came upon them. It is apparent that even those who saw the Ark being built and heard warnings from Noah were not fazed by the clear indications that God's judgment was coming. The Day of the Lord will come upon the world like a thief in the night (1 Thessalonians 5:2; 2 Peter 3:10). While they are saying "peace and safety", then destruction will come upon them suddenly (1 Thessalonians 5:3).

Genesis 6:4-5 gives us a picture of what life was like on the earth in the days of Noah, leading up to the flood.

"The Nephilim were on the earth in those days, and also afterward, when the sons of God came in to the daughters of men, and they bore children to them. Those were the mighty men who were of old, men of renown. (5) Then the LORD saw that the wickedness of man was great on the earth, and that every intent of the thoughts of his heart was only evil continually."
Genesis 6:4-5

Verse 5 tells us that the wickedness of man was great on the earth. This of course would have contributed to people being oblivious to the warning signs of coming judgment that were around them. Their hearts were filled with evil thoughts and intentions.

Verse 4 speaks of something that has sparked much interest and controversy within Christian circles. The Nephilim were giants that lived on the earth in the days leading up to the flood and to some degree in the days after the flood. The Hebrew word for Nephilim means giants and also speaks of "a bully" or "a tyrant". The mere existence of giants creates much interest and many questions. The explanation of how the Nephilim came into existence adds to the interest and has stirred some controversy between Bible teachers.

We are told here that "the sons of God came in to the daughters of men and they bore children to them." Some have identified the "sons of God" as angelic beings who forsook their proper abode and took upon themselves human flesh. Those who hold to this understanding interpret "daughters of men" as simply human women. Others have identified the "sons of God" as men from the lineage of Seth and the "daughters of men" as women from the lineage of Cain.

I believe that the first interpretation is true. The term "sons of God" is used elsewhere in the Old Testament to speak of angelic beings. (see Job 1:6, Job 2:1 and Job 38:7) The term is never used elsewhere to refer to the lineage of Seth. Also, the fact that the offspring of these unions were giants would seem to indicate something beyond normal human unions. In the New Testament there are passages that appear to refer back to this time in Noah's day and actions of the "sons of God", showing them to be angels.

> *"And angels who did not keep their own domain, but abandoned their proper abode, He has kept in eternal bonds under darkness for the judgment of the great day,"*   *Jude 1:6*

> *"In* (spirit) *which also He* (Jesus) *went and made proclamation to the spirits now in prison, (20) who once were disobedient, when the patience of God kept waiting in the days of Noah, during the construction of the ark, in which a few, that is, eight persons, were brought safely through the water."*
>   *1 Peter 3:19-20*

If "the sons of God" are fallen angelic beings then the days of Noah that preceded the flood also included the blending together, or union, of human beings and fallen angelic beings. When we look at verse 4 and verse 5 of Genesis 6 together, it appears that what opened the door for this possibility was the level of evil and wickedness that filled the earth at that time. Could this sort of thing happen again in the last days?

We discussed earlier in chapter 9, the increase of wickedness on the earth in these days leading up to the 2nd coming of Christ and the judgment of God that will come at the time of the Day of the Lord. This increase of wickedness would appear to parallel the days of Noah, leading up to the flood judgment that came upon the earth at that time.

Much of this chapter will focus on the possible spiritual dimension of the last days related to what happened during the days of Noah. Admittedly, one cannot state definitively that what the Bible is referring to when it says, "as in the days of Noah" includes the spiritual dimensions we will discuss. If we limit our understanding of "as in the days of Noah" to the wickedness on the earth and evil in the hearts of people, we can see that the time we live in now fits this description.

If the phrase "as in the days of Noah" does include the opening of a door to the spirit realm by the evil and wickedness at that time, then we may have indication of where a number of current trends may lead. If this is the case, it may very well be connected to the signs, false wonders and deception that will be prevalent at the time when the lawless one is revealed.

Fascination With Alien Life - Open Door to Deception?

I believe that there are many things that people believe today that may open the door to a new level of deception that will grip the world in the last days. Many of these beliefs are even held by numerous scientists.

In earlier chapters we looked at some of the deceptive beliefs that many are embracing today. These include the theory of evolution that is the foundation for many other deceptive beliefs. Denying God as creator and denying mankind's unique place in creation opens the door to many other lies. We looked at the idea of "directed panspermia" proposed by Dr. Francis Crick which postulates that life was seeded on the earth in the past by advanced alien beings. We also looked at the idea of the "multiverse theory" which promotes the idea that there are millions of universes and that travel from one to another might be possible through a wormhole.

We looked at the strange combination of high tech science and eastern religion at CERN, the European Organization for Nuclear Research. CERN has produced dramatized videos that reveal their belief that they may be able to open up a wormhole for travel from this dimension, or universe, to other dimensions or universes.

Man's fascination with alien beings and spiritual beings beyond the bounds of earth is nothing new. The popularity of programs and movies such as Star Trek, Star Wars, Avatar and E.T. show that interest in such things is high.

Towards the end of the last century the New Age Movement grew significantly and promoted the idea of a Spiritual Hierarchy, including a messianic figure some referred to as the Lord Maitreya. This Lord Maitreya had supposedly come from another realm or dimension to lead mankind into the new age of Aquarius.

It is not surprising that according to polls, the majority of the population now believe in intelligent alien life forms and a great percentage of people believe that aliens will at some point contact us here on earth. A 2021 New York Post article says, *"The majority of Americans believe in aliens, and we really do think they come in peace. According to a Pew Research study, about 65% of people said they think there is intelligent alien life on other planets. An even stronger majority of about 87% said they don't believe UFOs are a security threat at all or only represent a minor one."* [1] The article also cites a 1997 CNN/Time poll which found that 80% of Americans thought that the government was hiding knowledge of the existence of extraterrestrial life forms. [2]

Another 2021 "Study Finds" article states, *"According to a new study, alien conspiracy theorists are now the alien conspiracy majority! A survey of 2,000 adults in the United Kingdom finds six in 10 now believe it's only a matter of time before Earth becomes the target of an alien invasion."* [3]

Thousands of reports have come from people around the

---

[1] https://nypost.com/2021/07/07/most-americans-believe-in-aliens-new-study-reveals/

[2] ibid

[3] https://studyfinds.org/ufo-alien-invasion-inevitable/

world who claim to have encountered aliens, or at least seen UFOs here on the earth. These reports have come from average people as well as from pilots, radar operators and intelligence community personnel. I do not believe that all of these reports are fake. I believe, as do many other Bible teachers, that many of these reports are real, but rather than being encounters with aliens from another planet, they are encounters with demonic entities, disguising themselves as alien beings from somewhere beyond earth.

Man's Search for Alien Life in Space

You may recall that the 7th prediction of the World Economic Forum's 8 predictions for what the world will be like in 2030 stated, "You could be preparing to go to Mars. Scientists will have worked out how to keep you healthy in space. **The start of a journey to find alien life?**" There is, without question, a growing number of people who are interested in connecting with someone or something beyond the earth. Billionaires are spending huge sums of money to develop privately owned companies to explore space and to take people from earth to other planets. Many believe that this will be a key in helping mankind maintain life here on earth. Could this be a setup for a great deception?

In 2021 and 2022 billionaire Jeff Bezos' Blue Origin space program successfully launched four different space tourism missions, taking small groups of passengers into space and back. Blue Origin has now signed a contract with NASA to launch a 2024 interplanetary mission to Mars. One article said of this, "The Washington company announced two science initiatives supporting humanity's efforts to push outward into the cosmos." [4]

Also in July of 2021, Virgin Galactic, owned by billionaire Richard Branson, successfully launched a similar tourist mission, taking a small group of people into the edge of outer space and

---

[4] https://www.fastcompany.com/90851250/how-blue-origin-is-ramping-up-plans-for-interplanetary-missions

back. On their website Virgin Galactic describes their company this way, "We are the world's first commercial spaceline, and our purpose is to connect people across the globe to the love, wonder and awe created by space travel." [5]

Not to be outdone, Elon Musk's SpaceX company sent 4 passengers into space in September of 2021 for 3 days. SpaceX has worked in conjunction with NASA and as of February of 2023 has launched over 200 missions according to their website.[6] The company was founded in 2002 to revolutionize space technology, with the stated goal of reducing space transportation costs to enable the colonization of Mars.

In addition to all of these private endeavors, China's Mars rover named "Zhurong" successfully landed on Mars in May of 2021 and has since transmitted pictures of the planet back to earth.

The interest in space exploration and potential alien civilizations has grown exponentially over recent years. Another scientific connection to this whole fascination with alien and spiritual beings comes out of the deeply held beliefs regarding evolution and the resulting time tables proposed for the development of the universe and of life on earth. A 2020 article in The Guardian, was entitled "Scientists say most likely number of contactable alien civilisations is 36 - New calculations come up with estimate for worlds capable of communicating with others.

The article states, *"Basically, we made the assumption that intelligent life would form on other [Earth-like] planets like it has on Earth, so within a few billion years life would automatically form as a natural part of evolution,"* [7]

---

[5] https://www.virgingalactic.com/

[6] https://www.spacex.com/launches/

[7] https://www.theguardian.com/science/2020/jun/15/scientists-say-most-likely-number-of-contactable-alien-civilisations-is-36

It also says, *"there are likely between four and 211 civilisations in the Milky Way today capable of communicating with others, with 36 the most likely figure."* [8]

The "SETI" ("Search for Extraterrestrial Intelligence") Institute was formed in 1984. SETI works in cooperation with NASA and uses high tech instruments to continually monitor space for visible or audible signs of alien life.

With all of this increased effort in connecting with alien life it would seem that the world is ripe for demonic deception, with demonic entities posing as some type of highly evolved alien life form. Could this be a part of the end time deception that the Bible warned of? Second Corinthians 11:14 says that Satan disguises himself as an angel of light. With the world actively looking for highly evolved, intelligent beings from somewhere beyond the earth, it would seem that satanic entities in disguise might find an opportunity to deceive the masses.

In the days of Noah the wickedness was so great that it appears to have somehow created an opportunity for fallen angels to abandon their proper abode and take some form of human flesh upon themselves, interacting with and affecting humanity. If this is the case then the Nephilim, or the giants referred to in the Bible were actual offspring that resulted from the union of human women and fallen angels. Since the last days will be as the days of Noah, could this sort of thing happen again and be a part of the deception of the last days? I don't believe we have the answer to this question, but we do see both increased wickedness and great interest in finding some sort of intelligent life forms from beyond the earth, in the world today.

Revelation 12 tells us that a time is coming when Satan will be cast down from heaven onto the earth. Since he is a deceiver, a liar, and one who disguises himself, might he appear to the world at that

---

[8] ibid

time in disguise, seeking to lead the entire world astray?

Artificial Intelligence and the Transhuman Movement

Another related development in the world today is the growing interest in creating transhuman beings. This involves the blending of humans with computer technology and/or artificial intelligence. The desired results in this blending would be superhumans, capable of incredible intellectual and physical feats. The fact that this idea has been around for a while can be seen in the t.v. series that ran from 1973-1978 entitled, "The Six Million Dollar Man", which depicted a man with bionic implants, capable of superhuman feats. Transhumans have also played a major role in the Star Trek series.

Wikipedia describes transhuman in this way. *"Transhuman, or trans-human, is the concept of an intermediary form between human and posthuman. In other words, a transhuman is a being that resembles a human in most respects but who has powers and abilities beyond those of standard humans. These abilities might include improved intelligence, awareness, strength, or durability."* [9]

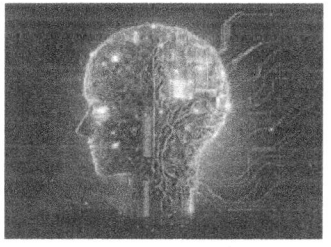

An additional Wikipedia article entitled "Transhumanism" adds this. *"Some transhumanists believe that human beings may eventually be able to transform themselves into beings with abilities so greatly expanded from the current condition as to merit the label of posthuman beings."* [10]

A 2018 Guardian article was entitled "No death and an enhanced life; Is the future transhuman?" It stated, "The aims of the transhumanist movement are summed up by Mark O'Connell in his book To Be a Machine, which last week won the Wellcome Book

---

[9] https://en.wikipedia.org/wiki/Transhuman
[10] https://en.wikipedia.org/wiki/Transhumanism

prize." *"It is their belief that we can and should eradicate ageing (sic) as a cause of death; that we can and should use technology to augment our bodies and our minds; that we can and should merge with machines, remaking ourselves, finally, in the image of our own higher ideals."*[11]

The subtitle of Mark O'Connell's book "To Be a Machine" is "Adventures Among Cyborgs, Utopians, Hackers, and the Futurists Solving the Modest Problem of Death." Wow, solving the modest problem of death! That reminds me of one of the first quotes in all of history, "you will surely not die" (Genesis 3:4).

A 2017 Forbes article entitled, "Transhumanism And The Future Of Humanity: 7 Ways The World Will Change By 2030" gives details of some of the advancements in the transhuman movement that are in the works for the next few years.

The article explains, *"The coming years will usher in a number of body augmentation capabilities that will enable humans to be smarter, stronger, and more capable than we are today. Wearables will be one form of body augmentation, but they will far surpass the fitness trackers of today. In the future, we can expect the arrival of contact lenses that can take pictures or video, universal language translator earbuds that allow us to communicate anywhere in the world, and exosuits that increase physical strength. We will also see increased use of implants ranging from brain microchips and neural lace to mind-controlled prosthesis and subdermal RFID chips that allow users to unlock doors or computer passwords with the wave of a hand."*[12]

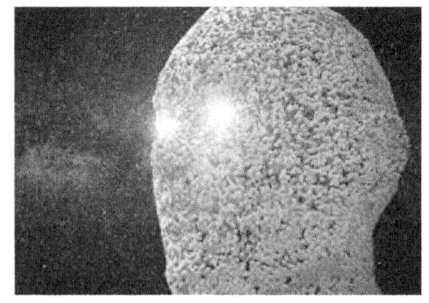

---

[11] https://www.theguardian.com/technology/2018/may/06/no-death-and-an-enhanced-life-is-the-future-transhuman
[12] https://www.forbes.com/sites/sarwantsingh/2017/11/20/transhumanism-and-the-future-of-humanity-seven-ways-the-world-will-change-by-2030/?sh=5a34804d7d79

The article continues and makes these statements. *"These body augmentation capabilities will give rise to humans that are more resilient, optimized and continually monitored."*[13] *"Both wearable and implantable brain-machine interfaces (BMIs) are in development from organizations that include Elon Musk's Neuralink, Facebook, and DARPA."* [14] (Notice above that transhumanism will give rise to humans that are 'continually monitored'.)

Numerous internet articles can be found that speak of the current development of 6g networks. The goal is to have 6g working and available by 2030. 6g technology will allow nanosensors within the human body to monitor health, and nanodevices to function inside the body, including brain-computer interface devices. 6g will allow for greatly increased wireless communication through novel Terahertz bands with ultra-high data rates. While 5g networks have allowed for self-driving cars and smart cities, 6g will allow for holographic technologies, Extended Reality technologies and IoB, the internet of bodies.[15] [16]

Even casual internet research concerning transhumanism reveals that there are many ethical concerns that have been expressed in regards to where the transhumanism movement may take humanity. The technological advances certainly have an upside, but the potential for misuse becomes greater as well. In light of our discussion in this chapter, it is easy to see how the merging of human intelligence with artificial intelligence, human strength with robotic strength, and human abilities with technological advances, could lead to a time of decreased reliance upon God and more reliance upon superhuman abilities.

The increased use of artificial intelligence, or "AI" is not limited to the transhuman movement. Chatbots like "ChatGPT",

---

[13] ibid
[14] ibid
[15] https://www.researchgate.net/publication/336846261_6G_Wireless_Communications_Future_Technologies_and_Research_Challenges
[16] https://www.elanafreeland.com/post/6g-transhumanism-iob-by-2030

developed by "OpenAI" have emerged, enabling users to have robotic programs write papers for them on specific topics. Bias and the censoring of politically incorrect ideas have already been identified in such chatbots, increasing concerns that the controlling of every narrative by a specific group of people could take another step forward with this new technology. Elon Musk has recently indicated that he is calling on artificial intelligence researchers as he considers creating an alternative chatbot to combat the "wokeness" found in current versions.[17] The development of artificial intelligence technologies could provide wonderful advancements for mankind, or could move mankind further from dependency upon God.

In Genesis 11 the people said "come let us build"! They had intentions of building their own kingdom apart from God. This was not a good thing! Today, the same mentality is seen throughout the world, especially within the movement toward a global system. We saw in chapter 12 that the European Union has revealed something of their heart by choosing the Tower of Babel as their model. We read earlier in this chapter that one of the goals of transhumanism is to deal with the problem of death. We have also seen that there is now a push to expand our horizons beyond the earth to other planets along with a growing expectation that we will connect with highly evolved alien life at some point. Mankind, apart from Christ, continues to seek to build a future without dependency on God.

All of this may merge together as a part of the massive deception the coming antichrist will bring upon the people of the earth when he is revealed. As in the days of Noah, wickedness abounds, life goes on without thoughts of coming judgment, and it appears that doors may be being opened to allow greater satanically inspired deception to impact humanity.

---

[17] https://www.chron.com/news/local/article/elon-musk-chatgpt-woke-ai-17815678.php

CHAPTER 20

Matthew 24
and The Seals of Revelation

Matthew 24-25 records what it is typically called "The Olivet Discourse". Here Jesus responds to three questions posed to Him by His disciples as they left Jerusalem and went up with Jesus to the Mt. of Olives. In Matthew 24:1 the disciples had pointed out the Temple buildings to Jesus while they were in the city. Jesus responded to them in verse 2 and told them that the day was coming when all of those buildings would be destroyed.

As they arrived on the Mt. of Olives the disciples asked Jesus 3 questions, about the destruction of the buildings in Jerusalem, and about the sign of His coming, and about the end of the age.

> "As He was sitting on the Mount of Olives, the disciples came to Him privately, saying, "Tell us, when will ① these things happen, and what ② will be the sign of Your coming, and ③ of the end of the age?"
> Matthew 24:3

It is important to note that the first question was specifically about the destruction of the city of Jerusalem. The second and third questions were about the sign of His coming and of the end of the age. Jesus answers all of these questions together so it is important to note that some of what He describes within His answer was fulfilled in 70 A.D. when the Roman armies destroyed the Temple of God and the city of Jerusalem, while other aspects of His answer describes events that will take place in the time leading up to His 2nd coming and the end of the age. Some of the things He describes probably have a dual fulfillment, first in 70 A.D. and then again in a different but similar way at the end of the age.

Within Jesus' answer are descriptions of events that will lead to His 2nd coming which is found in Matthew 24:29-31. Jesus' 2nd coming that is described here in Matthew 24 appears to be the same coming that is described in Revelation 19 as He comes in glory to defeat His enemies at the time of the battle of Armageddon. It is also referred to in Zechariah 14.

In this chapter we will look at something that is especially interesting. There appears to be a parallel between the first six seals that are opened in the book of Revelation and the events that Jesus describes in Matthew 24:4-31.

Before we look at that I want to point out that there is a common tendency to assume that all of the seals, trumpets and bowls of wrath spoken of in the book of Revelation are fulfilled during the Great Tribulation. This is not something that comes from any directive of Scripture. Jesus actually described the timing of the Great Tribulation very specifically in Matthew 24:15-21. He said that it comes <u>after</u> the abomination of desolation, which according to Daniel 9:24-27 happens in the middle of a 7 year period of time. Then in Matthew 24:22 Jesus specifically says that this Great Tribulation period will be cut short for the sake of the elect. That means that the Great Tribulation is a period of time, less than 3 ½ years, just before the 2nd coming of Jesus. The seals, trumpets and bowls of wrath spoken of in the book of Revelation refer to more than this specific period of time.

To see the first six seals of the book of Revelation we need to look at Revelation 6:1-17 where Jesus breaks the seals of the book.

*"Then I saw when **the Lamb broke one of the seven seals,** and I heard one of the four living creatures saying as with a voice of thunder, "Come." (2) I looked, and behold, a white horse, and he who sat on it had a bow; and a crown was*

*given to him, and he went out conquering and to conquer. (3) When **He broke the second seal**, I heard the second living creature saying, "Come." (4) And another, a red horse, went out; and to him who sat on it, it was granted to take peace from the earth, and that men would slay one another; and a great sword was given to him. (5) When **He broke the third seal**, I heard the third living creature saying, "Come." I looked, and behold, a black horse; and he who sat on it had a pair of scales in his hand. (6) And I heard something like a voice in the center of the four living creatures saying, "A quart of wheat for a denarius, and three quarts of barley for a denarius; and do not damage the oil and the wine." (7) When **the Lamb broke the fourth seal**, I heard the voice of the fourth living creature saying, "Come." (8) I looked, and behold, an ashen horse; and he who sat on it had the name Death; and Hades was following with him. Authority was given to them over a fourth of the earth, to kill with sword and with famine and with pestilence and by the wild beasts of the earth. (9) When **the Lamb broke the fifth seal**, I saw underneath the altar the souls of those who had been slain because of the word of God, and because of the testimony which they had maintained; (10) and they cried out with a loud voice, saying, "How long, O Lord, holy and true, will You refrain from judging and avenging our blood on those who dwell on the earth?" (11) And there was given to each of them a white robe; and they were told that they should rest for a little while longer, until the number of their fellow servants and their brethren who were to be killed even as they had been, would be completed also. (12) I looked when **He broke the sixth seal**, and there was a great earthquake; and the sun became black as sackcloth made of hair, and the whole moon became like blood; (13) and the stars of the sky fell to the earth, as a fig tree casts its unripe figs when shaken by a great wind. (14) The sky was split apart like a scroll when it is rolled up, and every mountain and island* *were moved out of their places. (15) Then the kings of the earth and the great men and the commanders and the rich and the strong and every slave and free man hid themselves in the caves and among the rocks of the mountains; (16) and they *said to the mountains and to the rocks, "Fall on us and hide us from the presence of Him who sits on the throne, and from the wrath of the Lamb; (17) for the great day of their wrath has come, and who is able to stand?"*

Revelation 6:1-17

So here is what is revealed within the first six seals in Revelation 6 and what these symbols appear to represent.

1) White Horse - False Christs & False Prophets
2) Red Horse - War
3) Black Horse - Famine
4) Ashen Horse - Death
5) Martyrs Seen in Heaven
6) The Wrath of God Being Poured Out in Judgment

Now if we look at what Jesus said in Matthew 24:4-31, we find all of these same things described in different terms, but in the same sequence.

1) **False Christs & False Prophets - (Matthew 24:5)** *"For many will come in My name, saying, 'I am the Christ,' and will mislead many."* (He added emphasis to this by also referring to this in verse 11 and in verses 23-25)
2) **Wars & Rumors of Wars - (Matthew 24:6)** *"You will be hearing of wars and rumors of wars. See that you are not frightened, for those things must take place, but that is not yet the end."*
3) **Famine - (Matthew 24:7)** *"For nation will rise against nation, and kingdom against kingdom, and in various places there will be famines and earthquakes."*

4) **Death - (Matthew 24:5-7)** It can be assumed that many would die from the wars, famines and earthquakes spoken of in verses 5-7. In Revelation 6:8 we are told that the massive amounts of death that come at this time are caused by "the sword" (war), and "famine", plus "pestilence" and "wild beasts". Plus, the death of believers through persecutions are referred to in verse 9.
5) **Martyrs - (Matthew 24:9)** *"Then they will deliver you to tribulation, and will kill you, and you will be hated by all nations because of My name."* Revelation 6:9-11 gives more detail, showing these martyrs in heaven crying out for justice and receiving robes of white.
6) **The Wrath of God Poured Out As Jesus Comes Again to the Battle of Armageddon (Matthew 24:27-31)** *"For just as the lightning comes from the east and flashes even to the west, so will the coming of the Son of Man be. (28) "Wherever the corpse is, there the vultures will gather. (29) "But immediately after the tribulation of those days the sun will be darkened, and the moon will not give its light, and the stars will fall from the sky, and the powers of the heavens will be shaken. (30) "And then the sign of the Son of Man will appear in the sky, and then all the tribes of the earth will mourn, and they will see the Son of Man coming on the clouds of the sky with power and great glory. (31) "And He will send forth His angels with a great trumpet and they will gather together His elect from the four winds, from one end of the sky to the other."* Note the reference to the vultures in verse 28 which appears to be a reference to the gathering of people to the battle of Armageddon where birds are called upon to come and eat the flesh of the fallen. (see Revelation 19:17-18) Note the darkening of the sun and moon in verse 29, which is seen as well in Revelation 6:12. Note the shaking of the heavens in verse 29, which is seen as well in Revelation 6:13-14.

When we look at these passages and see a consistent listing of events leading up to, and included in, the 2nd coming of Jesus, we are reminded of the surety of these prophetic words of Scripture from nearly 2,000 years ago.

As we have seen in previous chapters, these prophesied precursors of the coming of Christ have happened, or are all happening now, indicating that the 2nd coming of Jesus Christ is drawing near. False christs, false prophets, wars and rumors of wars, famines and pestilences, as well as the persecution and killing of Christians, can all be identified in the days that we live in now.

This should remind us to be awake and alert, looking forward to the coming of Jesus!

I want to make one further note here before closing this chapter. In my book, "Rapture First or Rapture Later, and Why It Matters", I dedicate an entire chapter to examining how the Bible describes "the Day of the Lord". In that examination of Scripture we see that the darkening of the sun and moon, and the shaking of the heavens is the consistent biblical description of the beginning of the day of the Lord. As we saw here, these important signs that the day of the Lord has come are seen in both Matthew 24:29 and in Revelation 6:12-14 as a part of the sixth seal.

CHAPTER 21

Spiritual Battles

When looking at the world we live in today it is critical to remember a very important truth proclaimed in the Bible! In Ephesians 6:12 we are told.

> *"For our struggle is not against flesh and blood, but against the rulers, against the powers, against the world forces of this darkness, against the spiritual forces of wickedness in the heavenly places."*
> *Ephesians 6:12*

There certainly are layers of cause and effect involved in the developments of last days, world changing events. There are economic plans, political and governmental aspirations, personal ambitions, and more that all are involved in moving the world forward toward a global system. Behind all of these influences is another layer of cause and effect that is where the real battle lies. Ephesians 6:12 reminds us of the reality of the spiritual realm and of the ongoing battles that are taking place in this realm. As Christians, we must keep this in focus! Our true enemies are not people! Our enemies are satanic, demonic spirits! Our battle is in the spiritual realm and the outcome of these spiritual battles is what determines the course of world events in the natural, physical realm.

We must remember two key points about the spiritual and natural realms, and what we see happening in the world we live in.

First of all, behind the attempts we often see in the natural realm to weaken and destroy nations, to destroy moral standards, to weaken and destroy families, to create a global system to control all of humanity, to discredit and destroy biblical truth, and to promote false narratives to instill fear and bring about obedience among masses of people, there are satanic and demonic spirits at work to advance these attempts!

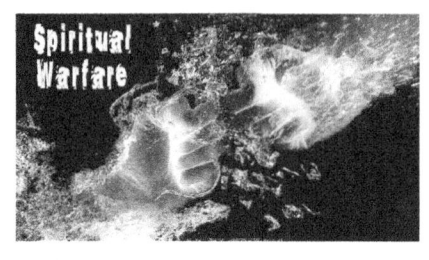

Secondly, and more importantly, God is all-powerful and the sovereign ruler of all things in the spiritual and physical realms. Some things happen in the natural realm because His judgments are involved, allowing Satan's purposes to advance, in order to call humanity to repentance and dependency upon God.

Notice in Ephesians 6:12 that there is a description of evil spiritual forces in terms that indicate different levels of authority and influence. We are told that our struggle is against -

1) "the rulers" (KJV says "principalities")
2) "the powers"
3) "the world forces of this darkness" (KJV says "the rulers of the darkness of this world")
4) the "spiritual forces of wickedness in the heavenly places"

It is difficult to clearly define the difference between all four of these described levels of satanic and demonic powers, but it is easy to see that this is a real, and organized enemy army that wages war against people who are created in the image and likeness of God.

The Bible speaks to us about how we should fight this spiritual battle. Notice what we are told in 2 Corinthians 10:3-5.

> "For though we walk in the flesh, we do not war according to the flesh, (4) for the weapons of our warfare are not of the flesh, but divinely powerful for

> *the destruction of fortresses. (5) We are destroying speculations and every lofty thing raised up against the knowledge of God, and we are taking every thought captive to the obedience of Christ,"*
>
> *2 Corinthians 10:3-5*

We are told that we do not war according to the flesh! We must learn to fight spiritual battles to impact things in the natural realm! We are told that we have weapons! These weapons are not of the flesh or physical weapons. These weapons are spiritual weapons that we use to fight spiritual battles! Included in these weapons are prayer, fasting, worship, God's Word, humility and dependency upon God!

In the passage from Ephesians 6 where we find verse 12, we find additional information about how we are to engage in spiritual battles.

> *"Finally, be strong in the Lord and in the strength of His might. (11) **Put on the full armor of God**, so that you will be able to stand firm against the schemes of the devil. (12) For our struggle is not against flesh and blood, but against the rulers, against the powers, against the world forces of this darkness, against the spiritual forces of wickedness in the heavenly places. (13) Therefore, take up the full armor of God, so that you will be able to resist in the evil day, and having done everything, to stand firm. (14) Stand firm therefore, having girded your loins with truth, and having put on the breastplate of righteousness, (15) and having shod your feet with the preparation of the gospel of peace; (16) in addition to all, taking up the shield of faith with which you will be able to extinguish all the flaming arrows of the evil one. (17) And take the helmet of salvation, and the sword of the Spirit,*

which is the word of God. (18) With all prayer and petition pray at all times in the Spirit, and with this in view, be on the alert with all perseverance and petition for all the saints,"

We are told that we have been supplied with armor as well. This armor is designed to enable us to stand in the evil day and to stand firm against the schemes of the devil! The various parts of this armor are listed for us here as well.

1) Truth (to gird your loins) (v.14)
2) Righteousness (as a breastplate) (v.14)
3) The Gospel of Peace (as shoes - prepared to go) (v.15)
4) Faith (as a shield to extinguish the evil one's fiery darts) (v.16)
5) Salvation (as a helmet) (v.17)
6) The Word of God (the sword of the Spirit) (v.17)
7) Intercessory Prayer (v.18)

We are told to take up this armor, or to put it on for protection during battles, and for victorious weaponry. In practical terms, think of it this way. You and I need to -

1) Fill our lives with the truth of God's Word
2) Walk in the path of Christ's Righteousness (Live in Holiness)
3) Prepare to share the Gospel of Peace with others
4) Grow in our Faith in God and His ability to protect us and provide for us
5) Come into the Salvation Christ offers us through faith in Christ
6) Learn to speak God's Word, using it as a sword to impact things within spiritual battles, and
7) Pray faithfully and regularly in the spirit for ourselves and for others in the body of Christ!

Behind everything that we have described in this book is a spiritual battle. As the 2nd coming of Christ draws near, Satan knows that his time to destroy people, who are created in the image and likeness of God, is limited. Therefore, the battles intensify and the need for Christians to follow the instructions of the Bible increases.

I remind myself often of this important truth. The battles we are facing in the last days are not against flesh and blood! The true battle is not with a group of "elites", with international organizations, with news media outlets or with a political party. The battles we are facing in the last days are spiritual battles and must be fought with spiritual weapons! We must pray, worship, fast, read and study the Word of God, speak the Word of God, speak the mighty Name of Jesus, live by faith, live in holiness and spread the love of Jesus Christ with lost people, whom Jesus died for!

I have been encouraged by a number of things related to this in the past few years, even as so many things in the natural realm have been disheartening. In 2020 there were at least 3 different prayer and worship gatherings in Washington D.C. In the fall of 2020 Rev. Franklin Graham led a Prayer March and Jonathan Cahn led a prayer and repentance meeting called "The Return", both in Washington D.C. and both involving tens of thousands of Christians, coming together to pray for the nation and the world. A few weeks later Sean Feucht led a worship gathering of about 35,000 believers in Washington D.C. called "Let Us Worship". The "Let Us Worship" gatherings also took place in cities across America. Numerous other online and live prayer, worship and fasting movements have also emerged. God hears and answers prayer! I am convinced that the greatest way to combat deception and movements to strip humanity of freedoms, in these days is through prayer! The battle is a spiritual battle and will only be won by spiritual means!

As I write, news of revivals breaking out across America and beyond has been very encouraging! God, in His mercy can certainly do wonderful things in the lives of people, bringing believers into times of revival, and unbelievers into salvation, even during times when trouble and difficulties abound!

Some recent songs about the power of the Name of Jesus have also emerged that remind us to speak the Name of Jesus over our world, over our nation, over our states, communities and neighborhoods, over our schools, over our churches, and especially over our families!

We are in a spiritual battle but "greater is He who is in you, than he who is the world!" (1 John 4:4)

Israel, Globalism
and The 2nd Coming of Christ
(Understanding Current World Events
in Light of Bible Prophecy)

SECTION 2
What Has God Promised?

CHAPTER 22

God's Plans For the Last Days

Throughout most of this book we have focused on things happening around the world that show the advancement of last days agenda of the kingdom of darkness. We've looked at the increase of immorality, the abundance of wars and rumors of wars, the great numbers of false christs and false prophets, and the increasing levels of deception found throughout the world. We've seen all that is taking place to weaken America and to remove it as a superpower in the world. We looked in detail at the plans and efforts to establish a global system. We've seen that there is no evidence to suggest that this global system will be based on the fear of the Lord, dependency upon God, and the worship of God. Instead, this movement toward a global system appears to be motivated by the same spirit as the ancient attempts at building the tower of babel.

It is important that we see and understand these things. It is important that we see how the prophecies in the Bible concerning the last days are coming to pass. It is important that we recognize that the fulfillment of these prophecies indicates that the 2nd coming of Jesus is approaching. It is important that we understand from the warnings of Scripture about these matters, our need to prepare our hearts for the things coming upon the earth. Jesus said, "Behold, I have told you in advance."

In this chapter I want to shift gears of talk about God's plans for the last days. While Satan has plans to deceive the world and set the stage for his coming antichrist, the Bible also indicates that God has plans and purposes for the last days as well! To only look at the progression of the plans of the kingdom of darkness would not be healthy for believers. It is critical that we recognize that God has plans and purposes that He will accomplish in the last days and that we can be a part of!

God's Love For Humanity (The End Time Harvest)

There are many indications in the Bible that God's love for the lost will impact much of what happens in the last days. God's nature is love! 1 John 4:8 and 1 John 4:16 specifically state that "GOD IS LOVE!" John 3:16 tells us that God so loved the world that He gave His only begotten Son! Luke 15 is an entire chapter dedicated to emphasizing God's great love for lost souls. In this chapter Jesus tells the parable of the lost sheep, the parable of the lost coin, and the parable of the prodigal son. The chapter begins with tax collectors and sinners gathered around Jesus and the Pharisees and scribes criticizing Jesus for interacting with sinners.

God's character does not change in the last days! His love and His heart for lost souls will continue to impact the world, though He will eventually pour out His judgment and wrath upon this sinful world. Failing to see God's heart for the lost will skew a person's view of the last days.

In 2 Peter 3:9 we see how God's heart for the lost impacts the last days.

> *"The Lord is not slow about His promise, as some count slowness, but is patient toward you, not wishing for any to perish but for all to come to repentance."*
> *2 Peter 3:9*

The context of this passage is clearly referring to His promise to come again. The patience of God and His desire to see all repent and none perish, is the reason Jesus has not yet returned!

James 5:7-8 also makes it clear that there will be a harvest of souls in the last days as God patiently waits for this precious harvest. He instructs His followers to wait for the early and latter rains that will help ripen and prepare this great harvest.

> *"Therefore be patient, brethren, until the coming of the Lord. The farmer waits for the precious produce of the soil, being patient about it, until it gets the early and late rains. (8) You too be patient; strengthen your hearts, for the coming of the Lord is near."*
>
> *James 5:7-8*

Based on the context of this passage the call to "be patient" and to "strengthen your hearts" is partly referring to believers facing sufferings being patient in endurance until the Lord comes again. Nevertheless, the text also clearly makes reference to the same thing that 2 Peter 3:9 speaks about. God is patient because of the precious harvest of souls that it appears will be brought in during the last days.

The Outpouring of God's Spirit Upon All Flesh

On the day of Pentecost, when the Holy Spirit was first poured out upon the church, Peter stood and preached to thousands of people who had gathered to observe and listen to what was going on. During his message that day he quotes a prophetic passage of Scripture from the book of Joel. He says that what was happening on that day of Pentecost was a fulfillment of what the prophet Joel wrote, as recorded in Joel 2:28-32. Peter's words are a part of Scripture so we know they are true, but Joel's emphasis on "the day of the Lord" in Joel 2 appears to indicate that what took place on the day of Pentecost was only an initial, partial fulfillment of Joel's prophetic words. Initial and subsequent fulfillments of prophetic Scriptures is common. Even Jesus quoted part of Isaiah 61:1-2 in Luke 4:18-21 and said the prophetic words of Isaiah were being fulfilled by Him at that time. He stopped short of quoting all the words of Isaiah 61:1-2 though, because the last portion which includes "and the day of vengeance of our God". He did this because this part of the prophetic passage refers to what He will do at the time of His 2nd coming in the future. With this in mind notice what Acts 2:16-21 says.

> *"but this is what was spoken of through the prophet Joel: (17) 'And it shall be in the last days,' God says, 'That I will pour forth of My Spirit on all mankind; and your sons and daughters shall prophesy, and your young men shall see visions, and your old men shall dream dreams; (18) Even on My bondslaves, both men and women, I will in those days pour forth of My Spirit and they shall prophesy. (19) "And I will grant wonders in the sky above and signs on the earth below, blood, and fire, and vapor of smoke. (20) 'The sun will be turned into darkness and the moon into blood, before the great and glorious day of the Lord shall come. (21) 'And it shall be that everyone who calls on the Name of the Lord will be saved."* Acts 2:16-21

Notice in this prophetic passage from Joel 2 and from Acts 2, that God has promised to pour out His Spirit upon all flesh in the last days. The "last days" is a period of time that began with the death and resurrection of Jesus and will continue until He comes again. There was a measure of an outpouring of God's Spirit at the beginning of the last days on the day of Pentecost. I believe there will be a greater outpouring of God's Spirit at the end of the last days, "before the great and glorious day of the Lord shall come". What a marvelous promise! He also says that during that time our sons and daughters will prophesy, our young men will see visions and our old men will dream dreams.

He says that this outpouring of His Spirit will be upon His bondslaves, both men and women. He says a second time that they will prophesy. In addition to these things He says that He will grant wonders in the sky above and signs on the earth beneath! All of this appears to take place just before the great and glorious day of the Lord. (I have an entire chapter in my book "Rapture First or Rapture Later and Why It Matters" dedicated to seeing how the Bible defines "the day of the Lord", and how it gives us greater understanding of the last days.) The conclusion of this prophetic passage gives us a great indication. It says, "And everyone who calls on the name of the Lord will be saved!"

This passage gives us great hope and great insight into God's plans and purposes in the last days. Satan's plans may be allowed to move forward so that the Scriptures may be fulfilled, but that will not prevent God Almighty from fulfilling His proclaimed plans and purposes in the last days!

As I write in the early part of 2023 there are many reports of revival breaking out in various places across the United States. At Asbury University in a small town in Kentucky, a typical morning chapel service on Wednesday, February 8th turned into a prayer and worship meeting that lasted for days and drew thousands of people from around the nation, and even other countries. Reports of salvations, healings and believers being revived abound.

The revival that began at Asbury University is spreading to other campuses and churches across the nation and in other parts of the world. Reports are surfacing of services lasting 2-3 days straight and more. A revival meeting was held in late February at Rupp Arena on the campus of Kentucky University. On February 8, the same day that the Asbury revival broke out, the administration of Oklahoma University approved a request allowing for a student-led service to be held in the football stadium on the campus of Oklahoma University on April 29th. Evangelist Nick Hall said that the stadium has only hosted two non football events in the past 50 years. Both of these events were music concerts, one by U2 and one by Toby Keith which was a tornado relief event.[1] Some people near Oklahoma University have been praying for decades for a Christian event to happen in the football stadium, and now, amazingly this event has been approved. It happens right at the time revival is spreading across America and "The Jesus Revolution" movie is being shown in theaters across the country, impacting many, as the movie tells the story of a great move of God's Spirit across America in the early 1970s.

Something wonderful is happening! Is it a true revival and spiritual awakening that will sweep over the nation, bringing transformation and the salvation of millions of souls? Time will tell. Hopefully, by the time you are reading this book, you will be smiling because you will already know the answer to that question. Hopefully, this will be a time when the sovereign God of heaven pours out His Spirit and brings a mighty, transforming revival!

A Mighty Witness

Another indication that God will accomplish great things among the nations during the days leading up to the 2nd coming of Christ, is the prophetic words concerning a mighty witness for Christ in the last days.

Just before Jesus ascended into heaven His disciples asked Him, "is it at this time You are restoring the kingdom to Israel?" Jesus answered their question this way.

> *"He said to them, "It is not for you to know times or epochs which the Father has fixed by His own authority; (8) but you will receive power when the Holy Spirit has come upon you; and you shall be My witnesses both in Jerusalem, and in all Judea and Samaria, and even to the remotest part of the earth."*
> *Acts 1:7-8*

Jesus made it clear that it was not for them, nor for us, to

---

[1] https://www.youtube.com/watch?v=BiOZ7HN1kEI

know the specific times the Father has set. Jesus then stated two things He wanted His disciples to understand about the future. The first thing was that they would receive power when the Holy Spirit comes upon them. The second thing was that they would be His witnesses throughout the world.

Jesus has had witnesses on the earth, ever since He returned to heaven, and gave His disciples this charge in Acts 1:8. As believers in Christ, we are called to be His witnesses. This is more than just by spoken word. It involves a life that bears witness to the reality of Who Christ is and what He accomplished through His death and resurrection. The Greek word for "witnesses" found in Acts 1:8 and elsewhere is "martus" which is also the word for "martyr". Our witness for Christ involves faithfulness to Christ, even when it means the giving of our life for the sake of Christ and His Kingdom.

In Revelation 11:3-13 we see a prophetic passage indicating that God will anoint His two witnesses for 3 ½ years in the days just prior to the 2nd coming of Christ. Verse 3 says, "And I will grant authority to my two witnesses, and they will prophesy for twelve hundred and sixty days, clothed in sackcloth." The fact that they are clothed in sackcloth may be an indication that they are mourning over the evil things that are taking place across the world. Verses 5-6 speak of the things they will do during these days.

> *"And if anyone wants to harm them, fire flows out of their mouth and devours their enemies; so if anyone wants to harm them, he must be killed in this way. (6) These have the power to shut up the sky, so that rain will not fall during the days of their prophesying; and they have power over the waters to turn them into blood, and to strike the earth with every plague, as often as they desire."*   Revelation 11:5-6

Notice that they prophesy, which is not always foretelling the future. Prophesying can also refer to speaking the truth boldly under the anointing or unction of the Holy Spirit. These witnesses may very well do both as they warn people of the soon coming day of judgment and proclaim the way of salvation through Christ. During the ordained days of their prophesying they have power and authority to defeat any who come against them, prevent rain from falling, turn bodies of water into blood and strike the earth with plagues as often as they desire. We are not specifically told what the goal of their witnessing is, but it would appear from the other passages that we have already discussed, that their witnessing is designed by God to give people another chance to repent.

Much has been written and spoken about the possible identity of these two witnesses. It is important to note that what they do, and why they are provided by God at this critical time in history, is not dependent upon who they are. God's purposes in giving people the opportunity to repent are seen here, no matter who the two witnesses are.

Many have stated their opinion that the two witnesses are either Enoch and Elijah or Moses and Elijah. The view that Enoch and Elijah are the two witnesses is based on the fact that they are the only two people in the Bible that were caught up into heaven without dying. The view that Moses and Elijah are the two witnesses is based on the fact that Moses is the biblical representation of the law, and Elijah is the biblical representation of the prophets. Also, Moses and Elijah were seen speaking with Jesus on the mount of transfiguration. Also, the calling down of fire, turning the water to blood and striking the earth with plagues, are all seen in the Bible through Moses and Elijah.

There is another view of the two witnesses that has been held by various Bible scholars throughout the centuries. This view interprets the two witnesses in Revelation 11 to be representative not of two individuals, but of two groups brought together as Christ's witnesses in this critical time.

The only description or identification of the two witnesses that is given in Revelation 11 is found in verse 4.

> *"These are the two olive trees and the two lampstands that stand before the Lord of the earth."*

Revelation 11:4

The two witnesses are said to be "the two olive trees" and "the two lampstands (or candlesticks in the KJV)" that stand before the Lord of the earth. One Old Testament passage (Zechariah 4) and two New Testament passages (Romans 11:11-24) and (Revelation 1:12-20), use these symbolic terms of "olive trees" and "lampstands". Based on these descriptions, some have interpreted the two witnesses to be the church and the nation of Israel, or the church, consisting of Jewish and Gentile believers. I do not believe that an argument can be made that proves this view to be true, but it is what I believe the passage indicates. In Revelation 1:11-20 "lampstands" are specifically said to be "churches".

I have written an entire chapter in my "Rapture First or Rapture Later" book concerning the two witnesses.

If the two witnesses seen in Revelation 11 are representative of Jewish and Gentile believers in the church of Jesus Christ, or the church and the nation of Israel, then the last days involve a time of great ministry and witness by believers, not a time that is only defeat and hiding from the antichrist. If the two witnesses of Revelation 11 are representative of the church, then this passage would fit with what we saw in Acts 2 where the Lord proclaims that He will pour out His Spirit on His bondslaves, both men and women, and they will prophesy.

If the two witnesses seen in Revelation 11 are representative of the church, then the greatest days of ministry in the history of the church may be coming in the near future.

At the end of their time of prophesying the witnesses are killed by the beast but are then resurrected by God within the view of the whole world. If the witnesses seen in Revelation 11 are representative of the church, it is interesting that they are seen dead in Jerusalem, and then seen resurrected from Jerusalem. This would be an interesting correlation to what took place in Jesus' life during the time of His first coming.

If the witnesses seen in Revelation 11 are representative of the church, then their resurrection from the dead that is recorded in verses 11-12 would appear to be a part of the rapture, as described in other places in the New Testament. If this is the case it would probably indicate that not all believers, or not all of the church, are killed by the beast, but simply a substantial number. Some would still be "alive and remain until the coming of the Lord" as 1 Thessalonians 4:15 says.

If the witnesses seen in Revelation 11 are not representative of the church, but are Moses and Elijah, Enoch and Elijah, or two individuals not yet known, they still reveal a continuing effort by God in the last days to reach out to a lost world, and call them into repentance.

The Salvation of Israel

In Isaiah 43:1 God says to Israel, *"I have called you by name, you are Mine."* In Deuteronomy 14:2 He says, *"For you are a holy people to the LORD your God, and the LORD has chosen you to be a people for His own possession out of all the peoples who are on the face of the earth."* Israel is God's chosen people! We see this throughout the Bible.

In Deuteronomy 28 the Lord laid out blessings for Israel if they follow Him and obey His commandments. In this same chapter He also laid out curses that would come upon them if they did not follow Him and did not obey His commandments. He speaks in this chapter of them being scattered throughout the earth, but later being brought back to their homeland.

In previous chapters we looked at the awesome prophecies in the Bible concerning the nation of Israel and the Jewish people. We saw how the return of the Jewish people to the land of Israel, the blossoming of the land, and the reestablishing of Israel as a nation, are all signs of the end times and the nearness of the 2nd coming of

Jesus Christ. There is another important aspect of God's dealings with Israel and the Jewish people in the last days that is spoken of in Romans, chapter 11. From this chapter we understand that Gentiles have become a part of God's chosen family when much of Israel hardened their heart toward God and were cut off from Him as a result. The illustration of a natural olive tree with natural branches (Jewish believers) and unnatural branches (Gentile believers) is used to reveal what has happened in the blending of Gentile believers into God's family. Verses 19-20 speak of this truth in this way.

> *"You will say then, "Branches were broken off so that I might be grafted in." (20) Quite right, they were broken off for their unbelief, but you stand by your faith. Do not be conceited, but fear;" Romans 11:19-20*

We have seen the essence of this truth as a reality in the world for hundreds of years. Israel is God's chosen people from the beginning but because of their unbelief Gentiles have been grafted in through faith and have become a part of God's chosen people.

Another amazing aspect of the final days leading up to the 2nd coming of Jesus Christ is seen in something that Romans 11 prophesied about.

> *"For if you were cut off from what is by nature a wild olive tree, and were grafted contrary to nature into a cultivated olive tree, how much more will these who are the natural branches be grafted into their own olive tree? (25) For I do not want you, brethren, to be uninformed of this mystery--so that you will not be wise in your own estimation--that a partial hardening has happened to Israel until the fullness of the Gentiles has come in; (26) and **so all Israel will be saved;** just as it is written, **'The deliverer will come from Zion, He will remove ungodliness from Jacob.' (27) 'This is My covenant with them, when I take***

away their sins.'" Romans 11:24-27

Romans 2:28-29 reveals that God considers Gentiles believers as Jews inwardly. Therefore, within the church of Jesus Christ, Jew and Gentile believers are both considered as Jews in God's eyes. They are both considered to be God's chosen people! Galatians 3:28 says that in Christ there is neither Jew nor Gentile, for we are all one in Christ. Praise God!

Some may conclude because of this that the prophetic statements about all Israel being saved in Romans 11 do not speak about the Jewish people and national Israel. Yet, the whole point of Romans 11 is the distinguishing between Jew and Gentile, though both are grafted into the natural olive tree. With this in mind we should see the statements about the fulness of the Gentiles coming in, all of Israel being saved, and the deliverer coming from Zion to remove ungodliness from Jacob and to take away their sins, as a future promise concerning national Israel and the Jewish people.

One of the noticeable things happening in the world today is related to God's promises to Israel in Romans 11. Unprecedented numbers of Jews are now coming to know Jesus Christ as their Messiah!

It has been estimated that there were about 2,000 Messianic Jews in the world in 1973. (A "Messianic Jew" is a Jew who acknowledges Jesus (or "Yeshua") as their Messiah). According to "Jews For Jesus" there were over 350,000 Messianic Jews in the world as of 2021.[2]

Also, a website entitled "One For Israel" has been established to reach Jewish people with the good news of Who Jesus is and what He came to do for us all.[3] The website includes a page called "I Met Messiah" that is filled with testimonies of Jewish people who have come to place their faith in Jesus Christ as their Savior. Many other tools and resources are available on the site to assist Jewish

---

[2] https://jewsforjesus.org/learn/what-are-messianic-jews
[3] https://www.oneforisrael.org/about/

people in coming to faith in Christ. One amazing aspect of information found on the site is the report of how many Hebrew speaking people have viewed Hebrew testimonies and films. A graph on the site shows that though there are less than 12 million people in the world who speak Hebrew, "One For Israel" Gospel

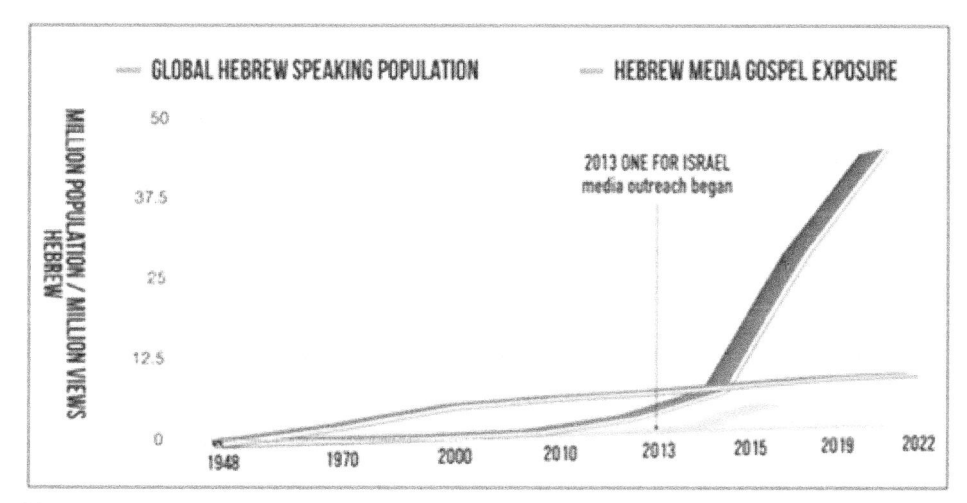

films in Hebrew have been viewed more than 50 million times. That's more than four views for every person who speaks Hebrew in the world.[4] The number of views has skyrocketed since 2013 when One For Israel began their media outreach. Something powerful is happening among Jewish people today but according to the Bible much more will occur before God's plans for the Jewish people are all completed!

The Morning Star Rising In Our Hearts

A number of years ago I was captured by a verse of Scripture found in 2 Peter, chapter 1. In this passage Peter is speaking of the fact that all the Old Testament prophecies concerning the coming of Jesus Christ, and the power that would be seen through Him, confirming that He is the Messiah, were confirmed on the Mount of

---

[4] ibid

Transfiguration as he and two other disciples saw Jesus glorified and heard the audible voice of God the Father bearing witness to Jesus being His Son. Peter encourages believers to pay attention to the Old Testament prophecies concerning Jesus, as well as to the words spoken by God the Father about Jesus on the Mount of Transfiguration. As he challenges believers to pay attention to the prophetic words which ground us with knowledge of Who Jesus is, Peter adds a statement that is very profound.

> *"So we have the prophetic word made more sure, to which you do well to pay attention as to a lamp shining in a dark place, until the day dawns and the morning star arises in your hearts."*   2 Peter 1:19

Notice that Peter refers to the prophetic word about Jesus, that was made more sure through the confirming words on the Mount of Transfiguration, as a lamp shining in a dark place. So, in the darkness of this sinful world, the light of Who Jesus is can bring light to us and can guide us and direct us!

It is here that Peter then makes a very interesting statement. He says, **"until the day dawns and the morning star arises in your hearts."** It is this statement that grabbed my attention years ago and led me to contemplate what Peter was saying.

It would appear that he is saying that our need to hold to Old Testament prophetic words about Jesus, and words that were spoken about Jesus on the Mount of Transfiguration, will continue until a future time when something will happen that will greatly increase our understanding of Who Jesus is. The words of the prophets and the words spoken on the Mount of Transfiguration about Jesus will still be our foundation for understanding, but this passage seems to indicate that a time will come when the presence of Jesus will rise in the hearts of His people in a profound way

As I pondered this verse I first thought of it in light of the truth that "the day of the Lord" is coming. Peter spoke of this in 2 Peter

3:10 when he said, "But the day of the Lord will come like a thief …" Paul has also spoken of this in 1 Thessalonians 5:2 when he said, "For you yourselves know full well that the day of the Lord will come just like a thief in the night." In Acts 2 Peter spoke of the promised outpouring of God's Spirit before the great and glorious day of the Lord. The day of the Lord is spoken of by many Old Testament prophets as well. The 2nd coming of Jesus Christ is a part of the day of the Lord, as He comes to judge this sinful world.

Peter spoke of a specific time in the future by saying, "when the day dawns." We can not say definitively what he was speaking about but I believe he was referring to the coming day of the Lord. In nature, each morning there is dawn, before the sun rises and the day officially begins. Dawn precedes the daytime.

Peter then said, "and the morning star rises in your hearts." In nature, the planet Venus is called "the morning star". During a portion of each year Venus appears in the evening sky just after sunset and is called "the evening star". Then for months each year Venus is seen in the predawn sky in the east as the brightest star in the sky and is then called "the morning star". For a number of months Venus can be seen for up to two hours before sunrise in the eastern sky. During this time "the morning star" can be seen rising in the eastern sky as a new day dawns. I have watched this occurrence before sunrise on a number of occasions. You can see the morning star rising over the course of an hour or so as dawn comes and darkness begins to give way to light in the eastern sky.

It would seem that Peter is referencing this common occurrence in the natural realm to speak of a spiritual reality that will occur at a future time. It is not uncommon for God to speak to us about spiritual truths through natural realities that we are familiar with. Jesus did this in His teachings. For instance, He spoke of grain harvests, the building of houses, and the appearance of the skies, to illustrate spiritual truths.

In Revelation 22:16 Jesus identifies Himself as the bright morning star.

> *"I, Jesus, have sent My angel to testify to you these things for the churches. I am the root and the descendant of David, the bright morning star."*
> *Revelation 22:16*

Could it be that Peter was indicating that there will come a time as the day of the Lord draws near, that Jesus, the bright and morning star will arise in the hearts of His people? Could it be that out of the darkest night, light will begin to come forth within Jesus' church, signifying that the day of the Lord is dawning and the Son of righteousness is about to appear? We certainly cannot state this as definitive doctrine, but Peter's words certainly fit what is seen every year in the natural world as the day dawns! If this is what Peter was indicating, it should be a source of great encouragement to believers living in the last days! If this is what Peter was indicating, it would fit well with Acts 2:17-21 that speaks of an outpouring of God's Spirit in the last days.

Another scripture that appears to fit with this understanding of 2 Peter 1:19 is found in Proverbs 4:18.

> *"But the path of the righteous is like the light of dawn,*
> *That shines brighter and brighter until the full day."*
> *Proverbs 4:18*

Could it be that while Satan promotes an agenda which increases sin and darkness throughout the world in the last days, that God will do wonderful things to purify His church and increase the light and presence of Jesus flowing through the lives of His people? I believe that the Lord has indicated in His Word that He will do great and mighty things in and through the lives of His people in the last days, as a witness to the nations!

CHAPTER 23

Jesus Christ Will Come Again!

Though we have focused primarily on world events in light of Bible prophecy, it is appropriate that we state clearly where all of the prophetic events of our time are heading. Jesus Christ is coming back to the earth to establish His eternal kingdom!

Probably the clearest statements regarding this in the Old Testament are found in the book of Daniel.

> *"In the days of those kings the God of heaven will set up a kingdom which will never be destroyed, and that kingdom will not be left for another people; it will crush and put an end to all these kingdoms, but it will itself endure forever. (45) "Inasmuch as you saw that a stone was cut out of the mountain without hands and that it crushed the iron, the bronze, the clay, the silver and the gold, the great God has made known to the king what will take place in the future; so the dream is true and its interpretation is trustworthy."*
>
> Daniel 2:44-45

> *"I kept looking in the night visions, And behold, with the clouds of heaven One like a Son of Man was coming, And He came up to the Ancient of Days And was presented before Him. (14) "And to Him was given dominion, Glory and a kingdom, That all the peoples, nations and men of every language Might*

> serve Him. His dominion is an everlasting dominion Which will not pass away; And His kingdom is one Which will not be destroyed."   Daniel 7:13-14

Zechariah 14:3-4 also speaks of the return of Jesus Christ to the earth as He comes to the battle of Armageddon.

> "Then the LORD will go forth and fight against those nations, as when He fights on a day of battle. (4) In that day His feet will stand on the Mount of Olives, which is in front of Jerusalem on the east; ..."
>   Zechariah 14:3-4

Job spoke prophetically of the 2nd coming of Jesus Christ.

> "As for me, I know that my Redeemer lives, And at the last He will take His stand on the earth."   Job 19:25

Isaiah also prophesied of the 2nd coming of Jesus Christ and of the fierce judgment He will bring upon the ungodly at that time.

> "For behold, the LORD will come in fire And His chariots like the whirlwind, To render His anger with fury, And His rebuke with flames of fire. (16) For the LORD will execute judgment by fire And by His sword on all flesh, And those slain by the LORD will be many."   Isaiah 66:15-16

There are other Old Testament passages that speak of, or allude to the 2nd coming of Jesus Christ. A much greater amount is said in the New Testament about the 2nd coming of Christ. The return of Jesus is one of the major themes proclaimed throughout the entirety of the New Testament. Twenty of the twenty six books of the New Testament have direct references to the 2nd coming of Christ with well over 50 passages addressing this important future event. I will certainly not include them all here but will focus on some that I believe are critical to our understanding of Christ's 2nd coming.

"But immediately after the tribulation of those days the sun will be darkened, and the moon will not give its light, and the stars will fall from the sky, and the powers of the heavens will be shaken. (30) "And then the sign of the Son of Man will appear in the sky, and then all the tribes of the earth will mourn, and they will see the Son of Man coming on the clouds of the sky with power and great glory. (31) "And He will send forth His angels with a great trumpet and they will gather together His elect from the four winds, from one end of the sky to the other."   Matthew 24:29-31

"Jesus *said to him, 'You have said it yourself; nevertheless I tell you, hereafter you will see the Son of Man sitting at the right hand of power, and coming on the clouds of heaven.'"
Matthew 26:64 (Quoting from Daniel 7:13-14)

"And as they were gazing intently into the sky while He was going, behold, two men in white clothing stood beside them. (11) They also said, "Men of Galilee, why do you stand looking into the sky? This Jesus, who has been taken up from you into heaven, will come in just the same way as you have watched Him go into heaven."   Acts 1:10-11

"... for I go to prepare a place for you. (3) "If I go and prepare a place for you, I will come again and receive you to Myself, that where I am, there you may be also."
John 14:2b-3

"For our citizenship is in heaven, from which also we eagerly wait for a Savior, the Lord Jesus Christ; (21)

who will transform the body of our humble state into conformity with the body of His glory, by the exertion of the power that He has even to subject all things to Himself."   *Philippians 3:20-21*

"For if we believe that Jesus died and rose again, even so God will bring with Him those who have fallen asleep in Jesus. (15) For this we say to you by the word of the Lord, that we who are alive and remain until the coming of the Lord, will not precede those who have fallen asleep. (16) For the Lord Himself will descend from heaven with a shout, with the voice of the archangel and with the trumpet of God, and the dead in Christ will rise first. (17) Then we who are alive and remain will be caught up together with them in the clouds to meet the Lord in the air, and so we shall always be with the Lord. (18) Therefore comfort one another with these words."
1 Thessalonians 4:14-18

"Then that lawless one will be revealed whom the Lord will slay with the breath of His mouth and bring to an end by the appearance of His coming;"
2 Thessalonians 2:8

"In the future there is laid up for me the crown of righteousness, which the Lord, the righteous Judge, will award to me on that day; and not only to me, but also to all who have loved His appearing."
2 Timothy 4:8

"Looking for the blessed hope and the appearing of the glory of our great God and Savior, Christ Jesus."
Titus 2:13

"So Christ also, having been offered once to bear the sins of many, will appear a second time for salvation without reference to sin, to those who eagerly await Him."   *Hebrews 9:28*

"Therefore be patient, brethren, until the coming of the Lord. The farmer waits for the precious produce of the soil, being patient about it, until it gets the early and late rains. (8) You too be patient; strengthen your hearts, for the coming of the Lord is near."
                                              James 5:7-8

"Therefore, prepare your minds for action, keep sober in spirit, fix your hope completely on the grace to be brought to you at the revelation of Jesus Christ."
                                                1 Peter 1:13

"Beloved, now we are children of God, and it has not appeared as yet what we will be. We know that when He appears, we will be like Him, because we will see Him just as He is."   *1 John 3:2*

"Behold, He is coming with the clouds, and every eye will see Him, even those who pierced Him; and all the tribes of the earth will mourn over Him. So it is to be. Amen."   *Revelation 1:7*

"And I saw heaven opened, and behold, a white horse, and He who sat on it is called Faithful and True, and in righteousness He judges and wages war. (12) His eyes are a flame of fire, and on His head are many diadems; and He has a name written on Him which no one knows except Himself. (13) He is clothed with a robe dipped in blood, and His name is called The Word of God. (14) And the armies which are in

heaven, clothed in fine linen, white and clean, were following Him on white horses. (15) From His mouth comes a sharp sword, so that with it He may strike down the nations, and He will rule them with a rod of iron; and He treads the wine press of the fierce wrath of God, the Almighty. (16) And on His robe and on His thigh He has a name written, "KING OF KINGS, AND LORD OF LORDS." Revelation 19:11-16

"He who testifies to these things says, "Yes, I am coming quickly." Amen. Come, Lord Jesus."
Revelation 22:20

Jesus Christ is coming again! When He comes He will bring judgment upon the world that will be following the antichrist and beast empire. When He comes He will destroy the antichrist and all of Satan's kingdom of darkness. When He comes He will bring salvation and reward to those who love Him and eagerly await His return. When He comes He will establish His kingdom of righteousness and He will reign forever and ever. When He comes He will bring peace on earth. When He comes we shall be like Him for we shall see Him as He is!

A part of Jesus' 2nd coming will be what we call the "Rapture" of the church, when the saints of God, both the living and dead, will be caught up together to meet the Lord in the clouds. What an awesome day that will be! The saints of God who are caught up to Jesus at the time of the rapture will return with Him to the battle of Armageddon, seen in Revelation 19. The timing of the rapture is a topic of much debate within the body of Christ. I am not addressing this debate within this book but have written extensively about it in my book, "Rapture First or Rapture Later: And Why It Matters". It is available on our website at localchurchapologetics.org. Though the timing of the rapture is in question, the surety of this catching away of Christians to be with Jesus forever is made very clear in Scriptures. (see Matthew 24:29-31; 1 Corinthians 15:21-23; 51-58; 1 Thessalonians 4:13-18 and 2 Thessalonians 2:1-3)

The Millennial Reign of Christ

We see a vivid picture of Jesus returning in glory and power to the earth in Revelation 19, defeating His enemies with the sword that comes out of His mouth. In Ephesians 6:17 we are told that "the sword of the Spirit" is "the word of God". Most likely, in Revelation 19 the sword that comes out of Jesus' mouth is probably a reference to His word. God created the heavens and the earth by His word in Genesis 1. John 1 says that Jesus is "the Word" and that all things were created by Him. Now, by His word Jesus destroys the works of darkness and brings peace on the earth.

In Revelation 20 we see that Satan is bound for 1,000 years and held captive in the abyss (or bottomless pit). Jesus then sets up His kingdom of righteousness and peace on the earth for 1,000 years.

> *"Then I saw thrones, and they sat on them, and judgment was given to them. And I saw the souls of those who had been beheaded because of their testimony of Jesus and because of the word of God, and those who had not worshiped the beast or his image, and had not received the mark on their forehead and on their hand; and they came to life and reigned with Christ for a thousand years."*
>
> *Revelation 20:4*

There are many who hold to an "A-Millennial" view, believing that Revelation 20 is simply symbolic of Christ reigning in the hearts of men and that there will be no literal 1,000 year reign of Christ on the earth. This seems untenable since there is nothing in the text to suggest that the 1,000 years that is spoken of numerous times in Revelation 20 is not literally 1,000 years.

There are also some who hold to a "Post-Millennial" view, believing that the church will establish the kingdom of God gradually on the earth, through the power of the Holy Spirit and that Jesus will then return to the earth after His church has established His righteous kingdom on earth. This also does not represent a straightforward reading of the text.

Revelation 20 describes a literal 1,000 years of Jesus reigning on the earth. Isaiah 11:1-10 appears to be describing this period of time when Christ reigns on earth bringing peace and righteousness. Within Isaiah's description he says it will be a time when the wolf will dwell with the lamb, the leopard will lie down with the young goat, the lion will eat straw like the ox, the nursing child will play by the hole of the cobra, and the earth will be full of the knowledge of the LORD, as the waters cover the sea.

After this 1,000 years we are told that Satan is released from his bondage in the abyss for a short time and that he again deceives the nations, or at least a substantial portion of them. (see Revelation 20:7-10) Satan and his armies are then defeated once and for all and the devil is thrown into the lake of fire to be tormented forever and ever. The next thing that is described in verses 11-15 is the white throne judgment when those who do not accept Christ and have rejected God's love and grace, will be thrown into the lake of fire.

The New Heaven and The New Earth

The last two chapters of the Bible in Revelation 21 and 22 describe the new heaven and new earth that seen as Christ says He is "making all things new". What a glorious description is found in Revelation 21:1-7!

> *"Then I saw a new heaven and a new earth; for the first heaven and the first earth passed away, and there is no longer any sea. (2) And I saw the holy city, new Jerusalem, coming down out of heaven from God, made ready as a bride adorned for her husband. (3)*

And I heard a loud voice from the throne, saying, "Behold, the tabernacle of God is among men, and He will dwell among them, and they shall be His people, and God Himself will be among them, (4) and He will wipe away every tear from their eyes; and there will no longer be any death; there will no longer be any mourning, or crying, or pain; the first things have passed away." (5) And He who sits on the throne said, "Behold, I am making all things new." And He *said, "Write, for these words are faithful and true." (6) Then He said to me, "It is done. I am the Alpha and the Omega, the beginning and the end. I will give to the one who thirsts from the spring of the water of life without cost. (7) "He who overcomes will inherit these things, and I will be his God and he will be My son."
Revelation 21:1-7

There are mysteries that still exist regarding the coming new heaven and new earth. For example, we see nations still existing outside the new Jerusalem with kings existing outside the city and bringing their glory into the city.

"The nations will walk by its light, and the kings of the earth will bring their glory into it." Revelation 21:24

One thing that is not a mystery is that those who are dwelling in the new Jerusalem will continually dwell in the tangible presence of God. His presence will perpetually light up the city.

"I saw no temple in it, for the Lord God the Almighty and the Lamb are its temple. (23) And the city has no need of the sun or of the moon to shine on it, for the glory of God has illumined it, and its lamp is the Lamb."
Revelation 21:22 23

Only those who have repented of their sins and trusted Jesus Christ as their Savior will be able to dwell in the new Jerusalem. That is those who have been cleansed from sin by trusting in the shed blood of Jesus Christ and whose names have been written in the Lamb's book of life.

> *"And nothing unclean, and no one who practices abomination and lying, shall ever come into it, but only those whose names are written in the Lamb's book of life."*   *Revelation 21:27*

> *"Blessed are those who wash their robes, so that they may have the right to the tree of life, and may enter by the gates into the city."*   *Revelation 22:14*

The only way to dwell with God for eternity is through faith in God's Son, Jesus Christ, Who died on the cross to pay the price for our sin and rose from the dead to give us eternal life. Jesus said in John 14:6, "I am the way, and the truth, and the life, no one comes to the Father but through me."

CHAPTER 24

All Things Together For Good

Whenever we look at the instability of the world we see around us today we are reminded of the prophetic descriptions of the world in the last days that we find in the Bible. Even though we know that the Bible foretold of these things, and even though we know that in the end Jesus Christ will return and establish His kingdom of righteousness and peace on the earth, we may ask why does God allow all of these things to come to pass? We may ask why doesn't the Lord just take believers in Christ home to be with Him and be done with this whole difficult and evil time?

One answer to these questions has to do with the heart of God for the lost. He is not willing that any should perish. He wants all to come to repentance and salvation. We will look at this answer in greater depth in the next chapter.

Another answer is found in a very familiar passage of Scripture found in Romans 8:28.

> *"And we know that God causes all things to work together for good to those who love God, to those who are called according to His purpose."*
>
> *Romans 8:28*

This verse has been a source of comfort and strength to many when life brings about circumstances and trials that we often do not understand. Refocusing on the truth that God has plans and purposes that He is accomplishing in our lives, even when our situation seems confusing and unexplainable, brings us hope and comfort. Faith in God's ability to work all things together for our good is the key to walking through difficult times without giving into despair. Our focus, when we consider this verse of Scripture, is almost always our personal lives and our particular circumstances.

Recently, while contemplating questions about why God's people are subject to living through the difficulties of the last days, this verse came to my mind and I saw it in a new light.

Just like we do not see the full picture of what God is accomplishing in our individual lives when we walk through times of difficulty and trial, we look at the world today and do not see the full picture of what God is accomplishing in His people.

Just as it is true that God is causing all things to work together for good in the individual lives of those who love Him and are called according to His purposes, it is also true that God is causing all things to work together for good corporately within His church in these last days.

Why does God give authority to the beast of Revelation 13 authority for 3 ½ years? Why does God allow great deception to fill the earth in the last days? Why are many Christians martyred in the last days according to the Bible? Why does God allow an ungodly global system to gain power in the last days and why does God allow a time to come about when no one can buy or sell unless they have the mark of the beast?

If you hold to a Pre-Trib view concerning the coming rapture of the church these questions may not seem as pressing, but the reality is, even if the Pre-Trib rapture position is correct, portions of these last days difficulties will be faced by believers in Christ before the rapture, and all of these things will be faced by some called "the saints" during the great tribulation. If you hold to a Post-Trib or Pre-Wrath view concerning the coming rapture of the church, these questions are hard to ignore. (See my book "Rapture First or Rapture Later And Why It Matters" for a detailed biblical study on the timing of the rapture and other issues of biblical eschatology.)

Here's the bottom line! If God has ordained that these things will take place in the last days, and if God has ordained that His people face many of the difficulties of the last days, then it is better for us to face these things than to not face these things! God causes all things to work together for good to those who love Him and are called according to His purpose! We can rest in this and face tomorrow with great assurance in our hearts!

In Romans 8, the next verse gives us great insight into what is meant by "for good" and "according to His purpose" in verse 28. This is true for our individual lives and it is true for the corporate body of Christ as well.

> *"For those whom He foreknew, He also predestined to become conformed to the image of His Son, so that He would be the firstborn among many brethren;"*
> *Romans 8:29*

Being conformed to the image of His Son! Becoming more like Jesus! This is God's purpose for you as a child of God and for me as a child of God! God, in His sovereignty, causes everything in our lives to work together to make you and I more like Jesus! This is "good" that goes beyond making us comfortable or happy in the moment. This is "good" that has eternal ramifications and benefit!

This is true for all of us in the body of Christ in regards to the things that will occur in the last days. It is for our good! Ephesians 5:27 says that Christ will present to Himself His church "in all her glory, having no spot or wrinkle or any such thing; but that she would be holy and blameless." The end times and all that occurs within the fulfillment of Bible prophecies will be used by God to purify the body of Christ!

In Daniel 12, the prophet Daniel speaks of the events of the last days including the abomination of desolation, times of distress, and persecution of believers. In verse 10 he gives insight into what will be accomplished during this time.

> "Many will be purged, purified and refined, but the wicked will act wickedly; and none of the wicked will understand, but those who have insight will understand."
> Daniel 12:10

There is no question that throughout history believers have been purged, purified and refined by times of difficulty, trial and persecution. Many passages of Scripture confirm this truth and declare that great reward comes to those who suffer with Christ. Here are two passages that remind us of this.

> "But to the degree that you share the sufferings of Christ, keep on rejoicing, so that also at the revelation of His glory you may rejoice with exultation."
> 1 Peter 4:13

> "The Spirit Himself testifies with our spirit that we are children of God, (17) and if children, heirs also, heirs of God and fellow heirs with Christ, if indeed we suffer with Him so that we may also be glorified with Him."
> Romans 8:16-17

God promises that He will never leave us nor forsake us! (Hebrews 13:5) As the last days unfold we may very well find His presence to be more sweet and restful than we have ever experienced before. We may find our intimacy with Christ growing sweeter, our faith growing stronger, and our character growing deeper as we experience these days! Most importantly, **we will become more like Jesus as God causes all things to work together for good in our lives!**

Israel, Globalism
and The 2nd Coming of Christ
(Understanding Current World Events
in Light of Bible Prophecy)

SECTION 3
How Should We Then Live?

CHAPTER 25

Ready For Eternity

As we have seen throughout the chapters of this book, Bible prophecy is being fulfilled at this time and the 2nd coming of Jesus Christ appears to be very near. So the question for each of us becomes, "how should we then live"?

The answer to this question undoubtedly begins with making sure that we are ready to face eternity beyond this life! To die, unprepared for eternity is the greatest error any person can make!

The Bible states clearly the reason that Jesus has not yet returned.

> *"The Lord is not slow about His promise, as some count slowness, but **is patient toward you, not wishing for any to perish but for all to come to repentance.**"*   2 Peter 3:9

God does not want anyone to perish! God wants everyone to repent of their sins and put their trust in His Son, Jesus Christ for salvation!

The message of the entire Bible revolves around God's love for each of us and His plan of redemption for mankind! At the very beginning of the Bible we see that God created man in His own image and likeness! God gave man authority and dominion over all the earth and the created things on the earth. God clearly created man unique with the purpose of being His sons and daughters for eternity. Psalm 139 speaks of this truth as well.

"For You formed my inward parts; You wove me in my mother's womb. (14) I will give thanks to You, for I am fearfully and wonderfully made; Wonderful are Your works, And my soul knows it very well. (15) My frame was not hidden from You, When I was made in secret, And skillfully wrought in the depths of the earth; (16) Your eyes have seen my unformed substance; And in Your book were all written The days that were ordained for me, When as yet there was not one of them. (17) How precious also are Your thoughts to me, O God! How vast is the sum of them!" Psalm 139:13-17

Each of us is created by God and known by God! We are a unique person, with DNA different from any other person. We are known by God as a unique person that no one else can replace. He loves each of us as an individual and has a purpose for us both in this life and in eternity!

Though each of us are created by God we have been separated from God by our sin. We see how this happened to Adam and Eve in Genesis 3. We see this is true for all of us in Romans 3.

"As it is written, "There is none righteous, not even one;" (12) All have turned aside, together they have become useless; there is none who does good, there is not even one." Romans 3:10, 12

"For all have sinned and fall short of the glory of God," Romans 3:23

Romans 3:20 also makes it clear that none of us can be saved by our own good works or by attempting to fulfill the law of God. We may measure up in comparison to other people, but we could never measure up to the holiness of God by our own goodness and good works. The law was not given to save us but rather to reveal our sin to us and our desperate need for a Savior!

> *"Because by the works of the Law no flesh will be justified in His sight; for through the Law comes the knowledge of sin."* Romans 3:20

The good news, the greatest news in all of history, is that God still loves us and He made a way to save us from our sin. He made a way so that we can receive the gift of eternal life from Him and spend eternity with Him! God made a way for us to be saved by sending His Son, Jesus Christ to die on the cross for our sin! Jesus took our punishment and paid the price for our sin as He suffered on the cross for us! He defeated death for us through His resurrection from the dead so that we can now have eternal life through faith in Him!

> *"For God so loved the world, that He gave His only begotten Son, that whoever believes in Him shall not perish, but have eternal life."* John 3:16

> *"All of us like sheep have gone astray, Each of us has turned to his own way; But the LORD has caused the iniquity of us all To fall on Him."* Isaiah 53:6

> *"For Christ also died for sins once for all, the just for the unjust, so that He might bring us to God, having been put to death in the flesh, but made alive in the spirit;"* 1 Peter 3:18

To be forgiven of our sin, saved from the condemnation that sin brings, and to receive the free gift of eternal life, we must turn away from our sin and turn in faith to Jesus, accepting Him into our life by faith as our Savior and as our Lord!

> *"For by grace you have been saved through faith; and that not of yourselves, it is the gift of God; (9) not as a result of works, so that no one may boast."*
> Ephesians 2:8-9

> *"They said, 'Believe in the Lord Jesus, and you will be saved, ...'"*   *Acts 16:31*

> *"That if you confess with your mouth Jesus as Lord, and believe in your heart that God raised Him from the dead, you will be saved; (10) for with the heart a person believes, resulting in righteousness, and with the mouth he confesses, resulting in salvation."*
> *Romans 10:9-10*

The most important response to realizing that you are living in the last days is to prepare your heart for eternity! Apart from faith in Jesus Christ no one will be saved and spend eternity with God! Salvation cannot be earned! It is a free gift from a loving God!

> *"For the wages of sin is death, but the free gift of God is eternal life in Christ Jesus our Lord."*   *Romans 6:23*

> *"But God demonstrates His own love toward us, in that while we were yet sinners, Christ died for us."*
> *Romans 5:8*

> *"Jesus *said to him, 'I am the way, and the truth, and the life; no one comes to the Father but through Me.'"*
> *John 14:6*

Some complain and say it is not right for Jesus to say that He is the only way of salvation. They want to cling to the idea that there are many paths to salvation and to God. Jesus stated clearly that He is the only way to God!

Think about it for a moment. If there are many paths to God then at some point there must have been a conversation between God the Father and Jesus, God the Son that sounded something like this.

"Hey Son, I've been thinking about man and his sin problem

that separates him from us. I know there are many ways that a person can be forgiven of their sin and spend eternity with us. Still, I was thinking it might be good for you to become a man, let them beat you, scourge you, tear your flesh apart, put a crown of thorns on your head, drive nails in your hands and feet, spit on you, mock you and crucify you on a cross to take the punishment for all of their sin. That way there would be one more way for people to be saved. You know, kind of like going to the ice cream shop and picking out your favorite flavor. They would have another flavor choice in picking out their favorite plan of salvation. What do you think?"

That doesn't make sense does it! God would never have given His Son for us if there was another way. If we could save ourselves in any other way, Jesus would not have left heaven and experienced a horrible death on our behalf to save us. He came to save us because there is no other way!

Jesus died a brutal death on the cross, taking our sin upon Himself to make a way for us to be redeemed and brought back to God our Creator. Through faith in Jesus Christ we can become children of God!

> *"But as many as received Him, to them He gave the right to become children of God, even to those who believe in His name,"* John 1:12

The same Bible that prophesied all the things we see happening in the world today is the same Bible that reveals this wonderful plan of salvation that God has brought to us through His Son Jesus! This plan is revealed from Genesis in the Old Testament, all the way through to Revelation in the New Testament!

Hundreds of prophecies in the Old Testament about the coming Messiah (the anointed one) were fulfilled in the person of Jesus Christ. He changed the world so much that our calendars date back to the time of His birth! All of history is divided into the years before He came and the years after He came!

In my book "Faith & Reason Made Simple" I speak of the areas of evidence which confirm that God is our Creator, the Bible is God's Word, and Jesus is Who the Bible says He is! The evidence is overwhelming for anyone willing to look at it with an open mind and heart! Salvation through faith in Christ is factual and real!

The question really comes down to the decision each of us make about Who Jesus is and whether or not we will turn away from our sin and turn in faith to Jesus as our Lord and Savior.

You can know that you have the gift of eternal life and that you will spend eternity with God when you die! You can know this! Eternal life will not come by your good works or by you being good enough on your own. It is through faith in Jesus Christ that you can know assuredly that you are saved and have the gift of eternal life!

This is the most important issue for every person's life! Where will you spend eternity? If you are ready to turn from your sin, turn from your trust in self, and turn in faith to Jesus, you can pray the prayer listed here, or a similar prayer. If you pray sincerely God will hear you, forgive you, and give you the gift of eternal life.

Dear Jesus, I know that I have sinned. I ask you to forgive me of all my sins. I believe that you took the punishment for my sin upon yourself as you suffered that horrible death for me on the cross. I turn away from sin and turn to you. I invite you to come into my life. I ask you now to be my Savior and the Lord of my life. I confess with my mouth that you are Lord! Please give me the gift of eternal life. I give you all of my life. Please cleanse me and make me your child for eternity. Thank you so much! I love you Jesus! Amen!

Praise God! If you just prayed that prayer and invited Jesus Christ into your life I welcome you to the family of God! I encourage you to get involved in a church that preaches the Bible, get baptized in water to express your faith in Christ publicly, and begin reading your Bible and praying each day! God bless you!

CHAPTER 26

Awake, Alert and Sober Minded

Maybe the most often cited directive in Scripture for believers living in the last days is the directive to "be awake and to be sober minded." It is seen in many passages dealing with the last days.

Jesus spoke about this a number of times both directly and through parables as a part of what we call "The Olivet Discourse", found in Matthew 24-25, Mark 13 & Luke 21.

> *"Therefore **be on the alert**, for you do not know which day your Lord is coming. (43) "But be sure of this, that if the head of the house had known at what time of the night the thief was coming, he would have been on the alert and would not have allowed his house to be broken into. (44) "For this reason **you also must be ready**; for the Son of Man is coming at an hour when you do not think He will." Matthew 24:42-44*

During this same Olivet Discourse, Jesus tells the parable of the ten virgins in Matthew 25:1-13. The meaning of this parable is clear as it is stated in verse 13.

> *"**Be on the alert** then, for you do not know the day nor the hour." Matthew 25:13*

In Mark's gospel, the Olivet Discourse is recorded in chapter 13 and it includes these instructions.

> **"Take heed, keep on the alert**; for you do not know when the appointed time will come. (34) "It is like a man away on a journey, who upon leaving his house and putting his slaves in charge, assigning to each one his task, also commanded the doorkeeper to stay on the alert. (35) "**Therefore, be on the alert**--for you do not know when the master of the house is coming, whether in the evening, at midnight, or when the rooster crows, or in the morning-- (36) in case he should come suddenly and find you asleep. (37) **"What I say to you I say to all, 'Be on the alert!'"**
> Mark 13:33-37

This consistent directive to be alert and to be ready for the coming of Christ is not limited to the gospels. Other passages in the New Testament also include this directive.

> "Now as to the times and the epochs, brethren, you have no need of anything to be written to you. (2) For you yourselves know full well that the day of the Lord will come just like a thief in the night. (3) While they are saying, "Peace and safety!" Then destruction will come upon them suddenly like labor pains upon a woman with child, and they will not escape. (4) **But you, brethren, are not in darkness, that the day would overtake you like a thief; (5) for you are all sons of light and sons of day. We are not of night nor of darkness; (6) so then let us not sleep as others do, but let us be alert and sober.** (7) For those who sleep do their sleeping at night, and those who get drunk get drunk at night. (8) **But since we are of the day, let us be sober,** having put on the breastplate of faith and love, and as a helmet, the hope of salvation."
> 1 Thessalonians 5:1-8

In this passage we are told that "the day of the Lord" will come as a thief in the night. Though many books and movies have misinterpreted this passage as "the rapture" will come as a thief in the night, it is actually "the day of the Lord" that will come like a thief. The world will be spiritually asleep, crying peace and safety, when sudden destruction will come upon them as Jesus returns and the judgment of God is poured out upon a sinful world.

There is a sharp contrast drawn in this passage between those in darkness and those who are sons of light or sons of day. Those who are in Christ and are not of the darkness are directed to be sober and alert as the day of the Lord draws near. Those who are in Christ will be able to recognize that the judgment of God is coming and will be able to stay awake and alert spiritually.

> "Therefore, **prepare your minds for action, keep sober in spirit**, fix your hope completely on the grace to be brought to you at the revelation of Jesus Christ."
> 1 Peter 1:13

> "The end of all things is near; therefore, **be of sound judgment and sober spirit** for the purpose of prayer."
> 1 Peter 4:7

> "Behold, I am coming like a thief. Blessed is the one who **stays awake and keeps his clothes**, so that he will not walk about naked and men will not see his shame." Revelation 16:15

Staying awake, alert and sober minded involves keeping your mind and spirit in touch with the Holy Spirit of God and listening to His promptings and instructions. The Holy Spirit lives within us and is our teacher! If we listen to Him He will give us the understanding we need about the times we are living in. He will also guide us in making decisions. Those who are caught up in this world and out of touch with God's Word and God's Spirit, are asleep spiritually and in a drunken stupor spiritually. 1 Peter 4:7 tells us that being of sound judgment and sober spirit is for the purpose of prayer. Being men and women of prayer in the last days is critical!

Ephesians 5 does not specifically address the end times but it does give instructions consistent with the instructions in the end times passages we have looked at. Verse 8 says, "For you were formerly darkness, but now you are Light in the Lord; walk as children of Light." The chapter speaks of not participating in the deeds of darkness in this world. Then it gives these instructions.

> *"For this reason it says, "Awake, sleeper, And arise from the dead, And Christ will shine on you." (15) Therefore be careful how you walk, not as unwise men but as wise, (16) making the most of your time, because the days are evil."*   *Ephesians 5:14-16*

As the 2nd coming of Christ approaches believers in Christ must be awake, alert and sober minded!

CHAPTER 27

Attached To the Heart of God

This may be the most important chapter of the entire book!

What should our heart desires look like in the last days? What should our attitude be toward the world? What should our priorities and actions reveal?

Studying end times issues can actually be detrimental if the result is believers taking up attitudes and priorities that are contrary to the heart of God!

In this chapter I want to look at the heart of God and see that the Bible has revealed to us what our focus should be in the last days as we see the 2nd coming of Christ approaching. If we are among those who will be alive and remain when He comes again, we should recognize the value of this privilege God has entrusted to us. We should make sure that we are found serving Christ faithfully when He comes again!

Let me begin this search for the right heart attitude in the last days by describing two heart attitudes that are quite prevalent, and are not in line with the heart of God.

The Bunker Mentality

The first is the bunker mentality. This heart attitude recognizes that very difficult times are coming upon all those who live upon the earth. Therefore, it responds by proposing to accumulate plenty of food, guns and ammo to weather the storm and make it safely until Jesus comes again. Of course this may look a bit different in different people and may be embraced in varying measures, especially the guns part, but the essence is that of a bunker mentality.

This heart attitude involves taking your mind off of the great commission that Jesus has given us and focusing on self preservation. Some have become consumed with this heart attitude. Beware! This is not in line with the heart of God! At its core, this heart attitude is selfish, unloving and uncaring. This heart attitude has lost sight of a lost world that needs Jesus!

Certainly, concern for providing for one's family in difficult times is a good thing. That would include preparing for a bad storm or preparing for difficult times of persecution and trial. Using wisdom in having some extra food on hand if possible, in case of an emergency is prudent. These concerns and preparations must be tempered though! If they begin to dominate a person's priorities they are not in balance and are not biblical. When our concerns for self preservation separate us from the heart of God, we have moved from that which is prudent to that which is fleshly and out of God's will for His people.

The Escape Mentality

The second heart attitude I want to address involves an "escape mentality". In this case a believer determines to just look for the rapture of the church as an escape from this world without concern for those left behind on the earth. I believe that dogmatic "Pre-Trib" rapture teaching can contribute to this heart attitude.

A heart that is alert and ready for the coming of Jesus, and a heart that anxiously awaiting the return of the Savior is a good thing and a biblical thing. Still, it is not a good thing when we begin to focus only on wanting to get out of here to avoid hardship. This is not in line with the heart of God and is not biblical.

Aren't you glad that Jesus wasn't looking for an escape when it came time for Him to suffer and die on our behalf? He could have escaped all of it. Notice what He said to His disciples in the garden of Gethsemane when the soldiers came to take Him captive.

> *"Or do you think that I cannot appeal to My Father, and He will at once put at My disposal more than twelve legions of angels?"*   Matthew 26:53

He could have escaped but He chose to be concerned about our salvation, rather than His own comforts. He did this because He had His mind set on the goal, our salvation.

> *"Fixing our eyes on Jesus, the author and perfecter of faith, **who for the joy set before Him endured the cross**, despising the shame, and has sat down at the right hand of the throne of God."*   Hebrews 12:2

Looking forward to the rapture, whether it happens before, during, or after the great tribulation period is a normal and good thing. If we lose sight of our calling and of God's heart for the lost because of our focus on the rapture, that is when an "escape mentality" becomes a problem. We don't know when we will be raptured and we don't know what we may or may not face. We do know that we must stay connected to the heart of God! This is what will ensure us facing the last days properly!

God's Heart for the Lost

Perhaps the greatest theme in all the Bible is the love of God for lost souls. God's grace and mercy are unfathomable. An entire chapter is dedicated to this theme. In Luke 15 Jesus told three separate parables to emphasize this truth. The chapter begins with Jesus spending time teaching tax collectors and sinners. When criticized for this He told these three parables. In Luke 15:3-7 he tells the parable of the shepherd who leaves the ninety nine sheep, safe in the fold, to search and find the one lost sheep. In Luke 15:7 He concludes this parable by saying, *"I tell you that in the same way, there will be more joy in heaven over one sinner who repents than over ninety-nine righteous persons who need no repentance."*

In Luke 15:8-10 He tells the parable of the lost coin and concludes it in verse 10 by saying, *"In the same way, I tell you, there is joy in the presence of the angels of God over one sinner who repents."*

Finally, He tells the parable of the prodigal son in Luke 15:11-32 which clearly shows the deep and abiding love in the heart of God the Father for lost souls. Jesus concludes this parable in verse 32 by saying, *"But we had to celebrate and rejoice, for this brother of yours was dead and has begun to live, and was lost and has been found."*

God's loving heart toward the lost is seen in the most famous of all Bible verses.

> *"For God so loved the world, that He gave His only begotten Son, that whoever believes in Him shall not perish, but have eternal life."*   John 3:16

This wonderful truth is seen in many other passages including these examples.

> *"But God demonstrates His own love toward us, in that while we were yet sinners, Christ died for us."*
> Romans 5:8

> *"But God, being rich in mercy, because of His great love with which He loved us, (5) even when we were dead in our transgressions, made us alive together with Christ (by grace you have been saved),"*
> Ephesians 2:4-5

> *"In this is love, not that we loved God, but that He loved us and sent His Son to be the propitiation for our sins. (11) Beloved, if God so loved us, we also ought to love one another."*   1 John 4:10-11

There is also a passage that specifically connects God's loving heart for the lost with understanding about the timing of Christ's return. 2 Peter 3 deals with the 2nd coming of Jesus Christ and the day of the Lord in which the judgment of God will come upon this sinful world. In verse 4 we are told that mockers will come and mockingly ask, "where is the promise of His coming?" The response to this question is found in verse 9.

> *"The Lord is not slow about His promise, as some count slowness, but is patient toward you, not wishing for any to perish but for all to come to repentance."*
> 2 Peter 3:9

So it is God's desire for all to be saved that is the reason that Jesus Christ has not already come again. God is patient! God loves the lost! Consistent with this truth is the statement that Jesus made concerning the last days in Matthew 24:14.

> *"This gospel of the kingdom shall be preached in the whole world as a testimony to all the nations, and then the end will come."* Matthew 24:14

Clearly, the determining factor in the timing of the 2nd coming of Jesus Christ is God's great love for the lost and His patient waiting for their repentance unto salvation. As we saw in a previous chapter, He also says that He will pour out His Spirit and show signs and wonders in the heavens and on earth before the great and glorious day of the Lord, and everyone who calls upon the name of the Lord shall be saved! (Acts 2:17-21)

With these things in mind let's return to the thought of being attached to the heart of God in the last days. It is absolutely clear in Scripture that the Lord has ordained that those who come to know Jesus Christ as their Savior also come to take up His mission to reach the lost with the good news of salvation. In 2 Corinthians 5 believers are described as ambassadors of Christ.

> *"Therefore if anyone is in Christ, he is a new creature; the old things passed away; behold, new things have come. (18) Now all these things are from God, who reconciled us to Himself through Christ and **gave us the ministry of reconciliation**, (19) namely, that God was in Christ reconciling the world to Himself, not counting their trespasses against them, and **He has committed to us the word of reconciliation. (20) Therefore, we are ambassadors for Christ, as though God were making an appeal through us; we beg you on behalf of Christ, be reconciled to God."***
>
> 2 Corinthians 5:17-20

Verse 17 speaks of the wonderful truth that in Christ we are a new creature! Verse 18-20 explains that being a new creature in Christ involves stepping into His mission, His purposes, and His heart. He has given to us the ministry of reconciliation! He has committed to us the word of reconciliation! God is making His appeal to the lost to be reconciled to Him, through us! We are ambassadors for Christ! An ambassador is someone who is sent to a foreign land to represent the leader or ruler of their homeland within that foreign land. An ambassador is to do their best to act and speak on behalf of the leader of their homeland so that their being there is as though the leader were actually there in person. Think about what this means!

Would it not seem strange if the very ones who have been given the ministry and word of reconciliation, the very ones who are making an appeal to the lost on behalf of God, separated themselves from the task before it is complete?

Consider also what Jesus said in Luke 6:40.

> *"A pupil is not above his teacher; but everyone, after he has been fully trained, will be like his teacher."*
>
> Luke 6:40

If we are truly disciples of Jesus Christ we will become like Him. His heart is to reach the lost! He is not consumed with self preservation or with escaping personal suffering. He gave His all to reach the lost and to save them. As disciples of Christ, our heart in the last days must not turn away from His heart!

In Acts 1:8-11 we read Jesus' last words to His disciples before He ascended into heaven. They asked Him if it was at this time that He was going to restore the kingdom to Israel. He tells them that it is not for them to know the timing of these things. Then He gives them instructions to guide them, and all believers, until He comes again. We also see that as He leaves two angels appear to the disciples and speak to them. Adding their words to what Jesus had just told the disciples reveals a powerful message.

> *"But you will receive power when the Holy Spirit has come upon you; and you shall be My witnesses both in Jerusalem, and in all Judea and Samaria, and even to the remotest part of the earth." ... (11) They also said, "Men of Galilee, why do you stand looking into the sky? This Jesus, who has been taken up from you into heaven, will come in just the same way as you have watched Him go into heaven."* Acts 1:8, 11

The message of Jesus to His disciples then, which applies to we who are His disciples today, is that we are not to be wrapped up in the timing of the establishment of His eternal kingdom, but we are to receive power when the Holy Spirit comes upon us, and we are to be His witnesses throughout the world! The angels then ask the disciples why they are gazing up into the sky. It seems as though the angels are saying here, Jesus will return in His perfect timing just as He has left, but you need to go ahead and get busy pursuing what He has instructed you to do. Receive power and be witnesses throughout the world! These instructions remain until He comes again! We need to stay connected to His heart and His mission!

The Parable of the Talents and The Final Judgment

In Matthew 25 Jesus teaches us important things we need to understand about living in the last days. The context of these passages is the 2nd coming of Christ seen in Matthew 24:27-31. In Matthew 25:14-30 Jesus tells the parable of the talents. The lesson of this parable is clear. God has given each of us resources and giftings to use to accomplish His purposes until Jesus returns. When Jesus returns we will give an account for how we used those resources and giftings. Did we help to expand the kingdom of God by reaching people with the good news of Jesus' salvation or did we focus on self preservation and hide our resources and giftings?

Then in Matthew 25:31-46 Jesus speaks of the final judgment. In this passage He speaks of the nations, (which would seem to apply to individuals as well) who respond to the needs of people around them, and the nations, (which would seem to apply to individuals as well) who do not respond to the needs of people around them. "I was hungry, and you gave Me something to eat; I was thirsty, and you gave Me something to drink; I was a stranger, and you invited Me in; naked, and you clothed Me; I was sick, and you visited Me; I was in prison, and you came to Me." Then the powerful explanation of what this means is given. "When you did it to the least of these my brethren you did it unto me!"

How we should live in the last days is made very clear in the Bible! We must stay connected to the heart of God! We must love the lost! We must do our part to share the gospel with a lost world! We must be His ambassadors and His witnesses! We must show His love and compassion to people around us in need! He is not willing that any should perish but that all would come unto repentance! We must not allow ourselves to be disconnected from His heart and mission!

Keep On Loving! (Keep the Fire Burning!)

One of the warnings that Jesus gave about the last days in Matthew 24 has penetrated my mind and heart in a substantial way. I have considered it many times over the past few years. Whenever I think about it and remind myself to respond to it, I immediately feel a difference in my heart attitude toward life and toward other people. In Matthew 24:12 Jesus gave this warning about the last days.

"Because lawlessness is increased, most people's love will grow cold." Matthew 24:12

Lawlessness has certainly increased in the world in the past 50 years. The increase of immorality is all around us. It seems as though mankind continues to move further and further from the fear of the Lord and a reverence for His laws and commandments. Unbelievably, we have even reached a point where people are openly calling for lawlessness, encouraging the removal of funds for law enforcement officers. The warning Jesus gives in Matthew 24:12 is twofold. First of all, lawlessness will increase. Secondly, most people's love will grow cold! It is the second part of Jesus' warning that I want to consider here.

I believe that the warning that "most people's love will grow cold" applies to people who are practicing lawlessness, but also applies to people who are perplexed and angered by the increase of lawlessness all around them.

Over the past few years I have often considered these warnings of Jesus and prayed that the Lord would help me to continue to love people. I have reminded myself in those moments that this is God's will, for me to love people! It has been in these moments, after praying this prayer, that I would immediately feel a difference in my attitude toward life and toward others.

It is amazing how easy it is to forget that we are called to love people! We are called not to just love our family and friends. We are called to love our enemies! We are called to love people who are living in lawlessness and who are promoting things we strongly disagree with. The greatest of all the commandments is to love God with all of your heart, your soul and your mind, and to love your neighbor as yourself! (Matthew 22:37-39)

1 Peter 4:7-8 reminds us of the need to stay fervent in our love for one another in the last days.

> *"The end of all things is near; therefore, be of sound judgment and sober spirit for the purpose of prayer. (8) Above all, keep fervent in your love for one another, because love covers a multitude of sins."*
> *1 Peter 4:7-8*

Romans 13:8 says, *"Owe nothing to anyone except to love one another; for he who loves his neighbor has fulfilled the law."* 1 Corinthians 13 gives a detailed explanation of the character of love, including the fact that love is patient and kind, not selfish and not offended. Love bears all things, believes all things, hopes all things, and endures all things! Love never fails!

You can't walk in love and walk in bitterness! You can't walk in love and walk in self preservation mode! You can't walk in love and be more concerned about escaping than seeing others saved from eternal damnation!

Praying for protection and provision is biblical but not to the extent of ceasing to be concerned for others. What is God's plan for believers in the last days? His plan is for believers to stay connected to His heart! His heart is for believers to love one another and love the lost that He so desperately loves and wants to save!

CHAPTER 28

Be Heavenly Minded!

In the last chapter we focused on what our heart attitude should be in the last days in regard to living this life, attached to the heart of God. This chapter deals with another aspect of a proper mindset in the last days. This mindset does not contradict what we discussed in the last chapter. Rather, it compliments and adds to what we discussed in the last chapter.

Have you ever heard a statement that sounds something like, "He is too heavenly minded to be of any earthly good." I think statements like this are not grounded in biblical truth. Actually the Bible says that we should be heavenly minded.

In the last chapter we referred to Hebrews 12:2 which says this about Jesus. "Who for the joy set before Him endured the cross, despising the shame, and has sat down at the right hand of the throne of God." Notice that Jesus looked to future joy and by doing so gained the strength He needed to complete the earthly task He was to fulfill. He then took His place at the right hand of the Father, to continue to intercede for those He died for on the cross. In this we understand that having a view of the future beyond this life can strengthen us to fulfill God's plans for us in this life. Being heavenly minded is what gives us the strength to continue to love others and serve as Christ's ambassadors in this life!

Notice what we are told in the following passages.

> "Therefore if you have been raised up with Christ, **keep seeking the things above**, where Christ is, seated at the right hand of God. (2) **Set your mind on**

the things above, *not on the things that are on earth. (3) For you have died and your life is hidden with Christ in God. (4)* ***When Christ, who is our life, is revealed, then you also will be revealed with Him in glory."*** *Colossians 3:1-4*

"Therefore, prepare your minds for action, keep sober in spirit, ***fix your hope completely on the grace to be brought to you at the revelation of Jesus Christ."***
1 Peter 1:13

*"****Looking for*** *the blessed hope and the appearing of the glory of our great God and Savior, Christ Jesus,"*
Titus 2:13

"For our citizenship is in heaven, from which also ***we eagerly wait for a Savior****, the Lord Jesus Christ; (21) who will transform the body of our humble state into conformity with the body of His glory, by the exertion of the power that He has even to subject all things to Himself."* *Philippians 3:20-21*

Just as Jesus fulfilled His call to endure the cross, though He despised the shame of it, by focusing on the joy set before Him, we should diligently fulfill our call to love people and share the gospel of Jesus to others, by keeping our heavenly future with Christ in view. Being heavenly minded and committed to the work at hand is much different than being focused on escaping hardship to the point of turning away from the call to love others and faithfully do what we can to reach the lost with the message of God's love and salvation. When trials and persecution come for the sake of the gospel, remembering God's promises for our future can give us courage and strength to continue loving and serving faithfully. Being heavenly minded in the last days is a very good thing!

CHAPTER 29

Leaning Into the Grace of God

I think that if we are completely honest, the thought of living through all the things described in the Bible concerning the last days, scares us at least a little, if not a lot. It is important that we face those fears and allow faith to overcome them, so that we do not sin by allowing fear to dictate our words, decisions and actions, rather than faith in Christ!

Throughout this book I have avoided getting into a discussion about when the rapture will take place in relation to the great tribulation. This is mostly true because I focused on this extensively in my last book. Also, the timing of the rapture is not a determining factor for most of the things that this book deals with. Fulfilled Bible prophecy concerning what the world will look like in the days leading up to the 2nd coming of Jesus is easy to see in the world today and is not dependent upon the timing of the rapture. Our responses and priorities as believers in the last days are not dependent upon the timing of the rapture.

I will state one thing emphatically here. I believe that it is critical for believers to prepare their heart for both possibilities! We should be prepared to be raptured at any time. We should also be ready to face the things the Bible describes concerning the great tribulation, including the persecutions and martyrdom that is described in the book of Revelation and elsewhere, that will come upon "the saints".

With this in mind I ask that you read this chapter with the mindset that we are "the saints" that the Bible says will endure with perseverance the great tribulation that Jesus spoke of in Matthew 24 and the difficulties that the book of Revelation speaks of, especially in Revelation 13. If we are raptured before many of those things come about, and another group of "saints" endure those times, we still need to realize that the Bible talks about "the beginning of birth pangs". A "Pre-Trib" rapture does not ensure believers from enduring any hatred by the world or persecution from the spirit of antichrist that is already in the world. The reality is, believers in many parts of the world, if not most parts of the world, are already facing this hatred and these afflictions.

I believe that ignoring the changes taking place in the world and the increasing hostility toward the things of God is a mistake and is dangerous. Any belief or doctrine that results in ignoring the consistent directive of Scripture to be awake, alert and sober minded is misguided.

With these thoughts as a backdrop, before ending this book I want to share information with you that I consider to be critical for believers living at this time in history.

Leaning Into the Grace of God

The grace of God involves one of the major themes of the Bible. "Grace" means "unmerited favor" or "undeserved favor". It speaks of God giving us things that we do not deserve, while "mercy" speaks of God not giving us things that we do deserve like judgment and punishment.

When we think about grace, we tend to think about salvation, and we ought to do so. We receive salvation from God by grace. We have not earned it and we do not deserve it.

> ***"For by grace you have been saved through faith;***
> *and that not of yourselves, it is the gift of God; (9) not*
> *as a result of works, so that no one may boast."*
> Ephesians 2:8-9

*"For all have sinned and fall short of the glory of God, (24) **being justified as a gift by His grace** through the redemption which is in Christ Jesus;"* Romans 3:23-24

Salvation comes to us by God's grace. It is important for us to realize though that God's grace that He gives to us freely is not limited to salvation by grace. We receive many other things from God by grace! Actually, we haven't earned anything that we receive from God. Everything we receive from God is by His grace!

In a discipleship book that our ministry has published entitled "Faith & Reason Discipleship" there is a lesson that deals with salvation by grace. Attached to that lesson is a supplement page listing verses throughout the New Testament that speak of things that we have received by God's grace. The list reveals over 30 different things that we as believers have received by God's grace.

Actually, every moment of our life we are experiencing God's grace. Life is a miracle from God! Each heartbeat directed by a brain signal, each time we swallow successfully because of a flap called the epiglottis that protects our windpipe, each second that involves another batch of multiple trillions of newly produced proteins within our body, we are experiencing the grace of God without our notice!

God's grace is available to us for provision, protection, power, purpose, and more in the last days. We need to learn to lean into His grace!

We have grown so accustomed to having everything in life covered and protected, we have grown callus to the fact that we can trust God for the things we need. Most of us have life insurance, health insurance, car insurance, house insurance, workman's compensation insurance, retirement funds, etc. With all of this protection we tend to not be conscious of the fact that God is watching over each of us and providing for us every moment of our life. These things are not evil and God uses them to provide for us and protect us, but if they are removed from us, He is still there to protect us and provide for us!

Leaning Into the Grace of God for Provision

Jesus spoke of our need to consider God's provisions during the Sermon on the Mount in Matthew 6:25-33. He said, "do not be worried about your life, as to what you will eat or what you will drink; nor for your body, as to what you will put on." He went on to remind us that God takes care of every little bird and every flower of the field. He also reminds us that our Father in heaven is aware of our needs and we are of more value to Him than birds or flowers.

In the book of Exodus we read of the children of Israel's 40 year journey through the wilderness before they entered the promised land. We are told that God provided manna each morning for them to eat, quail each evening for them to eat, and water from a rock for them to drink. This of course was for a group that was probably around 2 million in size. We are also told that God caused their clothes to not wear out for 40 years and their sandals to not wear out for 40 years, all while traveling through a desert. Wow, now that is provision! These things are written to us for more than just historical value. These things are also written to us to inform us that God is very capable of providing for us in these days, during difficult times that appear to be approaching. If the mark of the beast comes, and we as believers are not able to buy or sell, God is more than capable of providing for us supernaturally!

Think also of the feeding of the 5,000 with 5 barley loaves and 2 fish. Matthew 14:21 says that the 5,000 were men, and that this number did not include the women and children who were there. So actually it was probably more like 20,000 who were fed.

In Matthew 17 Peter is asked if Jesus pays a certain tax. When Peter asks Jesus about it, Jesus tells Peter to go to the sea, throw in a hook, catch a fish, and look into the mouth of the first fish he catches. Inside the mouth of the fish there was a coin valued at the proper amount to cover the tax in question for both Jesus and Peter. Why is this story in the Bible? I believe it is another example for us to learn from, revealing that God is our supernatural provider.

We need to learn to lean into God's grace for provision! We may experience a shift in how provision comes to us. If our means of provisions that we have experienced are taken from us, God will still be there!

Leaning Into the Grace of God for Protection

Jesus protected His disciples from a violent storm at sea more than once. He spoke to the winds and waves and they obeyed Him.

In 2 Chronicles 20 King Jehoshaphat and the nation of Israel were threatened by a vast army described as a "great multitude". After praying, God tells them that He will fight this battle for them. They send the singers and worshippers ahead of their army as they head out to face this great multitude. God causes the enemy to kill one another and Israel is protected without them fighting the battle.

In 1 Samuel 17 we read of God anointing David to kill a lion and a bear with his hands, and Goliath the giant with a sling.

The book of Daniel is the most prophetic book related to the end times of any Old Testament book. I do not believe that it is a coincidence that the book is divided evenly. The last 6 chapters are filled with prophecies concerning what will take place in the last days. The first 6 chapters though are filled with historical accounts of God's miraculous protection shown multiple times to His servants during a time when their nation had conquered and taken captive. What a reminder that even when ungodly pagan rulers ascend to power, God is able to protect His people supernaturally and bring attention to His great power!

In chapter 1 Daniel, Shadrach, Meshach and Abed-nego are given permission by a pagan captain to eat only the food allowed within God's law, as opposed to the king's appointed food. After a test period it is clear to the captain that they are stronger and healthier than others and they are able to continue to obey God's law in their dietary choices.

In chapter 2 King Nebuchadnezzar has a dream that is revealed to Daniel by God, along with the interpretation of the dream. Daniel's life is spared, along with many others, because of this supernatural revelation from God. As a result the pagan king proclaims, "Surely your God is a God of gods and a Lord of kings". Another result is that Daniel, Shadrach, Meshach and Abed-nego are all promoted to positions of great influence and authority.

In chapter 3 Shadrach, Meshach and Abed-nego refuse to worship the king's statue. As a result they are thrown into the fiery furnace. In the fiery furnace they are fully protected and Jesus is seen walking inside the furnace with them. When they come out of the furnace unharmed the king proclaims, "I make a decree that any people, nation or tongue that speaks anything offensive against the God of Shadrach, Meshach and Abed-nego shall be torn limb from limb and their houses reduced to a rubbish heap, inasmuch as there is no other god who is able to deliver in this way."

In chapter 4 King Nebuchadnezzar has another troubling dream. God gives Daniel the interpretation of the dream. After it is fulfilled as Daniel had said and the king is humbled before God, the king worships and honors God publicly.

In chapter 5 King Nebuchadnezzar's grandson is now ruling. He sees the handwriting on the wall and Daniel interprets the writing. The interpretation comes true that very night and Daniel is again honored in the midst of a pagan king.

In chapter 6 Darius the Mede, who is now king, is tricked by evil men into making a decree that no one can pray to anyone except for him for 30 days, knowing that Daniel prays every day to God. Daniel is thrown into the lion's den but is supernaturally protected and kept safe. As a result another pagan king publicly honors God as King Darius proclaims, "I make a decree that in all the dominion of my kingdom men are to fear and tremble before the God of Daniel; For He is the living God and enduring forever, And His kingdom is one which will not be destroyed, And His dominion will be forever."

Everything about the circumstances in Daniel 1-6 would have suggested that nothing good could happen to God's people and God's servants. Yet, because of God's supernatural protection, God's servants were spared and God was publicly honored and worshiped by pagan kings and pagan nations.

We need to learn to lean into the grace of God for protection! The safest place to be in the last days will be in the center of God's will, trusting in His grace for protection!

This doesn't mean that no believers will be persecuted or no believers will die as martyrs for their faith. According to Bible prophecy we know there will be many who will die for their faith. Even then God's grace will be there! Years ago I was watching a Christian film about John Huss, a courageous man of God who stood for truth in the early 15th century and was burned at the stake because of his stand. I knew that he was going to die at the end of the film but had this thought in my mind, "I hope he dies singing". I thought this because I knew that this would encourage me in my faith that God's presence is with believers in a special way when they give their life to stay true to Jesus and His truth. Sure enough, at the end of the film as they tied John Huss to the stake, and the flames around him began to rise, the film ended with him singing praises to God. Like Stephen in Acts 7 who saw Jesus in heaven as he was stoned for his faith, John Huss obviously was surrounded by the Lord's presence as the flames engulfed his body!

Leaning Into God's Grace for Power and Courage

I would guess that most of us feel that we do not have the strength to do well in facing difficult things that we have never faced before. We recognize our fears and weaknesses. The good news is that God gives grace for this as well. When we are weak He is strong and we are fearful He gives us courage to face those things that are the cause of our fears. 2 Corinthians 12:9 speaks of God's power being perfected in our weaknesses.

"And He has said to me, "**My grace is sufficient for you, for power is perfected in weakness**." Most gladly, therefore, I will rather boast about my weaknesses, so that the power of Christ may dwell in me."

2 Corinthians 12:9

2 Timothy 1:7 tells us that God has not given us a spirit of fear, but of power, and of love, and of a sound mind! This verse gives us assurance that we can overcome fear through the power of the Holy Spirit, Who lives within us.

A number of years ago Corrie Ten Boom, who was a holocaust survivor, and a powerful minister of the gospel, wrote a letter to express her concerns about believers not preparing their hearts to face trials and tribulations. Within the letter she includes a memorable moment in her childhood. With persecution arising during the days leading up to World War 2 Corrie was conscious of the fact that she may face great persecution for her faith. She was very concerned that she would not have the courage to give her life for Jesus if she needed to. She talked to her father about her concerns. Here is her description of that conversation.

> *"When I was a little girl, ... I went to my father and said, 'Daddy, I am afraid that I will never be strong enough to be a martyr for Jesus Christ.'"*
>
> *'Tell me,' said Father, 'When you take a train trip to Amsterdam, when do I give you the money for the ticket? Three weeks before?'*
>
> *'No Daddy, you give me the money for the ticket just before we get on the train.'*
>
> *'That is right,' my father said, 'and so it is with God's strength. Our Father in Heaven knows when you will need the strength to be a martyr for Jesus Christ. He will supply all you need - just in time...'"*

God's grace is available to give us power, strength and courage in the time that we need it.

We see this truth exemplified in the life of the Apostle Paul. In Acts, chapter 14 Paul is preaching in the city of Lystra. In verses 19-20 we read of something that Paul did that can only be accounted for by supernatural grace.

> *"But Jews came from Antioch and Iconium, and having won over the crowds, they stoned Paul and dragged him out of the city, supposing him to be dead. (20) But while the disciples stood around him, he got up and entered the city. The next day he went away with Barnabas to Derbe."* Acts 14:19-20

No human being is courageous enough after being stoned by a mob, dragged out of the city, and left for dead, to get up and reenter the city to finish preaching their sermon! Only the grace of God can explain these actions!

We need to learn to lean into God's grace for power and courage in the last days! It is available!

Leaning Into God's Grace for Purpose

Beyond provision and protection, is the issue of God's grace that is available to us to bring purpose in life. Having purpose in life is connected to God's grace for power and courage. God's will for the life of a believer is more than survival. We are here for a purpose and a plan. Each of us has a divine destiny established before we were born and written out by God while we were still in our mother's womb. Living in the last days does not change this truth of Scripture. For each believer who finds themselves living in the days that lead up to the 2nd coming of Christ, a destined purpose for their life has been established! God's grace is available to bring those purposes to fulfilled reality.

> *"For consider your calling, brethren, that there were not many wise according to the flesh, not many mighty, not many noble; (27) but God has chosen the*

foolish things of the world to shame the wise, and God has chosen the weak things of the world to shame the things which are strong, (28) and the base things of the world and the despised God has chosen, the things that are not, so that He may nullify the things that are, (29) so that no man may boast before God."
1 Corinthians 1:26-29

Notice in this passage of Scripture that God loves to use those who do not have special intellect, special strength, or special position to accomplish His purposes. By doing this He brings attention to His power and wisdom that works through common vessels to ensure that the world's attention is directed back to Him. In this way more are drawn to know Him.

This truth can be illustrated by looking at the eight authors of the 27 books of the New Testament.

1) Matthew - (A tax collector) Tax collectors were despised and considered to be the low life of society.
2) Mark - (Known as John Mark in the book of Acts) According to Acts 15 John Mark has the distinction of being known as the guy who deserted Paul and Barnabas during a ministry trip. Acts 15:38 says that John Mark "had deserted them in Pamphylia and had not gone with them to the work."
3) Luke - (Gentile Physician) In the beginning days of the Christian church being Jewish, as opposed to being a Gentile was a significant thing. All of the pillars of the New Testament church were Jewish. Luke would have been considered an outsider to many in that day.
4) John - (Disciple of Jesus and brother of James) James and John were disciples of Jesus but are seen in Mark 13 presenting this request to Jesus. "Grant that we may sit, one on Your right and one on Your left, in Your glory." Their request caused the other 10 disciples to be indignant with them. Pride was obviously an issue here and is seen in other

places as even at the time of the last supper the disciples are seen arguing about who among them was the greatest. Wow!
5) Paul - (Formerly Saul of Tarsus) Saul was a vicious, hateful persecutor of believers who even was a part of the imprisonment and killing of Christians.
6) Peter - (Disciple of Jesus) Peter denied Jesus multiple times after Jesus was taken captive, the night before His crucifixion. Then in Galatians 2 Paul indicates that at Antioch he confronted Peter face to face because of his hypocrisy. Peter had been eating with the Gentile believers until Jewish leaders came. He then held himself aloof from the Gentile, fearing the party of the circumcision.
7) James - (Brother of Jesus) It appears that James did not believe in Jesus until after His resurrection from the dead.
8) Jude - (Brother of Jesus) It appears that Jude did not believe in Jesus until after His resurrection from the dead.

I have purposely addressed the less admirable aspects of these men's qualifications to illustrate a point. Despite the glaring flaws and weaknesses of these men, God used them in many great ways, including using them to write the entire New Testament. In the end they were all great men of God, but they were all common, flawed men, with weaknesses. God loves to extend His grace into the lives of ordinary people to raise them up to accomplish His purposes.

This pattern is not limited to Bible times. Another illustration of this truth is seen in the modern day Pentecostal movement. The start of the modern day Pentecostal movement is typically traced back to the 1906 Azusa Street revival in Los Angeles. The congregation that began to experience this pentecostal outpouring, and subsequently shared it with many who came to experience this move of God, was a very humble group, meeting in a very unimpressive building, led by a very humble pastor.

According to a wikipedia article on the Azusa Street Revival the building that housed the 1906 revival was rented for $8.00 per month. A newspaper referred to the downtown Los Angeles building as a "tumble down shack".[1] It was approximately 60 feet long and 40 feet wide, totaling 2,400 square feet, sided with weathered whitewashed clapboards. Some of the benches were simply planks put on top of empty nail kegs. There was no elevated platform, as the ceiling was only eight feet high.[2]

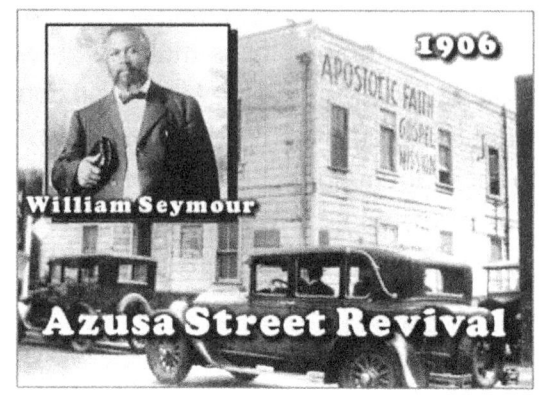

The pastor of the Azusa Street Revival was Rev. William Seymour. He was described as a one-eyed 34-year-old son of freed slaves.[3] After Brother Seymour arrived in California in February of 1906 he was invited to speak at a local church, where he preached about speaking in tongues as the first biblical evidence of the inevitable infilling in the Holy Spirit. His message was rejected by the Holiness Church Association of Southern California. A week after his message, the church he had preached at was padlocked.

A group of people began to attend Bible studies with Brother Seymour and in April of 1906 they rented the building on Azusa Street. This was the beginning of a revival that changed the world in unfathomable ways!

According to a Pew Forum analysis of estimates from the Center for the Study of Global Christianity, as of 2011 there were an estimated 584,080,000 Pentecostal and Charismatic Christians in the world.[4] That is over ½ billion people! All of this from a shack of a building in a humble congregation led by the son of freed slaves.

---

[1] https://en.wikipedia.org/wiki/Azusa_Street_Revival
[2] ibid
[3] ibid
[4] https://www.pewresearch.org/religion/2011/12/19/global-christianity-movements-and-denominations/

The impact upon the world that has resulted from this revival with such humble beginnings would have been unimaginable in 1906 for those who were a part of what God was doing in them and through them. God loves to work in these marvelous ways.

As we saw in an earlier chapter, even today there are stirrings of revival with humble beginnings that are spreading across America and other nations.

In Romans 12 we are told of gifts that God has given to each of us.

*"Since we have gifts that differ **according to the grace given to us**, each of us is to exercise them accordingly:"*   *Romans 12:6*

God has given you gifts by His grace. You have not earned them and you don't deserve them. Still, they are given to you freely by a wise and loving Heavenly Father. Each of us living in the last days needs to identify gifts that God has given to us by His grace, and use those gifts faithfully until Jesus returns or until our life here on earth is ended.

God's grace has been available to us for much more than salvation throughout our lives. It has been easy to overlook His grace since we have had so many outward sources of security surrounding us. From Bible prophecies about the last days and from what we see developing in the world today, it appears that many of those external sources of security may cease to exist.

Leaning hard into the grace of God for provision, protection, power and purpose during these last days will serve to strengthen and purify us as believers!

Faith Overcoming Fear!

Is fear a sin? There is more than one answer to this question. The fear of the Lord is definitely a good thing. Built in fears, like the fear of touching a hot stove is a healthy thing.

On the other hand, fear that begins to dominate our life can be a sin that leads to many other sins. Notice the descriptive terms used to identify those who are condemned to the lake of fire in Revelation 21:8.

> *"But for the cowardly and unbelieving and abominable and murderers and immoral persons and sorcerers and idolaters and all liars, their part will be in the lake that burns with fire and brimstone, which is the second death."*   *Revelation 21:8*

Every one of the descriptive terms used are what we would expect except one. We would expect to see, "unbelieving", "abominable", "murderers", "immoral persons", "sorcerers", "idolaters", and "liars" listed. What we would not expect is the term used first in this list. The list begins with "the cowardly". Clearly fear can become sinful when it begins to dictate our life and determine our words and actions.

In Matthew 25 Jesus tells the parable of the talents. Among the servants who report to the master when he returns is the servant who had one talent. His response to his master is seen in verse 25. *'And **I was afraid**, and went away and hid your talent in the ground. See, you have what is yours.'* What was the master's response to this excuse? Did he give him a pass? We see his response in verse 26. *"But his master answered and said to him, 'You wicked, lazy slave, ..."* He goes on to take away the talent he has and to have the wicked slave thrown out into outer darkness. Fear is a serious thing that must be confronted, especially in the last days.

I believe that the greatest way to confront and overcome fear is to meditate upon the character of God and the promises of God. Using a Nave's Topical Bible it is helpful to see how abundant the biblical references are to the various aspects of the nature of God. If we look for references on the love of God, or the faithfulness of God, or the grace of God, or the mercy of God, we will find an extremely long list of passages that reveal these aspects of the nature of God. Notice the list below of references for the love of God as an example.

> **"Love of God" - General References**
> Deu 4:37; Deu 9:29; 1Ki 8:51-53; Deu 7:7-8; Deu 7:13; Deu 10:15; Deu 10:18; Deu 23:5; Deu 33:3; Deu 33:12; 2Sa 12:24; Neh 13:26; Job 7:17; Psa 42:8; Psa 47:4; Psa 63:3; Psa 78:65; Psa 78:68; Psa 78:61-62; Psa 89:33; Psa 103:13; Psa 146:8; Pro 15:9; Isa 38:17; Isa 43:4; Jer 31:3; Hos 11:1; Mal 1:2; Joh 3:16; Joh 5:20; Joh 14:21; Joh 14:23; Joh 16:27; Joh 17:10; Joh 17:23; Joh 17:26; Joh 20:17; Rom 1:7; Rom 5:8; Rom 9:13; Rom 11:28; 2Co 9:7; 2Co 13:11; Eph 2:4-5; 2Th 2:16; Tit 3:4-5; Heb 12:6; 1Jo 3:1; 1Jo 4:8-10; 1Jo 4:12-13; 1Jo 4:15-16; 1Jo 4:19; Jud 1:21; Rev 3:12; Rev 14:1
>
> **Love of God, exemplified**
> Gen 17:7; Exo 3:6; Gen 46:3; Exo 6:7; Exo 29:45-46; Exo 19:4-6; Lev 20:26; Lev 20:24; Lev 22:32-33; Lev 11:44-45; Lev 25:38; Num 15:41; Lev 25:23; Lev 25:42; Lev 25:55; Lev 26:12; Deu 4:20; Deu 4:34; Deu 4:37; Deu 9:29; 1Ki 8:51-53; Deu 7:7-8; Deu 7:13; Deu 10:15; Deu 14:2; Deu 7:6; Deu 23:5; Deu 26:18-19; Deu 27:9; Deu 28:9-10; Deu 29:13; Deu 32:9-12; Deu 33:3; Deu 33:12; 2Sa 7:23-24; 2Sa 12:24; Neh 13:26; Psa 4:3; Psa 31:19; Psa 31:21; Psa 42:8; Psa 47:4; Psa 48:9; Psa 48:14; Psa 50:5; Psa 50:7; Psa 63:3; Psa 73:1; Psa 74:2; Psa 70.65; Psa 78:68; Psa 78:61-62; Psa 81-13; Psa 89:33; Psa 90:1; Psa 100:3; Psa 79:13; Psa 95:7; Psa 103:4; Psa 105:6; Psa 114:2; Psa 135:4; Psa 148:14; Pro 11:20; Pro 15:9; Isa 5:7; Isa 41:8-10; Isa 43:1-4; Isa 43:7; Isa 44:1-2; Isa 44:21-22; Isa 48:12; Isa 49:13-17; Isa 51:16; Isa 54:5-6; Isa 54:10; Isa 62:4-5; Isa 63:7-9; Isa 65:19; Isa 66:13; Jer 3:14-15; Jer 10:16; Jer 12:7; Jer 13:11; Jer 15:16; Jer 31:3; Jer 31:14; Jer 31:32; Jer 32:41; Eze 16:1-14; Eze 34:31; Eze 37:27; Hos 2:19-20; Hos 2:23; 1Pe 2:10; Hos 9:10; Hos 11:1; Hos 11:3-4; Zep 3:17; Hag 2:23; Zec 1:14; Zec 2:8; Zec 8:8; Jer 30:22; Zec 13:9; Mal 1:2-3; Mal 3:16-17; Mat 18:11-14; Luk 15:4-7; Luke 15:11 27; Joh 14:21; Joh 14:23; Joh 16:27; Joh 17:10; Joh 17:23; Joh 17:26; Rom 1:7; Rom 5:8; Rom 8:31-32; Rom 8:39; Rom 11:28; 1Co 2:9; Isa 64:4; 1Co 3:9; 1Co 6:19-20; 1Co 7:23; 2Co 5:18-21; 2Co 6:16; 2Co 13:14; Eph 1:3-6; Col 3:12; Heb 11:16; Jam 1:18

Similar lists of references are found for the other aspects of the nature of God. Seeing who God is and saturating our minds and hearts with this knowledge can help us overcome fear by faith.

If we meditate upon the promises of God in His Word like "I will never leave you nor forsake you" and "my God will supply all your needs according to His riches in glory in Christ Jesus" we can strengthen our faith and overcome fear by faith.

Leaning into God's grace applies in this situation as well. None of us are tough enough to overcome fear on our own! None of us! We need to lean into God's grace and ask Him to give us faith, courage and strength to overcome fears within us!

Why was young David so much more courageous than all of the seasoned warriors in Israel's army? I believe it was because David had been spending time with God and meditating upon Who God is and what God had promised him. David faced Goliath, not with self-confidence but with God-confidence.

As we saw earlier in this chapter, 2 Timothy 1:7 tells us that "God has not given us a spirit of fear, but of power, and of love, and of a sound mind." We need to lean into this grace that God has given to us.

The message of the Bible is that God is an almighty, all knowing, loving, holy, just, righteous and wise God, Who wants us to put our faith and trust in Him. When we trust Him and put our faith in Him, it pleases Him! He wants to show His strength in us and He wants to bless us!

Living in the last days will provide opportunities for believers to grow in their faith in God. This is a good thing! As we learn to lean into His grace we can experience greater measures of life that is both biblical and fulfilling!

CONCLUSION

Lift Up Your Heads, Your Redemption is Drawing Near!

In Luke 21:25-27 we find a description of the time surrounding the 2nd coming of Jesus that is a bit different than what we find anywhere else in Scripture.

> *"There will be signs in sun and moon and stars, and on the earth dismay among nations, in perplexity at the roaring of the sea and the waves, (26) men fainting from fear and the expectation of the things which are coming upon the world; for the powers of the heavens will be shaken. (27) "Then they will see the Son of Man coming in a cloud with power and great glory."*
> *Luke 21:25-17*

A number of descriptions of the time surrounding the 2nd coming of Jesus Christ are listed here. Signs in sun, moon and stars, dismay among the nations, perplexing things in the seas, and the powers of the heavens shaken are all mentioned. Men's hearts will faint from fear and expectation of the things which are coming upon the world.

For the believers that are alive at that time there is an exciting, hopeful word found in verse 28.

> *"But when these things begin to take place, straighten up and lift up your heads, because your redemption is drawing near."*
> *Luke 21:28*

A key question related to this passage is what does "these things" refer to? "These things" may refer to what we read in verses 25-27. Then again "these things" may refer in a broader sense to the things listed earlier in the chapter like wars and rumors of wars, earthquakes in various places, and the persecution of Christians.

Though it is hard to determine the exact meaning of "these things", the basic meaning of the verse is clear. As believers in Jesus Christ see the signs of His coming appearing in the world they should lift up their heads, look eagerly with anticipation for their redemption that is drawing near!

The return of Jesus Christ to this earth is by far the most profound moment in history since His first coming! In His first coming He came to be a sacrifice for sin. In His second coming, He will come to bring to us the full measure of the salvation that He paid for when He came the first time.

> *"So Christ also, having been offered once to bear the sins of many, will appear a second time for salvation without reference to sin, to those who eagerly await Him."* Hebrews 9:28

We have seen throughout this book that the fulfillments of Bible prophecies concerning the time leading up to the 2nd coming of Christ are all around us. The signs of His soon coming appearance abound! He comes to bring salvation! He comes with great power and glory! He comes to bring victory over His enemies! He comes to establish righteousness and peace! He comes to be glorified among His saints!

In Revelation 22:7 Jesus says, "Behold, I am coming quickly!" In Revelation 22:12 Jesus says, "Behold, I am coming quickly, and My reward is with Me!" In Revelation 22:21 Jesus says, "Yes, I am coming quickly!"

And we say, "Amen, come Lord Jesus!"

Notice - Other books, video resources and audio resources by Rick are available at LOCALCHURCHAPOLOGETICS.ORG, including the resources shown here.

CONCLUSION - LIFT UP YOUR HEADS, YOUR REDEMPTION IS DRAWING NEAR

Video Resources and Audio Resources (Cont.)

A study of Biblical Eschatology, including the Day of the Lord, the Great Tribulation, the timing of the Rapture & more.

32 Discipleship Lessons to help believers understand and live out their New Life in Christ!

Rick has produced 2 family devotional books designed to teach Christian Apologetics to children in the home. "God's Creation Family Devotions" is for families with children 2nd grade and younger, while "Got a Moment Family Devotions" is for families with children 3rd grade and older.

Made in the USA
Monee, IL
29 August 2023